T0280028

A BRIEF HISTORY OF
HISTORY

A BRIEF HISTORY OF
HISTORY

—ɯ—

Jeremy Black

INDIANA UNIVERSITY PRESS

This book is a publication of

Indiana University Press
Office of Scholarly Publishing
Herman B Wells Library 350
1320 East 10th Street
Bloomington, Indiana 47405 USA

iupress.org

© 2023 by Jeremy Black

Manufactured in the United States of America

First printing 2023

Library of Congress Cataloging-in-Publication Data

Names: Black, Jeremy, author.
Title: A brief history of history / Jeremy Black.
Description: Bloomington, Indiana : Indiana University Press, [2023] |
  Includes bibliographical references and index.
Identifiers: LCCN 2022057913 (print) | LCCN 2022057914 (ebook) |
  ISBN 9780253066091 (hardback) | ISBN 9780253066114 (ebook)
Subjects: LCSH: Historiography—Philosophy. | History—Philosophy.
Classification: LCC D13 .B528 2023 (print) | LCC D13 (ebook) | DDC
  907.2—dc23/eng/20221206
LC record available at https://lccn.loc.gov/2022057913
LC ebook record available at https://lccn.loc.gov/2022057914

For Philip Waller
With thanks for friendship

CONTENTS

PREFACE

HISTORY—THE SENSE OF THE PAST, the stories we tell about it, and how we understand these stories—is a key point, purpose, and activity of all cultures. The very multiplicity of meanings of the word captures its significance. This book seeks to engage with the range of institutions and individuals who produced accounts of the past. In 2022, this purpose and process became more urgently present with Vladimir Putin's justification of the illegal Russian invasion of Ukraine by means of a perverse account of the histories of both countries. At a Moscow exhibition for the anniversary of Peter the Great's birth, Putin compared the war in Ukraine to Peter the Great's conquests in the Baltics: "You get the impression that by fighting Sweden he was grabbing something. He wasn't taking anything, he was taking it back. . . . Everyone considered it to be part of Sweden. But from time immemorial Slavs have lived there alongside Finno-Ugric peoples. . . . It is our responsibility also to take back and strengthen."[1]

Indeed, the age of revived nationalism that has become increasingly apparent from the 2010s is very much grounded ideologically in accounts of historicized nationhood. The exploration of this situation throws light on both past and present and provides a way to consider anew history and the identity of historians.

Unsurprisingly, these topics, the interrelationships of which contribute to the strength of each and all, have been annexed to the academic projects of understanding and explaining through creating abstractions and systems. That process, while useful, can also be misleading, not least as it can entail a degree of replication of the standard biases and hierarchies of academic life.

The intention here is somewhat different in several respects. I seek to introduce what history is through a retelling of the capacious forms that historical awareness has taken and in a way that resists excessive teleology, presentism, and a narrative of professionalism. From this comes a need to challenge the self-limiting ways in which *historiography* is normally historicized. Instead, I argue the need not only for a holism in the conception of what *history* has meant in the past but also for a democratic understanding of what historical consciousness involves. In the ensuing chapters, I draw attention to recurring motifs in the form of historical knowledge across time, not least by resisting modernizing accounts of historiography that ignore the continuities and cycles connecting modernity to earlier periods. I argue that the standard modernity and modernization of these are inherently flawed, not least because they downplay and even ignore other practices that also were present and would have been rival or alternative versions of modernity had they prevailed.

The key players here as historians, those who create and repeat accounts of the past, are families and governments, the latter particularly so in authoritarian systems or ones in which there is a strong state account of the past. The norms and narratives asserted in the latter can be highly misleading and lead readily to an opposition between false and true history. While that judgment can be readily made of state narratives, for example Putin's Russia, that should not imply that the accounts offered in university circles are free of bias. Indeed, the need to be cautious about some of the norms and narratives currently offered in Western universities is very much the theme of chapter 8. It can be read either in its present position, which is chronologically appropriate, or as a preliminary introduction.

This is a deliberately short book for a fast-moving situation, one that is of great relevance not only today but also for the perceptions that will help mold the twenty-first-century world.

ACKNOWLEDGMENTS

IT IS A GREAT PLEASURE to thank Kristofer Aller-
feldt, Julie Arliss, Joshua Bennett, Pete Brown, Bill Gib-
son, Crawford Gribben, Will Hay, Lothar Hobelt, Virgilio
Iliari, Luigi Loreto, Wanjiru Njoya, and Thomas Otte for
commenting on earlier drafts as well as Peter Wiseman
for providing insights on particular points.

A BRIEF HISTORY OF
HISTORY

ONE

INTRODUCTION

The Controversy of History

> The particulars of that dismal scene have been transmitted from father to son and are still spoke of with horror by the peasantry of that country, among whom the French nation is held in detestation to this day.
>
> —John Moore, British traveler, 1779, of the French pillaging of the Palatinate region of Germany by order of Louis XIV in 1689

"HISTORIES NOW" OR "The Present in the Past" is a theme that is ever more assertive when considering how we, in human societies, experience and discuss history. This issue has been pushed to the fore for me, writing in 2022, because of the use by Vladimir Putin of an account of Russian and Ukrainian history, outlined the previous year, as a justification for a brutal and aggressive war. This seemed a particularly disturbing instance of the use (and abuse) of history. This crisis also led to a reiteration of the frequently made distinction between true and fake news or true and false history, as done by Donald Trump in response to the presidential election of 2020 or by Simon Schama in the *Financial Times* of May 7, 2022. Each figure's assessment, however, is deeply flawed: the first, that of former president Trump, provides the creation of a false history, notably about the 2020 election, while the second offers a problematic guide to the subject of false history. Schama repeated the implication that there was somehow a contrast simply between a reprehensible authoritarian populism and a benign, unbiased liberalism. Instead, this book sees history as an ongoing conversation and, more specifically, as a response to such ideas, not least because there are populist as well as (separately) misleading or questionable dimensions to liberal historical narratives and to those that are nonliberal.

Turning to how Western academics tend to discuss the process of writing about history, the different character of accounts of historiography, in the sense of works about the presentation of history, is immediately apparent; and this is also true of the limitations of these works. First, works on historiography focus heavily, arguably excessively, on those writers defined as historians, those producers of formalized and coherent accounts of the past that can be presented as intellectual, as part of an intellectual progression, and as providing a shaped and distinct subject.

Second, there is a strong Eurocentricity in much of the coverage, with the story taken from the classical Greeks to modern Western historians, generally those who are German, French, American, and British. This combines an emphasis on intellectual speculation and academic processes, all generally within an Enlightenment and secular context. However sympathetic this context might be, not least to most readers of such works, the approach fails to engage with the broad nature of the historicizing consciousness and experience of historical thought. The idea of history and historians is frequently too narrowly constructed, as therefore are historical surveys of the subject. Although multiple historiographical approaches, if aptly summarized, can be refreshing, even enlightening, for the reader,[1] historiography, as a branch of modern intellectual history, is an approach that has little to offer the majority of those interested in the past.

The interest in the past, instead, has seen a democratization of historical experience. This attracts public attention and, separately, can also be seen replicated in museums, curricula, and other public-facing aspects of state historical activity and consciousness. There has always been interest in the "But what did they eat?" or "What did they wear?" approach to history, and this method has broadened out to include other branches of human activity. Presentations of the past can then be deployed to help make modern circumstances appear normative. Television has provided much of the impetus in capturing the often monochrome "everyday" life of the past, whereas film has tended to go for the full-color commanding heights of atypical narratives, whether in social rank or personal behavior.

Other genres have followed suit. Thus, detective novels, which very much began in the nineteenth century with crimes of the here and now, have broadened out to range across time, from antiquity to recent years. Some of the results captured the past, as with Agatha Christie's setting of a novel in ancient Egypt, *Death Comes as the End* (1944), one for which she deployed her strong connections among archaeologists. Most novelists, however, have not matched this presentation of the different. Yet, that does not mean that detective novels set in a past that is strongly reminiscent of the present are thereby less effective as novels. Indeed, Christie's sole historical novel has not been televised and does not appeal to many readers, in part because of a lack of points of ready access. It is too different.

In terms of its impact, Westernization has been unhelpful in the discussion of history more generally and, not least, in its wider application on the global scale. This is the case not just with content but also with process. The latter includes the most basic form of segmental chronology, that of ancient, medieval, early modern, and late modern or, for earlier, Stone, Bronze, and Iron Ages, the last maybe being since replaced by steel, plastic, and microchip ages. In turn, the Renaissance typology and progression of historical eras (classical, medieval, modern) was related to the Protestant proposal of early church, medieval church, and reformed church—that is, Protestant. The Marxist chronology similarly is one based on European history or, rather, an account of this history: progressing through feudal, bourgeois, and proletarian stages. Explanations of modernization have accordingly been framed in Western terms. Once question marks are attached to these terms, these explanations, and their application, however, then much that is accepted in the Western model becomes problematic or, at the very least, worthy of fresh scrutiny.

The need for further scrutiny has become more apparent as the historical world has changed and notably so over the last century. In particular, there has been the rise of a considerable number of independent states with their own narrative and sense of priorities, and, in some cases, a rejection of the external narratives, both Western and Communist, that were dominant and distorting, in the early decades of independence. Handling that variety helps ensure that there is no single way to approach the subject of this book. Moreover, that point is a matter of organization as well as content.

All choices made will inevitably attract debate. Yet, far from qualifying—or, still more, lessening—what is offered, that debate is a welcome process. Healthy to the historical discipline, debate undermines the norm in the historiographical literature, one that is, all too often, of an Olympian-style approach to the subject, as in x historian or y approach (generally, well close-to-uniformly, those of the author) are critical and deserving of more attention and others can be ignored. Furthermore, the subject is then assembled (or constructed) for discussion in terms of priorities reflecting and affirming these choices and the related priorities. Instead, debate should be welcomed at every turn and contention understood as inherently part of a world in which history, both the entire process as well as the specifics, is open to discussion.

Moreover, history, whether explicitly or implicitly, is politicized in at least a general sense of relating to political values, if not a narrow sense of being directly linked to assertive political partisanship. In consequence—both of the discussion mentioned in the last paragraph and of this politicization—there is also a variable fixing of historical consciousness, in part chronological, in part geographical, and in part thematic. To squeeze out this variety, in order to have a uniform approach—or, alternatively, one shaped in a clear dichotomy between, as it were, true and false, or with reference to clear and almost automatic political preferences—would be problematic but is a stance that is frequently adopted.

Separately, it is necessary to cover the many popular approaches to history as well as those of more elite groups, contexts, and forms, notably the culture of print, although, again, without there being any clear dichotomy between the popular and the elite. Indeed, in historiography, other than as interpretative suggestions, such dichotomies generally break down if applied rigidly. In practice, for all groups, history is a search for meaning and identity, and this search shapes collective as well as individual memory. In every society, memories are formed that mold the way we understand ourselves. We incorporate information beyond ourselves and our experience from the past in order to understand and interpret who we are and might be. This process involves our sense of who we are in terms of our history, which is part of the glue of society.[2] Shared narratives are very important to the cohesion of nations and of groups within, or between, them.

Narrative is a key term, because for "recovered time," or time that can be reclaimed through memory, direct or reported oral history is a vital backdrop throughout. In the case of most of time past, however, no such recovery is possible or, earlier, was possible other than through the oral accounts that remained. Instead, the past then has to be scrutinized through archaeology, as well as related subjects, such as surface geology. How best to understand the history and present of these periods is unclear, as is how far to do so within the formal structures of history as a subject, whether academic or not. Linked to this, comes the question of whether historiography should extend to geological time or even only to prehistoric time, and if so, how best to do so.

Material from the latter was (and is) certainly used in the historicizing of nations that has been central to much public history. This situation became prominent in the late nineteenth century and helped drive much interest in archaeology, both academic and popular. Separate "cultures" were discerned and mapped, and these cultures were then linked to later tribes and nations in a convenient, but often questionable, fashion.

This process, which spread as more states became independent, continues. The discovery in the Gaza Strip of the statue of a Canaanite goddess of love, hunting, and war from about 2500 BCE was proclaimed in 2022 as an assertion of lineage by Jamal Abu Rida, the director of the Ministry of Tourism and Antiquities in the Gaza Strip: "Such discoveries prove that Palestine has civilisation and history, and no one can deny or falsify this history. This is the Palestinian people and their ancient Canaanite civilisation."[3] In practice, this claim was scarcely value-free but was made in order to counterpoint Jewish/Israeli continuity, which is an established and vigorously argued political and archaeological theme in Israel.

Early human history is generally approached through archaeology. This can indicate much, although only infrequently the historical thought of past societies. Moreover, aside from the complexities of assessing surviving material, the archaeological database is generally very incomplete. Thus, the absence of sites in a given region may reflect incomplete or nonexistent field research. Since relatively few sites are ever excavated, archaeologists rely on material collected from the surface of a site for most regional information as well as to determine which sites are selected for excavation. In addition, later deposits can obscure earlier ones, while sampling techniques, not least generalizing from a few sites, pose significant issues, and it is difficult to project what is to be found beyond the limits of the actual excavations. More generally, modernity has a Janus-like relationship with archaeology: endowing it with identity, resources, and technological progress, while destroying sites at an ever more rapid rate, thus dramatically altering the database on which interpretations are offered by the archaeologist.

Technology has greatly increased the type as well as quantity of the available archaeological data, as with the consequence of the combination of photography and aerial survey. These have been particularly significant for archaeology, not least making it possible both to survey terrain that was otherwise difficult and to discover sites and information not visible on the ground, as in recent work in Amazonia. Yet, the historiographical context for this data very much includes the limitations of the material. Thus, the data yielded by aerial photography depends on a number of criteria, including optimum climatic and flying conditions, the suitability of the subsoils and modern crop rotations for yielding information, the absence of restricted flying zones, and the degree of historic and present-day damage and destruction owing to ploughing and construction. Droughts are particularly useful. These criteria mean that it is dangerous to assume that individual aerial surveys can yield comprehensive information.

Turning from archaeology, we find the engagement with history is (and was) all around us, from finding out about ancestors and places to considering how best to confront the legacies of past conduct. Because people see their identity as deriving in part from ancestors, ancestral memory was, and is, kept alive by a number of means: for example, in China and Japan, by including prayers and sacrifices to the dead as well as naming the living to recall past family members.[4] So also in other historical cultures. Modern genealogy, and television programs about the ancestors of celebrities and others, are part of the same process. The method may change, as well as the context—in the shape now of a widespread move away from religiosity, at least in much of the West, and the declining social significance of occasions such as christenings—but the goal of remembrance continues.

Governments, religions, community leaders, and historians, however defined, as well as other intellectuals, seek, and have sought, to mediate this process of understanding and representing the past. They commission or write accounts of the process, past and present, that reflect this perception and thereby seek to express what is normative to them. Normative is a matter for many not only of what appears central to the interpretation of a particular theme or period but also of what appears preferable in the past. Academics are not somehow separate to this process, nor apart from it, however much they may seek to be so or to present a philosophy of history in which they can be so.

In developing and applying these norms, there is an understandable tendency, and notably so in the case of governments, community leaders, and academics, to reflect current concerns and themes. For example, in the early 2020s, it may appear obvious to make Western-purchased and transported, African-provided slavery a key theme in historical work. It does not lessen that significance, nor indeed the many horrors of the slave trade and slavery, to point out that other narratives seemed just as obvious in their day and that other types of slavery have received relatively less discussion and might deserve more attention, both absolutely and in relative terms.

More generally, modern-day criticism of British imperialism is matched by earlier praise, accompanied by the sense that empire as a historical phenomenon was across time and therefore "natural." In their *Historical and Modern Atlas of the British Empire* (1905), C. Grant Robertson and J. G. Bartholomew, far from dating the British empire to the late Tudor period of maritime expansion under Elizabeth I (r. 1558–1603), saw a longer destiny: "Since the days of Boadicea [d. 60 CE] there is no period of our history in which the inhabitants of Great Britain have not been connected with or lived under a series of national and historic imperial systems . . . the theory and claims of the modern imperial crown are no pinchbeck [false metal] creation of the nineteenth century." The long procession of earlier imperial episodes gave modern British imperialism a legitimating history, one that made it appear natural. That assessment would be a different context to that generally offered now, on which see chapter 8.

Alongside the claims, explicit or implicit, for primacy on the part of academics, the reality is that a range of forces, drives, and elements are to the fore in a democracy of history—from government to family, religion to self— and, as a cause as well as a result, the historians are we ourselves, all of us. And thus also are our forebears. History, in this light, is the trust between the generations, a trust of understanding, and, related to this, the still present legacy of our predecessors. These are important psychological dimensions of history and key characteristics of social life. We approach, understand, and represent our past, the past, and the pasts of others and do so with all the energy, acceptance, and dissent that might be anticipated. That is the element, the inherent subjectivity of our action and response, a subjectivity we need to understand. In doing so, we need to consider how the situation has changed and will continue to change and the elements involved in each of these timeframes. Alongside the challenge of using any evidence without either being captured by its perspective, or imposing that of the particular observer, history can be seen as existing outside and independent of any documentary record.

For academic historians, there is, alongside national variations, a widespread commonality in the tension between empiricism, in the sense of knowledge and assessments founded on verifiable information, sources, and experience, and the wish to draw broader conclusions. The former is seen by many historians as a key distinguishing feature of their activity. It is deployed by other specialists who use the past, notably political scientists and sociologists, but historians tend to see their empiricism as both different and better. Empiricism, or rather a supposedly superior understanding and use of the sources, is also deployed to differentiate scholars from amateurs and the public. There is, however, a degree of self-serving in some of this argument, notably in the assertion of rank, prestige, and grant-monopolizing powers. Academe, its internal structures and role by aspiration, is a status system, if not what can be seen as a class one. Insiders are very well aware of this culture and practice, but only some who write on historiography give this dimension sufficient attention.

Lastly, empiricism is seen as a key differentiation of fact from fiction. Ironically, however, this approach has been criticized by those academics who have embraced postmodernism. There is also the key point that far from this distinction only being understood by academics, amateur historians, like public "consumers," are able to try to differentiate between fact and fiction while accepting all the difficulties of that proposition.

To that end, any focus on a small number of supposedly crucial historical thinkers, a Thucydides to Hobsbawm approach, is anachronistic and at times unintentionally humorous. That is also the case however much the list is updated, as would now be the case, in terms of gender, ethnicity, country of origin, and any other factor considered relevant. Indeed, both focus and upgrading are a somewhat dated and questionable method, one seen in past centuries as well as in the present, and therefore necessarily transient in the consequences. In one hundred years, for example, how many will consider Hobsbawm of much significance? Instead of engaging with historians as eminent figures in a pantheon (whether Western or global) of academics and other commentators, it is the far larger, more diffuse, and less consistent range of those who in fact produced history, considered as the presentation of the past, that is notable.

This is understandable in that more and more people now get their knowledge of the past from videos, podcasts, historical video games, and even heavy metal bands. Moreover, all of these are global. The most influential heavy metal bands, such as Iced Earth and Sabaton, have tens of millions of views and thereby influence historical memory more than any contemporary historian.

Furthermore, Chinese, Arab, and Turkish companies now produce, often in English, documentary films or historical soap operas regarding their histories, including encounters with the West: for example, the Crusades from the eleventh century on. Such accounts can have global reach, notably through Al Jazeera and Netflix.

Any emphasis, furthermore, is complicated by the extent to which accounts that were, and are, known to be fictional can be included. Examples include Henry Fielding's highly successful novel *The History of Tom Jones* (1749) or, indeed, more recently produced adaptations of this novel as well as generally more recently produced films and television programs. This inclusion is because they claim to be histories and depict the past or because they pretend to capture deep truths about humanity and its past. Fiction writers do not see themselves as ahistorical but as alternatively historical. This is an instructive response both to the continual element of historical fiction and to the shifting boundaries between fact and fiction.

A standard academic perspective on the subject, as well as being very much a version of the Whiggish, progressivist, teleological approach of history inevitably going in a certain direction, and a better one at that, is that of a focus on those who have allegedly "advanced" historical method. Yet, there is the need to understand a broader assessment of historical accounts and changes. This is the case for those who seek origin myths of the present, for those fascinated by the past, and for those seeking to validate specific views of the present and visions for the future. The collective character of historical work is particularly important in this respect, because individual views draw on aligning with those of others for their influence and tend to rely on the same factors for their content.

This wider ambit or collectivity extends to the way in which the recipients of these views have "agency," in that there is much evidence, as with past reading[5] or modern book groups (of both historical "fact" and "fiction"), cinema audiences, or website responses, that there is an independent, and often critical, response to what is "consumed." As such, the role of the overlapping groups of patrons, commissioners, authors, publishers, and teachers is often less influential, let alone directing, than might be envisaged while, conversely, that of "consumers" is greater. For universities, this approach extends to assessing the whats (and whys) of student perception and course choices, rather than solely those of the lecture givers. This approach to historiography has had insufficient attention. It certainly entails more difficulties in terms of sources and conceptually. Yet, that does not make the consumer approach to historiography nebulous or less significant.

This situation can also be seen with writing by children, as in Jane Austen's extensive marginalia on her brother's copy of Oliver Goldsmith's popular *The History of England* (1771) and in the unpublished (in her lifetime) *History of England* she herself wrote in 1791. In Austen's marginalia, Oliver Cromwell is referred to as a "detestable minister!" and God called on to bless those who helped Charles II to escape after the battle of Worcester of 1651,[6] a very different approach to that taken shortly before by John Adams when visiting Worcester, on which see the beginning of chapter 4. As is so often the case, it is unclear why one of those responses should receive more attention than the other. To offer only one of the two can provide a misleading view, especially if it is presented as normative.

Goldsmith's other works indicated the entrepreneurial possibilities of the historical work, as they included the *Account of the Augustan Age in England* (1759), *The Life of Richard Nash, a Recent Celebrity* (1762), *Dr Goldsmith's Roman History Abridged by Himself for the Use of Schools* (1773), and *An History of the Earth and Animated Nature* (1774), while he might have written the anonymous children's tale *The History of Little Goody Two-Shoes* (1765). The use of history apparently indiscriminately for fact and fiction captured the focus for the description on form rather than method and sources.

And so to the present focus. With the world's population at an unprecedented level—8 billion in 2023 and still, at least in aggregate global (as opposed to all-national) terms, rising rapidly. This size compares with 425 million in 1500, 1 billion in 1800, 2 billion in 1927, 3 billion in 1960, and 6 billion in 1999. As a consequence, the numbers of those "doing" history, if only solely "experiencing" and thus having to make sense of past events and developments, is greater than ever before. That should ensure a particular focus on the current situation, as should the probable increase of the global population to maybe 10.75 billion by 2100.

The potential for change offered by new technology should also ensure a focus on the current situation. The lessening of the dominance of print in the communication of views and information has been a striking feature of the last century, this lessening returning us, albeit in a very different form and context, to the preprinting variety of rapid and spontaneous verbal communication to close groups. This lessening has become more apparent from the 1990s with "social media," and the opportunities thereby offered to bypass earlier hierarchies of approval and authority. Such a bypassing was ironically seen in a different context with the development of book publication. "Social media" overlaps with earlier practices, as with that of publishing books online, but also moves on to other formats and methods.

The ready access of sophisticated (and unsophisticated) data tools is part of the process, as with methods of data mining, including by the use of artificial intelligence (AI). Thus, an AI system called Ithaca has been recently employed to analyze decrees from fifth-century BCE Athens, notably dating inscriptions and predicting what the missing bits contained.[7] Such methods can affect not only the content of historical research but also the means of historical discussion.

This book will adopt a historical approach in its consideration of the narration of the past as the foundation of collective identities. Considering historical thought, rather than written texts alone, enables us to overcome the specialized narrowness of historiography by extending the sources not only to other literary genres but also to iconography and, more generally, to the full social range of past narratives. Not least in terms of social and cultural resonance, these records express much better than academic history and the philosophy of history, ideas, and perceptions about collective identities, time, and the relationship between past, present, and future. This is linked to the practice of history not as a scholarly practice but rather as a prophecy about the past, that is, an explanation of the present sought in the past.[8]

Most of human history will be covered in the next chapter. We will then slow down to match the increasing history (in the sense of the scales offered by people and records), before focusing on the present, and then turning to the future in the concluding chapter. That the future is a cause and subject for most public discussion of history, as with the 2022 war in Ukraine, but not of academic work within that particular discipline, emphasizes the perspective adopted in this book. This perspective is that of the need to consider history as a continuation of past, present, and future, one of necessarily multiple interactions in perception and analysis. Let us turn first to origins.

TWO

—✕—

ORIGIN ACCOUNTS AND
SACRED TIME

It is the privilege of antiquity to mingle divine things with
human, and so to add dignity to the beginnings of cities;
and so if any people ought to be allowed to consecrate
their origins and refer them to a divine source, so great
is the military glory of the Roman People that when they
profess that their Father and the Father of their Founder
was none other than Mars, the nations of the earth may
well submit to this also with as good a grace as they submit
to Rome's dominion.

—Livy, *History of Rome* (27–9 BCE), Book I

THE ESSENTIAL COMPONENT OF HISTORY is the
origin account, that of individuals, families, communities,
and peoples, however defined. In a reflection of anthropo-
logical and sociological frequencies, these accounts take
different, but also repeated, forms. There is also a repetition of content: the standard approach taken in origin accounts, both in terms of narrative and psychologically, is
that of challenges overcome, a process that provides both

narrative and explanation and offers excitement and meaning. This approach links what are too often differentiated as secular and sacred approaches to the past. There are repeated themes of resolve, redemption, and providence, and all are related in a sense of history as having purpose, both specific and overriding, and as involving effort.

Far from being inconsequential in its setting or story, the past is the context for these accounts. To a considerable extent, indeed, the themes are timeless. This is because these accounts are repeated as constants of both human circumstance and divine intention. Furthermore, the past is repeated in this fashion in the collective imagination of the groups, whether as storytellers or as recipients. This is the essential continuity of history, one in which experience is assessed, incorporated, and repeated. This experience is not as some supposedly impartial grasping and repetition of an abstract notion of truth but, rather, as the product of an active process of engagement by those telling the story.

The medium, means, and emphasis of this engagement all vary. Nevertheless, the essentials remain, and they necessarily extend, as an integral part, to the group presentation of the history of others. This is true whether specific groups are at issue or a universal history of creation in time and space. The latter is a task that links religions of the past to all-engrossing secular philosophies of the present. To be valid, both religions and secular philosophies need to cover all of time or, apparently, feel that they should do so. This perceived requirement adds an important compulsion to provide a historiographical span and purpose that is very different to that offered by most academic historians.

With the infinities of universal history requiring interpretation and delimitation, it is not surprising that for most of history the key intermediaries in discovering purpose in time—past, present, and future as well as its signs and other evidence of purpose—were priestly figures. Across time, these figures represented a range of practices, with oracles being particularly significant, as were shamans and other "wise" individuals. Arguably, some modern intellectuals try to play the same role.

This range of intermediary was more complex in polytheistic religions, where it was necessary to consider and discuss the direct and intercessionary role of more gods or godly bodies as well as the potential for intercession with them offered by those able to claim to understand their purpose. This understanding could include the role of the past, not least past wrongs, in present events. Indeed, that was a frequent theme in mythology: the past established a need for redemption through the sacrifice represented by effort, and history was an account of this sacrifice. Metaphors were important to these histories, and there were cross-cultural comparisons, as, for example, with the tasks of Hercules. Furthermore, miracles and the marvelous demonstrated the impact on humans of divine power, support, and displeasure while underlining the extent to which time could be recast in order to show the workings of providence as well as to create a new paradigm of the possible for the future.[1]

The group identity of polytheistic religions, with their complex divine hierarchies and interactions, set a model for human action. For humans to serve the purposes of the gods, it was necessary to have exemplary virtues. Honor was the key spur in Homer's *Iliad*, the account

of an expedition by the Greeks to Troy that was composed in about 700 BCE for public recital and written
down probably in the sixth century, thus becoming a text
that could be reread in a process that reduces the authority of the divine muse who inspires the singer. Although
the gods played the leading roles in the story, pushing
to the fore those humans who could interpret their messages, nevertheless, humans in the *Iliad*, such as Achilles,
made choices—major choices—including in response to
divine injunctions. As a result, these humans took the
consequences.

Separately, there was a real, as well as symbolic, authority in being able to explain, and thus apparently determine, the past. This authority could include skepticism
about particular means for understanding past, present,
and/or future. A key example was skepticism about oracles, as with Quintus Curtius Rufus in his *Histories of
Alexander the Great* (first century CE), a work supposedly
being *All the Books That Survive of the Histories of Alexander the Great of Macedon*. Discussing Alexander the Great
cutting through the Gordian knot rather than unknot-
ting it, Rufus observed, "He either tricked the oracle or
fulfilled it."

Understanding the processes of time through wise
figures can be presented as unending, with modern historical interpretations offering versions in secularized
forms, focused on authority and power and helping affirm both. There was also a frequent continuation in the
approach taken by writers. Support for government was
the most common. For example, the *Kelāb-e Diārbakrīya*
(1469–1478) by Abu Bakr Tihrani, an administrator who
became the court historian of Uzun Hasan (r. 1452–1478),

the leader of the Aq Qoyunlu Turkish tribal confederation, provided a history of the dynasty after it overran Iraq and Iran. This history was important to Tihrani's more general role in creating the dynasty's royal ideology. Enforced changes in ruler or dynasty made this process particularly important, and, indeed, the Aq Qoyunlu were overthrown by the Safavids in the 1500s.

Yet more profoundly, time in the sense of context was not unchanging. Among the key aspects of note was the establishment of the concept of the past and of time thereby as a dividing theme, both to and within the past. Whether with the past as separate, and therefore as a repository of values and lessons, or as linked and capable of affecting the present, the guardianship of the past became more significant as an issue. Ownership of the past secured the future, and longevity implied divine sanction. This was notably so for how far the past could be reinterpreted and to what present end.

In addition, there were important technological and organizational changes, both of which affected not just the context for historical thought and reflection but also their content. Systems of presenting and recording time were established, while graphic and written records of time developed in both present and past, providing the dual purposes and spheres of history. The understanding of time as something that could be recorded was aided greatly by systems for handling numbers and presenting the results.

Religions played a major role in these processes as time became a coherent and explicable record of divine purpose and, linked to that, of the struggle between good and evil. This was the case for individuals and also for society as a whole. Moreover, this purpose literally led to the end of time for both, as death was given a meaning, in terms of the afterlife and also in apocalyptic ideas of the end of human existence. A different change of emphasis in the understanding of time was to come with the fall of polytheistic religions and their replacement by monotheistic ones. This change was of great importance in global history. It was one in which, alongside the top-down religious approach based on conversion, direction, the propagation of doctrine, and the establishment of new organizational structures, came those emphasizing public views and the extent to which they influenced developments, both formally and informally. There was no clear causal relationship between the top-down and popular approaches, but they overlapped, and each approach captures part of the situation.

In monotheistic religious cultures, relations between gods ceased to be a theme. This ensured that history more obviously became a matter of that between a god and humanity. This change could lead to more of an emphasis on the latter. While they tended to have beliefs and practices that did not lend themselves to compromise and incorporation in religious terms, monotheistic religious cultures were more likely to have public ideologies that tended toward unity, if not uniformity. Monotheism eliminated diversity in gods to a single intention for the world. It put an emphasis on the factors affecting compliance.

History, divine and lay, recorded the necessity for the religious outcomes of the then present, and the travails encountered on the way. This recording was an aspect of the degree to which history was an account of the activities of religious figures, not least proselytization and hagiography. In addition, there was perforce the need for historical accounts to respond to divisions between, and within, religions.

Aside from those directly wielding ecclesiastical roles, rulers were generally sacral figures. In the case of Rome and Japan, the rulers asserted their divinity, which was close to the divinely ordained legitimacy argued by most rulers. This situation continued across most of the world until the recent past—Japan, for example, in 1945. In Saudi Arabia, the ruler is the guardian of the holy places of Mecca and Medina. This situation also has echoes, however indirect, in some modern societies that do not claim to be monarchies, for example North Korea. As a consequence, it was unsurprising that in honoring gods, history was also long the project of celebrating rulers and dynasties.

In early recorded history, this was, for example, the case with Egyptian pharaohs and Chinese emperors, both of whom, differently, claimed the Mandate of Heaven. They visually imposed on viewers, not least through accounts of martial triumphs, as with the pharaohs. The celebration of the achievements of one ruler became a history available for his successors.

This valorization of rulers was seen more generally and was reflected in written records, as with the Greek monarchs and leaders involved in the Trojan War. Indeed, Greece was to be a key seedbed of historical writing, a situation it shared with China, in both cases reflecting the significance of a literary culture for the means of historiography and the survival of records accordingly. In each case, history became a means to record providential purpose, establish right and rights, and offer exemplary tales. Hecataeus of Miletus (ca. 550–ca. 476 BCE), the first known Greek historian, left a history that looks at the genealogies of families that claimed to be descended from gods and, although it survives only in fragments, reflects a skepticism about the "many and ludicrous . . . stories of the Greeks."

Religion, history, and statecraft were all linked, as with the Greek historians who followed. Thucydides's account of the Peloponnesian War of 431–404 BCE between Athens and Sparta remains of significance. He wanted his text to be of lasting value, although today that conflict is generally presented by international relations specialists as a somewhat timeless, decontextualized, and clear-cut secular discussion of the rise and fall of states, and Thucydides is cited accordingly. As with other cultures, that of Greece was involved, not simply in the production of historical works, but also in the response to them. Reasoning attracted attention. Thus, Herodotus began his history in about 425 BCE: "This is the display of the research of Herodotus of Halicarnassus, made so that human achievements should not fade with time, and so that great and wondrous deeds displayed by Greeks and barbarians should not be without lasting fame: my particular concern is the reason why they went to war with one another."

There were also variations. In contrast to, for example, Herodotus, Thucydides does not expressly invoke the wrath of the gods to explain why certain events occurred. There is, with Thucydides, moira (fate) as a sort of quasi-divine force, punishing hubris or acts that did not arise from *phronesis* (practical judgment or wisdom), but that is not like the religious underpinning that is in Herodotus and other works.

Texts could be declaimed so that literacy was not a requirement for access. They provided a density of narrative and explication not offered by the recording of triumphs in visual form. The latter, however, were symbolically resonant, as with the depiction of military victories in the stone friezes of Assyrian palaces or in temples of victory. An instance of the latter was that at Himera, a Greek settlement on Sicily, commemorating victory over the Carthaginians in 480 BCE; although, in turn, the Carthaginians destroyed the city in 409 BCE.

Matching the visual capture of action, speech and messages recorded in literary form provided immediacy. Thus, in his account of the Peloponnesian War, Thucydides has Nicias seek aid from Athens for the force at Syracuse in these terms: "Our fleet, as the enemy also have learned, though at first it was in prime condition as regards both the soundness of the ships and the unimpaired condition of the crews, is not so now ... the fleet of the enemy ... keeps us in continual expectation that it will sail against us."

Similarly, in his *Hellenica*, a continuation of Thucydides's account of the war, Xenophon, in recording the last stage of the conflict, noted the significance given to controlling the grain trade in these terms: "Agis, who could see great numbers of grain-ships sailing in to Piraeus [port for Athens], said, that it was useless for his troops to be trying all this long time to shut off the Athenians from access to their land, unless one should occupy also the country from which the grain was coming in by sea."

The conversion narratives involved in the triumphs of religions could play a comparable role to these descriptions of war, also providing excitement and explanation. Texts could be taken further forward by being given dramatic form, as in Greece or in traditional Japanese drama. The history of individuals could be dramatized, as also those of communities. This has remained a prime medium of historical exposition, one seen, moreover, across the visual arts. This process is to the fore with both cinema and television accounts of the past. Drama involves clear, indeed stark, choices rather than ambiguity or nuance. The latter tends to be less popular as an approach and style, however much it may be applauded in scholarship. Drama is the antecedent of television in its format and impact, and this helps explain the nature of television history.

Drama was not in some fashion distinct from religion, a situation prefiguring the major role of morality in modern popular accounts of history, notably, but not only, those of and on religion. This helped lead to drama in the presentation of divine purpose in history. Historical accounts were declamatory in their use of text, not least in public readings during religious ceremonies. Modern religions with a long timescale show this tradition, as with the Jews, for whom the Bible (for Christians this is the Old Testament of the Bible) was the historical record. It provided an account of the special relationship between God and the People of Israel and served as an account of the history of the latter. Group identity and purpose were the key themes in a text in which rulers were valorized insofar as they observed divine intentions and, in doing so, represented their people to God or, for other religions, gods. Thus, rulers such as David, Saul, and Solomon were all located in a history that in practice seemed to have no end.

The scale for most societies was similar to that of ancient Israel. In addition, there were imperial historical consciousnesses based on states with a far more far-flung

temporal potency, one encompassing a number of different peoples but based, at least initially, on one in particular. The differences bound up in the last sentence help
provide the contrasts between the contexts and contents
of historical imaginations. For example, there was a difference between republican and dynastic empires, notably
with Rome. More commonly, the difference was between
empires closely focused on one people, as with China, and
those that ranged more widely territorially or in terms of
the number of peoples encompassed.

In each case, government was in part a matter of ordering people. This process could entail using the people's
accounts of themselves and their history. For example,
the Romans, seeking to understand Gaul (France), which,
under Julius Caesar, they conquered between 58 and 50
BCE, used the tribal names they were offered. In turn,
these tribes retain a pull on French national consciousness, notably in the names of regions and in the characteristics called on by the people that lay claim to their legacy.
This is an aspect of an ancient past that has provided images, mythic or otherwise, that stretch to the present. This
process, however, involves a constant revalidation by later
generations. In large part, this is because the potency and
relevance of the ancient past are far from fixed.

A different form of influence from the past was provided by the use of established models of history writing, which came with an inbuilt authority. As such, there
was a very different practice to that in modern writing,
historical and otherwise, because the emphasis, instead,
now is on new approaches and novel perspectives. That
culture of analysis and explanation, however, can make it
less easy to understand the value, as well as need, in most

historical cultures for a continual use of past models and the assumptions that went with them.

So also with the reference to a classical age of religious activity, as in hagiographies (saints' lives) and other works. These works recounted long-distant episodes but ones supposedly that demonstrated readily transferable providential interventions. This characteristic added to their interest and significance to contemporaries.[2]

Explanation provided issues for writers, with a variety of expedients or devices developed. Thus, at the start of book II of his *Histories* (ca. 100–110 CE), Tacitus observed: "Fortune was already, in an opposite quarter of the world, founding and making ready for a new dynasty, which from its varying destinies brought to the state joy or misery, to the emperors themselves success or doom."[3]

Whatever the explanation, history as an official project, rather than as an individual or collective memory of subjects, focused on authority and power. Its framers therefore had to adjust to conflicts between those wielding power and claiming authority, divine or human, notably so when there were enforced changes in ruler or dynasty. Such changes were frequent in imperial systems, including those of China and Rome, but also more generally.

In China, histories had been submitted for imperial approval and written at least partially under imperial auspices since Sima Qian's *Shiji* (*Records of the Grand Historian*, ca. 94–91 BCE) produced under the Han dynasty (202 BCE–220 CE); and this work excludes much older mythologized "histories" of the "Golden Age" of the Shang dynasty of ca. 1600–1046 BCE. Written on bamboo slips, *Shiji* offered much on individual rulers, with accompanying moral judgments, but also thematic historical

sections on a number of topics, including the calendar and
astronomy, all contributing toward his project to write
all known history. During the Tang dynasty (618–907
CE), much thought was given to historical writing, and
the evolving formal system of producing history reached
its mature form. Although not fully practiced during the
Tang period itself, the Tang system of historical compi-
lation was adopted by all subsequent dynasties and was
followed to a greater rather than a lesser extent.[4]

The assertion of legitimacy was therefore a prime
purpose of history and a reason for the choice among
histories available. For example, the Merovingians, rulers of France from the fifth to eighth centuries—in background "barbarians" but in practice synthesizers—drew
on a range of traditions, including German, Roman, and
Christian ones. Roman and Christian traditions reflected
the situation in Gaul (France) that the Franks had taken
over in the fifth century with the fall of the Western Roman Empire, and these traditions were particularly useful
to the kings as they separated the rulers from the aristocrats by asserting that the dynasty had higher origins
than the aristocrats. The dynasty's distinguished origins
were presented as fact, as in the sixth-century *Decem Li-
bri Historiarum* (*Ten Books of History*), better known as
Historia Francorum, written by Gregory Bishop of Tours.
This provided an account of the Creation, the origins of
Christianity, the story of Saint Martin, and the beginning
of Gregory's see of Tours. Such a standard move from the
general to the particular might appear somewhat absurd,
but in practice, it is also the norm with modern world
histories.

This practice of claiming legitimacy by means of the mandate of success enjoyed by previous dynasties was important in Eurasia, as noted rulers, such as Alexander the Great (336–323 BCE) and Chinggis Khan (1206–1227 CE), left a heritage on which others wished to draw. Thus, Babur, the Mughal conqueror of North India in the 1520s, drew on family links with Chinggis. Conversely, other rulers who lacked such links sought to assert them as with Timur (Tamerlane, 1336–1405). He saw himself as Chinggis's heir and presented his key campaigns as trying to restore the Mongol position. In his eyes, his success as a conqueror had to be validated by such means.

The search for religious and dynastic legitimacy was not just a matter of Eurasian historical consciousness but also seen generally, as in the states of the Sahel in Africa. Thus, the Askia dynasty of Songhai in the sixteenth century CE both asserted its legitimacy and sought to demonstrate a lineage from the earlier empire of Mali, which had expanded from the mid-thirteenth century. The sources for the empire of Mali are more generally instructive as they show the significance of external accounts, in this case by Arab writers: Shihab al-'Umari, Ibn Battuta, and Ibn Khaldun.

China, Rome, the Mongol Empire, and other states saw divisions and agglomerations that posed repeated questions of historical identity, legitimacy, narrative, and outcome. Related to both divisions and agglomerations came the process of adapting to outsiders who rose to power and who then themselves had to adopt and adapt to existing narratives while preserving a degree of their indigenous historical account. This was seen with empires including China and, with its fall in the fifth century, the Western Roman Empire, as well as with smaller states.

In turn, this process was greatly complicated by the religious dimension of such inclusion and also in response to the very different imperialism offered by the extension of religions. For example, the life of Jesus, in the style of a German epic, was the subject of the *Heliand*, a ninth-century CE work in Old Saxon that may have been intended to help ground Christianity in newly converted territory conquered by Charlemagne. This conquest had involved much brutality, as well as the destruction of pagan religious sites, including sacred groves of trees, that offered continuity. Christian proselytism was used by Charlemagne to help validate his conquests.

The contrast between differing religio-historical accounts proved relatively easy to surmount in some cases, for example the barbarian invasions of Christendom mounted by pagans from the fifth to the tenth centuries. Others were difficult, notably the invasions from the seventh century CE made by Muslims. Although there were many instances of borrowing between the narratives and casts of different religions, the Muslims, unlike the barbarians, had a clear historical account that was not subject to ready incorporation by non-Muslim opponents. This was also the case with Islamic advances into South Asia.

At the same time, the extent to which conquest precluded continuity is a matter for debate. For example, it is difficult to distinguish between the consequences of the end of imperial Roman rule, which occurred in western Europe in the fifth century CE, and, on the other hand, the impact of the invaders. For example, there is considerable potential in a long-term approach that understands the Dark Ages in pre-Roman terms and therefore emphasizes the end of imperial Roman rule rather than the impact of the invaders. This approach involves viewing the earlier Romanization as overlying deeper rhythms of continuity in settlement, land use, and trade.

The interplay between deep structures and issues and, on the other hand, more limited episodes is a matter of scholarly debate for this and other periods. Another variable would be to see Hellenism as lasting not only into the Roman Empire but also, after being transformed by Christianity, into the Eastern Roman (Byzantine) Empire, with its capital at Constantinople, modern Istanbul. Yet in contrast to this stress on Greek influences, the lasting impact of Rome on that empire can also be emphasized.

A different aspect of continuity can be found in accounts of Christianization that downplay both abrupt change and top-down direction. Instead, these accounts emphasize, as for example in Egypt, a long process in which existing patterns of worship and belief were supplemented, as well as adapted, under the later Roman Empire. Christians practiced, as a consequence, a religion of amalgamation, as much conscious as not.

Complicating any overall historical consciousness other than in terms of variety, there was an interplay in the Christian Mediterranean between the drive for greatness, including unity within a greater whole, and the strength of regional and local particularism. The former drive and unity were separately presented by Christendom, Byzantium, and the Papacy, and they were to produce a clear consequence in the Crusades that began in the eleventh century CE. This situation, however, left much room not only for tension and disputes at the time but also for differences over historical interpretation. To a degree, the contemporary interplay, and notably the extent of particularism, drew on the decentralized power structure of the post-Roman Mediterranean, but looked at differently, this was also actually the power structure of the late-Roman Mediterranean. Separately, the very issue of continuity directs attention to the problems involved in defining the Dark Ages, which, in some lights, continued until approximately the close of the millennium. This is a more general issue in historical interpretation.

At the same time that these broad patterns developed, the central political questions of dynastic monarchies, Christian, Islamic, and otherwise—namely, the caliber of the ruler and the nature of the succession—ensured a large degree of unpredictability. This volatility went alongside the continuities and similarities offered by sacral monarchy, military leadership, ritual, and the legacies of imperial Rome, as did, even more so in terms of ensuring unpredictability, conflict from the seventh century CE between Christendom and Islam.

Alongside undoubted crisis and specific crises in the Mediterranean world during the Dark Ages, as well as more generally, there was both continuity and areas of new development, both aspects of the significant transition seen in these centuries. This transition qualifies (without destroying) the view that the rise of Islam decisively disrupted Mediterranean unity. Instead, the divisive impact of the conquests linked to this rise, and of the subsequent warfare it caused, can be qualified by reference to intellectual parallels and overlaps, not least of which were the role across the Mediterranean as a whole of Aristotelian philosophy and the extent to which the monotheistic religions influenced each other. Aside from trade between the Christians and Islamic worlds, there was also a shared continuity with aspects of their Roman inheritance.

On the Old Testament pattern, as well as that of other religions, assaults by outsiders could be presented as God testing his people. This, for example, was a key theme in Christian Iberia (Portugal and Spain) to explain the rapid Muslim conquest of much of it from 711. The explanations were religious, providential, and moral, in terms such as the coming of the Antichrist. The same pattern is also seen in the story of Roderic, the last Visigothic king, whose perpetration of rape played a central role in the idea of Muslim conquest as divine judgment, a theme reminiscent, in some respects, of the abduction of Helen in the *Iliad*. The story of Roderic might appear historical. However, in practice, alongside the point that such Muslim conquest was widespread in this period rather than being specific to Iberia, Visigothic failure was specifically due to Muslim strengths as well as to Visigothic divisions and other military commitments, including that against the recalcitrant Basques.

Nevertheless, episodes, such as this conquest of Iberia or the later (and lengthier) Crusades, could be fitted into long-standing patterns. This "fitting in" could be a way in which these episodes were experienced but could also clash with them. Religious interpretations were an instance of them. These interpretations proved potent, as with the Christian Reconquista (Reconquest) that eventually reversed the Muslim conquest of Iberia. The Cantabrian Mountains of northern Spain provided refuge for the

Christians, a refuge that served as the basis for a medieval Christian Iberia defined by war with the Muslims. Rejecting the latter culturally, as well as in political and religious terms, the Christians sought to assert continuity with the Visigoths and, through them, with the Romans. This was a process in part designed to strengthen the legitimacy of new political and ecclesiastical dynasties and institutions. Made at the time, these claims were burnished by history. Thus, Bishop Pelayo of Oviedo (r. 1098/1101–1130) claimed that the relics of major saints were brought north from the Visigoth capital, Toledo, in the time of the kingdom of the Asturias (ca. 718–910). His claims were untrue and were aspects of the truth by fabrication that was important to the assertion of continuity. Separately, the invocation of Visigothic law remained a standard procedure in courts in northern Iberia. The Christian north was also an area in which monasteries were established. Artistic motifs developed, and these were linked to patterns elsewhere in Christendom. Thus, Romanesque-style horseshoe arches featured in the churches built from the ninth century.

Like the tombs of religious figures, relics were a crucial form of legitimation. They were a physical manifestation of the "truth" of the organization legitimized by survival and ownership. Relics were a parallel with the revering of the skulls and bones of ancestors in many cultures, for example several in Oceania. The remains of the great Northumbrian holy man St. Cuthbert were translated into the new cathedral at Durham in 1104, while those of Edward the Confessor were ceremoniously translated to Westminster in 1163. The major victory at Ourique (1139) by Afonso Henriques (later Afonso I), a key episode in Portuguese history linked with the founding monarch, was attributed to Saint James, whose relics are in Santiago de Compostela. Moreover, in Christendom, the relics of saints were to continue to be legitimizing factors until notions of religious authority changed, which, in most cases, was only in the twentieth century. Elsewhere, as in Buddhism, with for example the Buddha's tooth at Kandy in Sri Lanka, relics remain significant. In Islam, so very much does pilgrimage.

The breath of divine support through the events of history could have redemptive power, particularly (although not for Muslims or Jews) in the reconquest for Christendom of Jerusalem in 1099 in the First Crusade.[5] Yet when events were very different—notably as with subsequent failures in the Crusades, specifically the loss of Jerusalem to Saladin in 1187—then the ongoing nature of time within the gates of apocalyptic purpose could take on a very different account. The story of time and the purposes of human history moved in a jerky fashion,[6] one that was beyond human ken but within the direction of God.

Hagiography and history were not separate categories, and chronicles, church, dynastic and urban histories, and saints' lives overlapped and were produced often in the same milieux and/or by the same people. To a degree, history and politics were tranches of theology. In providential cultures, the integration of miracles into explanations was insistent and at all levels. This was true of all religions. Prominent Christian cases included the role of Saint James in helping Spain's Christians defeat the Moors, notably at Clavijo (844), and the part of heavenly armies in the seizure of Antioch by Crusaders in 1098 after a difficult struggle with Seljuk Turks. There was an important physical legacy. Thus, in Portugal, Afonso I founded a major Cistercian monastery at Alcobaça in response to his vow to the Virgin in 1147 to do so if he was able to capture Santarem from the Muslims, as he did that year. In turn, the monastery of Santa Maria da Vitória was built from 1388 to 1434 in fulfillment of John I of Portugal's vow to the Virgin Mary to do so in return for his victory over invading Castilians at Aljubarrota in 1385. Having decisively defeated the Muslims at Salado (1340), Alfonso XI of Castile built a large monastery at Guadalupe in thanks to the Virgin of Guadalupe to whom he had prayed before the battle.

In turn, on a more general pattern with religious history, the verdict of battle could lead to the testing of religious identities including saints and, therefore, the upsetting of their histories. This was the case within religions as well as between them, while the two combined were an important narrative of history. Thus, the Norman conquest of England after the battle of Hastings in 1066 saw a takeover of the English church. Norman ecclesiastics were sometimes uneasy about the cults associated with their new monastic houses, especially about English saints unknown beyond their own localities, for whom little written evidence, in the form of saints' lives, was available. Paul of Caen, abbot of St. Albans from 1077 to 1093, was accused of slighting the tombs of his predecessors, whom he referred to as uneducated simpletons, but he did not eject the relics of the saints of St. Albans from the church. The abbots of Abingdon and Malmesbury were also skeptical, while Archbishop Lanfranc of Canterbury had to be persuaded that a predecessor, St. Alphege (Aelfheah), killed by the invading Danes in 1012, was worthy of veneration. Anglo-Saxon relics were sometimes tested by fire, as at Evesham, although those that survived the test, as did, in this instance, the relics of St. Equine, were reinstated in new shrines.

This unease about the authenticity of some relics was itself part of a wider Christian suspicion about saints whose existence was obscure and undocumented and thus an aspect of a new historical "proving." In terms of saints, there have been a number of different stages of "proving." As with much else in history, ideas, practices, and outcomes that to some were primitive or primitivist were no longer acceptable, only to be replaced by others that, in turn, could subsequently be considered deeply problematic.

In twelfth-century England, a sense of Anglo-Norman identity and continuity was consciously developed, with Englishness and Britishness now being seen not in a negative light as by the early Normans but, rather, as memorable bases for a glorious present. The historical perspective was in large part constructed by clerics who had personal links with Anglo-Saxon England. The cult of saints, like the emphasis on monastic and ecclesiastical history, necessarily sought continuity and therefore looked to the Anglo-Saxon past. In the work of Geoffrey of Monmouth (d. ca. 1155), Anglo-Norman England latched on to a British past, as in his *Historia Regum Britanniae* (ca. 1136), which traced events from the legendary founding of Britain by Aeneas of Troy's grandson, Brutus, a heritage also traced elsewhere.[7] Geoffrey of Monmouth also greatly developed the Arthurian legend: Arthur's father was now said to be a descendant of Constantine the Great, who had converted the Roman Empire to Christianity, as well as, somehow, a conqueror of the French and the Romans. By the early eleventh century, a measure of celebration of the pre-Norman past was in order. However, the position had been very different in the aftermath of the Norman Conquest. It was only once Norman rule was established that the focus could shift to adaptability and continuity.[8]

Politico-religious contrasts between societies generally took precedence over those of historical method, which more frequently tended to be shared. For the last, the chronicle was the key approach, whether in China or Christendom. Moreover, the pattern of such writing included that of commenting on earlier accounts. This was seen, for example, with Islamic and Talmudic (Jewish) commentary, the latter commentary on the Torah and on subsequent rabbinic disputation. It was also a feature of Christian legal interpretation and of the use of earlier classical historians in later accounts.

A differing form of chronicle, but one still with that basis, was provided in the oral historical traditions of societies that lacked writing, for example Australian dream narratives depicting ancestral stories and beings and New Zealand kin histories. These differently captured the identification of people with places that were to be so important to the historical consciousness. Many Maori names in New Zealand could be understood only through their connection with other names and places there. These connections commemorated events such as journeys and related to an oral world of stories. The attempt to depict the experience of a colonized population and to present the oral-historical tradition is easier in New Zealand than in most of the world: colonization is relatively recent and much of the indigenous population survives. The oral tradition is accessible, both from nineteenth-century European records and because it is still alive today, while there is a large degree of cultural and complete linguistic homogeneity among the Maori. The theme of how linkages between place and people had occurred was also important to other historical accounts, for example in Oceania.

Similarly, Icelandic sagas were old tales, from 850 CE onward, that were memorized and retold across the centuries and were commuted to writing in the forms now preserved from the twelfth century. The sagas record the life and strife of Iceland as well as the Norse Atlantic explorers. Written in the vernacular, they focus often on feuds and honor. The *Greenland* and *Erik the Red* sagas, which differ in their accounts of which explorer came first, were probably not written down until about 1300 and therefore reflect embellishment after the tenth-century events they discuss.

The situation is far less accessible in many areas, in part due to the fragmentary nature of the remaining members of the indigenous society and the extent to which the process of assimilation was pushed with great energy in the past. Linkages between places and peoples in the past would presumably have been the case for societies for which records are absent. Again, as an instance of the intertwining, in this case, of the spiritual with the human, landscape, and universe, like human and sacred time, were not understood or apparently treated as distinct or separate. Thus, the landscape included entrances to the underworld and tales of such journeys, as on the Pacific island of New Caledonia or a variety of European sites, such as Lake Avernus near Naples.

That many or most understandings and accounts of history were not reproduced in manuscript or print in no way decreases their accuracy or significance, although printing does make the creation of a readily repeatable version far easier. Despite the question of how best to use oral tradition (and also material evidence in the shape of archaeological artifacts), oral culture is not necessarily deficient as a means for constructing, describing, and analyzing chronological relationships. Indeed, it is the basis of the essential aspect of historical understanding, that of verbal culture, notably speech. Prior to the recent use of sound recordings, the taking down of such speech was patchy and scarcely based on systematic sampling. Yet this is the key way in which experience is recorded, ordered, and transmitted. It is not so much the first stage of history but generally the only stage and should therefore come foremost in the discussion of historical method and historiography.

Moreover, the written word of the past (and present) is scarcely autonomous from oral culture. Indeed, many written records are basically gossip, some reliable but much not. Both oral culture and the written material convey myths and remnants, the former deliberately presenting a particular narrative, the latter providing evidence, sometimes encoded within myth, from which a picture of what actually happened can be pieced together critically.

There is also the relationship between visual and written accounts. In societies such as ancient Egypt and Aztec Mexico, there were picture stories in cartoon-strip style that moved in time and place in what they were discussing. Individual cultures had histories that reflected social norms. Thus, the Inca of South America, the imperial power of the Andean chain in the fifteenth century, treated their histories as statements of sociopolitical

hierarchy and cosmology rather than as event-based histories.[9] Histories were compressed, actions were inherited, and past acts were recast in terms of contemporane-
ous political power structures.

The Inca method of recording history was through
the use of the *quipu* (also spelled *khipu*), knotted cords
that were mnemonic devices to jog the *quipu* recipient's
memory, although there is a lack of clarity on their usage.
As an instructive qualification of standard preferences for
accuracy, different Inca accounts told to the Spaniards
attributed the same conquest to different rulers and thus
Spanish chroniclers complained about discrepancies in
what they were told, which indeed was affected by the
Inca origin-myth and its relation to dynastic history.[10] In
addition, the conventional Inca history does not accord
with radiocarbon dates. The development of carbon-14
dating from 1947 proved especially significant. Scientific
archaeological methods such as pollen analysis proved
very important to the dating of prehistoric cultures. Such
dating is an instance of how early histories can be tested
as a result of recent technologies, this process being an
instance of historiographical variance.

The significance of such testing has been increased and
complicated by the variety in surviving sources. In particular, hunting and gathering communities are generally
poorly documented in the archaeological record, as are, to
a considerable extent, regions, such as Amazonia, where
state structures were poorly developed.

Although, within both parts of the world and on the
global scale, they might be similar in method, foundation myths were specific as to episode and place. They all
conveyed a form of magic. That might seem primitive,

but modern belief systems also have instructive logics. Saint Denis, the first bishop of Lutetia (Paris), was allegedly beheaded by the Romans around 250 on the hill of Montmartre before picking up his head and walking while preaching. According to tradition, he died at the site where a chapel was established by Sainte Geneviève in 475 and where the present Basilica of Saint-Denis stands. The first king to be buried in it was the Frankish Dagobert I, who died in 639.

Place existed and was understood in space and time. There was an important and mutually reinforcing analogy between ideas of time and those of space. Notions of distance and scale that are regarded as axiomatic in modern geographical culture were not present. Indeed, maps made in traditional cultures did (and do) not incorporate the abstract projection, coordinate geometrics, and measured space that we now associate with mapping. Instead, in the traditional spatial imagination, concepts of linearity, center and periphery, contiguity, and connectedness are far more relevant than coordinate locations in an abstract, infinite plane, which is the modern system. Memory, rather than surveying, was important to this mental mapping. This was a situation with a clear parallel with that in history. Linked to both, a high proportion of historical accounts were in the form of itineraries: journeys through time and space, for example *Exodus* in the Old Testament of the Bible or Homer's *Odyssey*. These provided accounts of overcoming adversity, which were another source of legitimation.

While peoples had different itineraries, converging and reflecting contrasting identities, there were also differences in terms of distinctive systems of recording time and therefore envisaging how it would be recorded. These systems were related, as human time sat within its divine counterpart. In the case of sacral monarchies, the combination was more direct and helped explain dating in terms of the regnal years of divinely mandated rulers, as in the fourth year of Egbert's reign. At the same time, these periods were connected to create the greater pattern of divine dispensation. This was done with the divine creation of continuing human time and also by taking chosen humans into an afterlife that was continuous until amplified and transformed by divine intervention to end human time. Thus, apocalyptic beliefs brought to a crisis views of indefinite time.[11]

At the same time, and again as with the case in the modern age, the theme of the identification of people with places had to incorporate the degree to which there was often the need for a synthesis, however partial and/or coerced, of differing traditions. This was seen, for example, with the advance of Islam into South Asia from the seventh century and also with the character and significance of the Buddhist tradition there. These were instances of the repeated extent to which the historical consciousness in particular areas was greatly affected by change in the shape of political events and the often related migration of peoples and religious practices.

Far from this being simply an aspect of the distant past, large-scale migrations linked to politics remain highly significant, as in the bloody partition of British India in 1947 into the states of India and Pakistan. Moreover, war and, separately, environmental pressures are likely to continue to cause large-scale population moves and more so in scale than in the past. These moves will create contexts for new, as it were, historiographic units, in the sense of political contexts within which accounts of history are created and disseminated. The political nature of this context will not necessarily be a new sovereign state, as were Israel and Pakistan in the 1940s, but may be a matter of significant ethnic groups that retain an identity within such states.

Discussion of changes in the character and nature of historical writing is greatly complicated by issues of source survival and signification. Surviving sources can include material from and/or evidence of lost originals, for example the *History of Babylonia* published in about 290 BCE by Berossus, an indication of what has been lost. There is also the need to argue from where there are no records of historical works, however indirect, a situation that can encourage forgeries. There are, moreover, differences as to the definition of such works and over how historical records can be assessed.

It is very easy to adopt a developmental model of historiography predicated in particular on the replacement of chronicles by the coverage of shorter periods of time, combined with a degree of secularization, in the shape of explanations of events that were not made in terms of direct interventions by divine figures. Yet, this approach arguably tells us more about current emphases in assessment, important as they are, than about past views. Moreover, as an account of modern attitudes, these emphases can be more valid in some settings than others. Related to this, the extent to which formal historical writings in the past captured a wider consciousness is unclear. Certainly, they were only read by a minority, not least because literacy was very limited. In addition, these formal historical writings in the past are open to different definitions, as, indeed, to a degree, are those of the present.

It is likely, instead, that, however difficult to access, the collective memory of communities was the key element, and that this was especially the case when there had been a violent past to assimilate. Indeed, it was probably in response to threats and rule that could be perceived as foreign that a sense of history was particularly clearly defined. In China, the long and brutal conquest by the Mongols in the thirteenth century provided the basis for a potent sense of difference in the fourteenth century when there was a successful rebellion against Mongol rule, even though the resulting Ming dynasty under its first ruler, Zhu Yuanzhang (r. 1368–1398), also sought to maintain links with the Mongol system as part of an attempt to draw on a number of backgrounds for support.[12] These varied aspects of response to conquest can also be seen in other episodes of rebellion.

Opposition to conquest was a key theme, as with the successful Japanese resistance to Chinese attack in the thirteenth century, or that of Scotland to rule from the king of England from the 1290s. How far such views were also present in literature was a matter of the local literary practice and culture, as well as of particular circumstances. The issues would have been given an additional level of antipathy had there been religious difference as well.

Thus, politics helped provide a background for historical awareness and that in the context of what can be presented as a solidarity amounting to protonationalism— a solidarity stretching across space and time. Yet, that same description can be applied, instead, to a "sectarian interest," possibly opposed to a nation-state or state or nation, although such an interest, in many respects, is also a protonation. Moreover, this concept of protonationalism risks suggesting a developmental, indeed teleological, model, one in which nationalism is regarded as a necessary stage in development from protonationalism, with the latter also giving nationalism a longer history and relevance. It might, instead, be more appropriate to see all aspects of large-group organization based on a sense of commonality and community as nationalistic, with the latter then taking different forms from antiquity onward.

The identity of the nation then becomes a key element of the present (whenever that is), an element that is grounded in the past and defined accordingly, although there was competition and rivalry in this definition of the nation. A focus on group ancestry was an important aspect of the identification and can be seen as more significant prior to the nineteenth century, when, however, ethnicity was intellectually a more developed concept. Contemporary and subsequent use could be readily made of the histories of these groups. For example, Saxo Grammaticus's late twelfth-century *History of the Danes* served to provide a valorous history in which accounts of an older Denmark defying demons and warlocks, holding off the Roman Empire, and dominating the Baltic could serve as a justification, by parallel, for then modern Denmark conquering the heathen Wends, resisting the orbit of Frederick Barbarossa (r. 1152–1190) and the Holy Roman Empire, and acting as a major Baltic power.

Group ancestry, a part of genealogy along with patriotism, was also a theme in the writing of history by the use with some writers of the vernacular. In France, writing in the vernacular became common from the mid-thirteenth century, with texts such as the *Histoire Ancienne* and the *Grandes Chroniques de France*. However, such a use was not necessary for protonationalism. Moreover, many independent nations were to continue to use the language of (former) opponents and past imperial rulers, as with English in America.

At the same time as the protonation, there was the existence of other types of history linked to particular individual and group identities. Urban history was a key instance, with distinctiveness, prestige, and rights, all variously bound up in historical accounts. There was also a clear need for origin accounts. In his *The Divine Comedy*, begun in about 1307, Dante Alighieri provided an account of the origins of the poet Virgil's home town, Mantua, an account that emphasized the vitality of individual origin myths and the role of the occult. Manto, the sorceress, is described as traveling and finding a marshy part of the Mincio valley where she settled: "In time the scattered people round about collected at that town, secure and strong by virtue of the marshland on all sides, where, over those dead bones, they built a town." In fact, less dramatically, the city was settled by the Etruscans in the tenth century BCE.

Similar accounts were also recorded for the origins of specific institutions, such as individual religious sites. They recorded events, spiritual and/or secular, in so far as the two were separable, and also sought to present their history in order to maintain privileges and gain new ones. Writings were produced in order to authenticate their holdings of lands and the credentials of their saints. These offered defense against secular power and other church authority.

There was also the particular identity of social groups, and the privileges and rights thereby pertaining, including those from groups previously dispossessed. This was not just a matter of landownership and, more generally, of rights to particular jobs and revenues, but also of the prestige and privileges of lineage. The antiquity of lineage was a key theme in family sagas,[13] one that looks toward current interest in family history. Indeed, in Britain, genealogy vies with military campaign accounts as the most popular forms of history, although they are both largely ignored by academics. Britain is far from alone, although the modern historiography of genealogy attracts very little interest, and comparative statements on the topic are largely impressionistic.

The socially skewed nature of the subject was more apparent in the past. Thus, in England, the College of Arms, founded in 1484, was the official heraldic authority, with power, delegated by the Crown, to judge relevant issues, notably determining disputes but also granting new coats of arms. It held heraldic visitations that legitimized family history through the authentication of pedigrees. In Venice, the oligarchic Patriciate, their name inscribed in the "Golden Book of Venice," controlled the Senate and government until the republic came to an enforced end in 1797.

The ancestor pride and dynasticism involved in genealogical history was amply seen with individual families, notably aristocratic ones. It was a way to assert links and past service. Thus, in 1685, proud of his Plantagenet descent, Henry, Seventh Duke of Norfolk, put up a memorial pillar at the site of the death in 1307 of Edward I in Burgh-by-Sands. Edward had been a warrior king and the celebration of valor was important for family history across all social ranks. Lethbridge's *Golden Book of India* (1893) authenticated the dynastic pedigrees of Indian ruling families.

Such celebration was also significant for groups including, as an aspect of an extended tribalism, nations. This celebration could draw on the supposed achievements of individuals. Thus, Rodrigo Díaz de Vivar, known later as El Cid, a Castilian noble (d. 1099) who, in practice, was a mercenary and then an independent entrepreneur of territorial power, became in the perspective of history a role model, as in the anonymous twelfth-century Castilian poem *El Cantar del Mio Cid*. A man who reflected the opportunities and opportunism of frontier society, fighting both Moors and other Christians, was turned into a heroic but virtuous warrior. His fame was to be commemorated across the range of genres, including in Pierre Corneille's play *Le Cid* (1636), in Jules Massenet's opera *Le Cid* (1885), in a 1961 blockbuster film, in a song in 1979 by the Spanish rock band Crack, and in a 2020–2021 Spanish television series as well as in various video games. Politics played a role, as in the major sculpture erected in Burgos, his burial site, in 1954. This was during the Franco dictatorship, and El Cid appeared an appropriate historical reference point as a warrior for Christianity that matched Franco's self-presentation; El Cid could be readily presented as heroic unlike the other (albeit fictional) famous Spanish knight of Miguel de Cervantes's creation, Don Quixote, the protagonist in the eponymous novel published in 1605–1615, a novel rich in ironies and not an appropriate reference point for Franco.

As is to be expected, evidence is patchy for the range of historical consciousness that existed prior to 1500 CE, the

period of this chapter. As one element, the continuities
of societies in a world operating within largely consistent technological constraints, and with strong dominant
ideologies and societies demonstrating great durability,
affected the content and setting of historical accounts.
These took a variety of forms. For example, buildings, notably major ones, were used throughout and often reused.
In Syracuse, the cathedral, still used today, was built by
the seventh century CE over the Temple of Athena, which
had been built in the fifth century BCE and incorporated
some of that building. Also in Italy, the Church of Sant'
Andrea in Orvieto, where Martin IV was crowned pope
in 1281, was built in the seventh century CE on the site of a
Roman temple built, in turn, on walls that were Etruscan.

Symbolic sites were found more generally, as in places
of coronation, which, for kings of Germanica from 936
until 1562, was Aachen, earlier the capital and place of
burial of the Frankish ruler Charlemagne (r. 771–814),
who had been crowned "Emperor of the Romans" in 800.
In the quest to restore the authority of the Roman Empire, Charlemagne had consciously sought to emulate the
Byzantine (Eastern) Roman Empire. In turn, his relics
were placed in a gold shrine in the building when Frederick II was crowned in 1215. This was part of the more
general process of endorsement by ritual and the white
magic of relics.

Charlemagne's court at Aachen, and his role as emperor, ensured that he cannot comfortably be annexed
to French history, although that has never stopped the
attempt, largely due to his prestige but in part because
his policies had an impact in what subsequently became
France. Later kings of France were to be given the Sword

of Charlemagne at their coronation and to be crowned with what was termed the Crown of Charlemagne, which was probably made for his grandson Charles the Bald. The last of the Carolingian dynasty (that of Charlemagne) of France was succeeded in 987 by Hugh Capet, a Carolingian grandson but not the dynastically most appropriate Carolingian. However, Capet was a more clearly French candidate and benefited from the role in identity provided by important local saints, notably Martin and Denis, with the prelates of northern France being his key supporters. These were to become national saints.

As a reminder of the variety of narratives and contexts even in the relatively confined case of Western European kingship, the Capetians offered a different legacy to the Norman and later Angevin kings of England, who were representatives of a type of monarchy in which the king was, first and foremost, "lord" and then administrator of a mass of wealth and power. In contrast, the Capetians derived their power from atavistic roots in tribe and nation and from laying an emphasis on the holiness of the king's person. Ancestors and epic leaders from the past appeared in the tomb effigies in the choirs of the Basilicas of Saint-Denis (Paris) and Saint-Remi (Rheims). The sacrality of the Capetian kings was emphasized by their anointment with the holy oil reputedly brought down from heaven by a dove for the anointing of Clovis (baptized a Catholic in 508) that thereafter miraculously reproduced itself.

This myth invested the Capetian kings with immense mystique, a mystique with which the English kings, who were short of origin myths, notably of links with the prestige of imperial Rome, could not compete, although, like the Capetians, they claimed the power of touch for the king's evil, the skin disease scrofula. At the same time, for both kings of France and of England, dynastic objectives were largely hereditary ones, not least in terms of prestige and rank. Moreover, English monarchs sought to adopt and adapt origin myths, history in the shape both of the past and of accounts thereof proving characteristically plastic or malleable. The Norman monarchs (r. 1066–1154) sought to claim the historical inheritance of Old English kingship, in part by their support of religious foundations linked to this kingship. This process was taken forward by the sponsorship of historical writing.

Later kings, especially Henry III (r. 1216–1272) and Edward III (r. 1327–1377), very much supported such activity and added fresh initiatives of their own. Edward used the Arthurian legend to provide the authority of age for his embrace of chivalric ideals. This was seen with the establishment of the Order of the Garter in 1348–1349 and the foundation of the College of St. George to serve the royal chapel in Windsor Castle. This chapel was rededicated to St. George, whom Edward chose as the patron saint for the order. Edward's sense of royal dignity was powerfully informed by mythological and historical models of knighthood and kingship. The set of great classical, biblical, and Christian heroes known as the Nine Worthies became a popular convention in literature and art during the fourteenth century.[14]

The linkage of saint and nation in the cult of St. George was intended to bring prestige and success and thus provided a form of white magic for nationalism, one that certainly still resonated for some during wartime in the twentieth century. In turn, Henry VI (r. 1422–1461, 1470–1471) sought to have the ninth-century king Alfred of Wessex canonized, while the fastest-growing cult in early Tudor England was that of Henry VI, to whom miracles were attributed and who was informally regarded as a saint and martyr.

The nature of monarchy interacted with the question of group identity or nationalism and the degree to which it could provide a historical consciousness as well as one derived from history. Nationalism is frequently discussed as a product of the last quarter millennium, not least with the argument that the sense of collective identity that existed within the framework of the earlier monarchical state took a different form from that to be found in the nineteenth-century nation-state with the theme of ethnicity more developed in the last. However, many of the characteristics of nationalism, including a collective name, shared history, a distinctive common culture, an association with a specific territory, and a sense of solidarity, can be seen earlier. For example, in England and France, Trojan ancestry was regarded as a way to argue that prestige and legitimacy did not derive from the Holy Roman Empire. Thus, classical history could be deployed against *Romanitas*, the legacy of Rome. The sharing of circumstances arising from events, however much real or imaginary, as well as the political cohesion created by a common ruler, were all important elements in a historically derived identity. This is what is at stake in much of the governmental use of history in the present day.

This process of historical identification can be seen with the fate of Magna Carta, the 1215 charter of English liberties that was a wide-ranging condemnation of King John's use of feudal, judicial, and other governmental powers, a condemnation that defined and limited royal rights.

Magna Carta was in effect an enormous list of everything that was wrong with government as John (r. 1199–1216) had applied it, notably arbitrary royal action. This agreement forced from the king by baronial opponents, was a limitation in written form of royal rights. It thereby came to be seen as a charter of liberties and a rejection of the "Norman Yoke." Moreover, Magna Carta had a long and lasting resonance, playing a key role in a narrative of the nation and was thus occasion and process, event and symbol—a combination that is of particular historical resonance. By creating a new relationship between the king and the law that was in effect England's first written constitution, Magna Carta asserted the importance of placing royal power under the law, and freemen were provided with some guarantees against arbitrary royal action.

Like many documents that came to be seen as foundational, Magna Carta was to acquire totemic significance, being cited by opponents of what was presented as arbitrary government power. This was seen, for example, in the extent to which the new state of America established in 1776 from thirteen British colonies drew on this relevant English history, just, of course, as some New World colonies that did not rebel also did. The English Common Law lawyers, such as Sir Edward Coke (1552–1634), chief justice of the King's Bench (1613–1616) and author of the *Institutes of the Laws of England*, who had played the leading role in discovering a new political role for Magna Carta in the early seventeenth century, were heavily involved in drafting the charters of the English colonies established in North America. The rejection of George III from 1775 to 1783 by many of the North American colonists was regarded as another instance of the opposition to King John, over a half millennium earlier, and thus a rejection of unwarranted royal power.

The transfer of the English historical account to that of British colonies was an aspect of the established pattern in which such accounts were applied within political and religious empires, however defined. The nature of the transfer has varied greatly through history, as has the context, notably whether there were settlement colonies and/ or wars of independence. Moreover, the extent to which there was a usable historical myth, and for whom, varied. This political project, however, was more significant than the focus on particular scholars that dominates standard historiography.

The hostility to the Norman Yoke was also very much seen in the later treatment of Magna Carta, a treatment that provided a lasting basis for an assertion of Englishness. This was not only a question of the seventeenth and eighteenth centuries. Echoes are still offered. A poll conducted for *BBC History Magazine*, and reported in its June 2006 issue, offered a choice of ten days for "On what historical day do you think Britain should celebrate British Day?" and elicited the highest response for Magna Carta Day, June 15. On March 12, 2014, Tim Berners-Lee, speaking on BBC Radio Four, called for a "Magna Carta–like Charter of Rights" to guarantee rights on the web. Also that year, at a time of concern over alleged Islamic penetration of secondary education, David Cameron, the prime minister (r. 2010–2016), ordered that every school pupil be taught the "British values" enshrined in Magna Carta, adding that its principles "paved the way for the democracy, the equality, the respect, and the laws that make Britain, Britain" and that he would make the eight hundredth anniversary the centerpiece of a fight back against extremism. It was as if Magna Carta was a foundation document and had become a substitute for a written constitution. This provided an indication of earlier processes for similar or other agreements, when evidence for such processes is limited.

The range of historical consciousness remains the case to the present. The evidence for this range and content is obviously in part a matter of what from the past and in the past, whether factual, fictional or in-between, attracts attention. A key source is that of legal cases, which usually in the past related to specific historical privileges rather than to general concepts of universal human rights. This situation ensured that the administration of justice offered a prime record of changing emphases in historical consciousness. However, as with the presentation of the workings of divine providence, the preservation of legal privileges was done within a context in which continuity was the main point: there was no, or scant, value attached to change through time and little to be gained through implying that it was possible.

If that situation is provided as an ancien régime of history, the designation is not intended to suggest anachronism or anything equivalent. Instead, a fitness for purpose is the key theme for the provision of historical opinion, albeit purpose owing much to the ideology and interests of those providing and receiving the histories in question. Rather than focusing on the methods employed by academics or, separately, the questions of relative accuracy, historiography can then be understood in part as a matter of changes in these ideologies and interests while allowing for the autonomy of those who provided the historical "product." The latter was not just a matter of formal historical writings but covered a range of cultural and social products and practices. Thus, contextual alterations for these products and practices—in the shape, for example, of the mass urbanization of the nineteenth century and the sociability and large-scale literacy it made possible—were key elements in the development of history in so far as the latter is understood as the discussion and understanding of the past.

Prior to that, changes in religious beliefs were the key element in the development of specific historical consciousnesses. Redemptive figures, such as Christ, Muhammad, and Buddha, offered a structuring of time. Thus, the standard Western narrative was the Christian timescale. This had the era before Christ's mission as laying a path to his ministry so that Rome, under whose rule Christ was crucified, could be written into a Christian story as the canvas across which providential history unfolded. This approach was important for how Christianity understood and presented history, especially history outside its own sphere, notably the preceding pagan world. Nevertheless, Christ's mission was a crucial historical moment in that history. It was to be followed by a period from the Resurrection that was a "vale of tears" until Christ's Second Coming, with no real chronological distinctions in this period.

As a result of this sense of continuity, what could later be seen as white magic was potent, and its celebration was valuable. For example, in the empire created by Charlemagne in 800 CE, imperial rule was seen as particularly sacral, not least due to the possession of relics such as the Holy Lance. This sacral character was an aspect of providential time, in that the idea of the *translatio imperii* (transfer of rule) represented the need to carry forward in the new empire those aspects of classical Rome under which the Christian message had been propagated and which, therefore, had a providential significance.

Seen as immortal, religious figures acted across time, and were celebrated in the arts as doing so. For example, in the Church of St Augustine in San Gimignano in Italy, Benozzo Gozzoli (ca. 1421–1497) painted in 1464–1466 a fresco showing Saint Sebastian intervening to protect the city against the 1464 plague epidemic. The church itself dates from the thirteenth century, while Saint Sebastian was a third-century Christian saint. Also seen with other religions, such direct references across time were very common and undermined any sense of time as linear or of past experience or relevance as separated from the present by time passing. The latter element of the continued immediacy of the past is also common with much of the current usage of the past. Again, this is the case irrespective of scholarly cultures and methods. The presentation of identity in terms of continuity sees this element particularly strong. So also do readings of the past to which historic claims are relevant or those with the popular usage of the past in which a form of alleged inherited guilt plays a role. It is fair to say that much of the modern Western scholarly approach to historiography is very different in its presuppositions and content, being secularist in ideology, tone, and value, as well as academic in setting and style.

That approach is not the sole discontinuity of relevance to our history. In terms of Christendom, there had been different Christian emphases at issue earlier. In particular, moving from any account of human time that presented the Apocalypse as imminent, entailed not simply postponing the millennial end of human time but also reconceptualizing development during the resulting period. In part, such a reconceptualization was not simply a matter of Apocalypse Postponed but also a product of a sense of the separateness of the past from the present.[15] This was a separateness that was very much qualified, if not resisted, in religions and, differently, both in fiction and in some of the sense, notably the popular sense, of what was entailed by history.

This separateness did not itself necessarily lead to the modern concept of a linear development through the present to an imagined future. Yet, there were instances of such ideas, as in the *Geography* (7 BCE), by Strabo, a wide-ranging Greek geographer (ca. 63 BCE–ca. 23 CE). Writing in an increasingly Roman-controlled wider Mediterranean, referring back to Plato, a key figure of Greek intellectual authority, he observed:

> Plato conjectures that after the time of the floods three kinds of civilisation were formed: the first, that on the mountain-tops, which was simple and wild, when men were in fear of the waters which still deeply covered the plains; the second, that on the foothills, when men were now gradually taking courage because the plains were beginning to be relieved of the waters; and the third, that in the plains. One might speak equally of a fourth and fifth, or even more, but last of all that on the sea-coast and in the islands, when men had been finally released from all such fear; for the greater or less courage they took in approaching the sea would indicate several different stages of civilisation and manners.

This relationship between civilization and the shore was different to that offered in the histories of societies in

Oceania. Yet, there was a common theme of the human relationship with perceptions of the environment.

Despite the linear development suggested by Strabo, cyclical theories of time, of a present rerunning of the past, and of a future returning to the present and/or the past, were long more dominant. Moreover, such assumptions are still to the fore in many societies, for example those in the Arab Middle East. These theories made sense of astronomical movements, of the seasons (which were so important to agriculture), and of creation and revival myths. The idea of the sacrifice and rebirth of god(s) was an aspect of these myths and thus central to the history offered.

In turn, cyclical ideas could be reworked in a surprising fashion. Thus, in his *A Brief Account of the Intended Bank of England* (1694), Michael Godfrey, argued that it would "enable the government and people of England to revive, recover, and transmit to posterity, the virtue, lustre, and wonted glory, of their renowned ancestors; and to lay a foundation of trade, security, and greatness within the kingdom, for the present and succeeding ages." Cyclical theories were also a reflection of the prominent role of the past as a source of legitimacy, authority, and reference: the past as context, frame of reference, and content. This role of the past, however, could entail a variety of references. Thus, the Italian Renaissance of the fifteenth century saw a strengthening of interest in, knowledge about, and the depiction of the achievements of pre-Christian classical thinkers, artists, and authors.

At the same time, there could be a melding of influences when referring to the past, a melding that, in turn, created a new frame of reference. For example, drawing on the up-to-date geographical information of the period, information greatly enhanced by the Renaissance and its emphasis on classical understanding, notably that the world was a sphere, Christopher Columbus (ca. 1451–1505) set sail westward in 1492, hoping to reach East Asia, the lands explored by Marco Polo, and raise money to retake the Holy Land from Islam. This goal was regarded as a crucial preliminary to the Second Coming of Christ and, thus, to the redemption of the Christian world. In his *Book of Prophecies*, compiled before his fourth voyage to the Caribbean, in 1502, Columbus argued that the end of the world would occur in 155 years and that his own discoveries had been foretold in the Bible. The latter was an instructive means of asserting personal significance. The contrast with the frame of reference today is notable, although it can leave narcissists at a disadvantage. Many, instead, now prefer to claim that they will be "vindicated by history," a notion, for example, employed by Tony Blair, British prime minister from 1994 to 2007, and Jacques Chirac, French president from 1995 to 2007.

Millenarian ideas similar to those of Columbus were voiced by other figures prominent in European exploration, such as Prince Henry the Navigator of Portugal (1394–1460).[16] For long, that approach was downplayed, and notably so by Anglo-American historians, because it did not match the idea of exploration as modern, rational, and progressive. Yet, as this issue suggests, the parameters adopted to locate past episodes can reflect intellectual assumptions and strategies that are as problematic as what can be attributed when discussing governments in the past more generally. *As* may be a qualitative term that goes too far, but possibly not; there is no real criteria available for assessing this in a timeless fashion.

Separately, returning to millenarian beliefs, their presence did not prevent the argument that it was necessary to think carefully about how choices in the present would work out. Doing so was a means to regard the past as having consequences but also as gone. That practice, however, was lessened by the cultural norms of a past presence or presence of the past, as with ancestors worship and religious perceptions.

To adopt a different approach, at once functional and ideological, history operated, in large part, as an aspect of community agencies for the assimilation of information, with the latter understood as derived from the past as much as the present. This process put an emphasis on the experience of the past and, linked to that, of memory. Such a practice, indeed culture, was encouraged by age-related hierarchies. Societies generally focused on the authority of older males, and these males wielded power in families, communities, and society as a whole, both secular and spiritual.

To suggest some shift, abrupt or other, from this situation to a modernity of empirically derived rational assessments, one predicated on an assumption of transformation through improvement across time, provides both a conventional way to approach modernity and a means to locate and historicize premodernity accordingly. However, that time view is a simplistic and only partial account of the modern; and (at once linked, but also separate) a caricature of the complexity and attitudes of earlier ages.

That emphasis on modernization is implicit, if not explicit, in some, or rather many, approaches to historiography and, indeed, in the designation of modernization as a means to approach the past and, therefore, the subject of history. In this approach, the governmental and popular failings in the approach to the past that can be described, if not castigated, are, in reality, frequently matched by the failings of academic and institutional practice. This is notably so in the adoption by many of a simplistic account of what does not match the apparent desiderata of historical modernization. Thus, for example, with the current emphasis on a modern typology of social and cultural history as deserving prominence and the comparative lack of interest in older historical interests and methods, such as constitutional history and philology. More generally, as history is about change over time, it is unsurprising that there is a tendency to equate it with modernization. However, the conceptual slippage represented by that tendency is flawed.

Focusing any discussion of history on modernization simultaneously provides a teleological account of change and a simplification, if not neglect, of the premodern, which in the standard Western account ends in about 1450–1500. However, this chapter has argued that the historical understandings shown during this very long period are not separate to those seen subsequently. Instead of fundamental change, there was/is much continuity from the premodern, and some of that has lasted to the present.

THREE

—៣—

PRINTING AND NEW
UNIVERSAL HISTORIES

CHANGE AS PROGRESS VERY MUCH is the standard
Western account for the period half a millennium ago.
Conventionally, in the Western approach, modernity was
a product of the fifteenth and sixteenth centuries. This historical depiction of change was indeed one seen from the
period itself. In this depiction, a number of developments,
each involving discontinuities and contrasts—including,
in particular, the Renaissance, printing, transoceanic
European voyages of exploration, and the Protestant Reformation but also the "rise of the middle class" and the
growth of capitalism—all presented as essentially Western, produced both transformative change and a sense of
transformation. As a consequence, although this shaping
was both incomplete and a process, rather than a moment,
the past became potent not as a source of reference but as
the record of what had been rejected.

In a key instance, the past, the period of Catholic hege-
mony, was presented by some Protestant commentators
as the medieval and, as a characteristic of that, the feudal and the Catholic; although, the later, in ecclesiastical

terms, Protestants claimed to return to the primitive church, bypassing what were presented as Catholic accretions. Indeed, the past presented guidance and legitimacy for the present, notably so in the case of the primitive church but also by studying recent centuries in order to justify the Reformation. This was also in line with the degree to which the Renaissance and Reformation saw a greater emphasis on literal rather than allegorical interpretations of the classics and scripture. Linked to this came an explicit engagement, as part of textualism, with both the accuracy and clarity of the text.[1]

The context for understanding history was far from static. Although the Reformation presented the Middle Ages as a Catholic dark age, the account of medievalism owed a lot to the cultural revolution of Humanism, a key element of the Renaissance, which took place in a Catholic context. This cultural revolution very much reflected an engagement with history. It took place through the philological restitution and artistic *imitatio* of the classical Greek-Roman age. In part, this was an instance of the creation of a mythical past, one that can be seen as historic in its pattern, but it also looked toward a later, more radical use of the idea of rebirth. Ten centuries were expelled from history in order to create a new beginning of revival. Indeed, the ancien régime that was to be assaulted from the late eighteenth century was in reality the "modern state" created in Italy in a republican form and in France in monarchical form.

Some Renaissance theorists, notably those who accepted the arguments of Copernicus on terrestrial motion, explained time as simply a product of the spatial rotation of the Earth, a dimension that was accordingly without particular relevance, including religious or other purpose. Other scientific accounts of time came to be offered. In his *Essay Concerning Human Understanding* (1690), John Locke constructed time as a psychological experience of duration with no necessary connection to spatial movement.

As the significance of time came to be more strongly asserted, so chronology was of greater interest. Moreover, printing made it easier to record events located in time. Handbooks of history became frequent, such as Peter Heylyn's *Microcosmus; or, A Little Description of the Great World: A Treatise Historical, Geographical, Political, Theological* (1621), and *The Great Historical, Geographical and Poetical Dictionary* (1640), the latter being the basis of Louis Moreri's *Le Grand Dictionnaire Historique* (1674).

The standard approach to modernity, that given at the beginning of this chapter, has the appeal of clarity but also many limitations, indeed flaws. It is too sweeping, underplays or even ignores the many elements of continuity, and is apt to be overly Western centric. Alongside the idea of the death of the past came the reality of its myriad vital remains, some of which have lasted to the present, notably the use of particular languages, as well as the continuance of historical narratives and explanations. These included specific accounts, whether of dynasties, territories, cities, or institutions (such as guilds), and also the many ways in which history continued to be reenacted, as in hierarchical structures and designations, processions, feasts, and church services. There were also interpretative structures of deep history, most obviously apocalyptic ones but also the ideas of cleansing and redemptive time, as with Noah's flood and nonbiblical equivalents.[2] These and other ideas challenged, but also helped link, divine and human time.

As such, the tensions between pasts and presents (the differing versions of both) could overlap with the parallels posed by different accounts of geography. Indeed, bringing areas of very different geography into contact through voyages of exploration and long-distance trade and conquest could mean the need to reassess more specific chronological accounts, not least as these encoded specific religious interpretations. A similar situation would presumably arise if future interplanetary contact brought cultures into some sort of relationship. Hitherto, this has been a matter of science fiction, most of which is forward looking into the future, often the distant future; although with some interesting instances set in the past or in the past as well as the future, for example with both Arthur C. Clarke's *2001: A Space Odyssey* (1968) and, repeatedly, with the *Dr. Who* television series (1963–). Separately, the idea of time travel across human society is very much located within fiction. Yet, as with other aspects of the relationship between fact and fiction discussed elsewhere in this book, there is a more complex interplay in practice, not least with historians sometimes providing in their writing a simultaneity of direct speech. Moreover, the "face of" approach to history, with the heavy emphasis on the citation of personal evidence, can entail taking the fiction of the past into the present, fiction in this case being an imaginative construction. If there were to be such an interplanetary encounter, then, assuming humanity survived, it would presumably augur in a new period of history and cause a radical shift in historiography.

Returning to the supposed onset of a very different modernity in the fifteenth and sixteenth centuries, it would not only be provocative but also instructive, as far as Western centricity is concerned, to begin an account of the period from the mid-fifteenth to the late eighteenth century, in a contrasting historical geography to the norm that is adopted. This would mean starting not with printing in the West (which, like gunpowder, had begun earlier in China), or the Renaissance (which, like Christendom, was the latest of several later renaissances detected by historians, notably in the late eighth to early ninth, tenth, and twelfth centuries), or the Reformation (the latest of several heterodox movements within Western Christendom) but, rather, with cultures outside Christendom that appeared more dynamic.

The key instance would be the Ottoman (Turkish) Empire, which succeeded in expanding greatly and lastingly in the fifteenth and sixteenth centuries. In this period, Ming China, in contrast, found it difficult to maintain success, while no dynasty in India, despite the very impressive expansion by the Mughals from the 1520s, matched the growth of the Ottomans. Ottoman historical consciousness was a fusion of providential mission, dynastic pride, and particular needs, notably those of supporting specific sultans. The religious role of the Ottoman rulers contributed greatly to their historical identity. This was notably so with the guardianship of the Islamic holy places, Mecca, Medina, and Jerusalem, all gained through the conquest, by Selim I "the Grim" (r. 1512–1520), of the Mamluk sultanate of Egypt in 1516–1517. On a more common pattern within Islam, the Ottoman Sultans claimed the position of Caliph and a form of primacy within Islam.

There was a similar linkage of sites, icons, and dynasties in other cultures. Thus, moving his capital from Chambéry to Turin in the 1560s, a "secular" choice for governmental and geopolitical reasons, Duke Emmanuel Philibert of Savoy-Piedmont also moved the Holy Shroud. This alleged relic of Christ's death gave the dynasty particular prestige. Italy is now a republic and the Shroud no longer a dynastic symbol, but it is still held and exhibited in the cathedral in Turin.

Somewhat differently to travel for religious purposes, a sense of history and of place converged in travel accounts that referred to particular places as being established historic sites. This practice, seen with tombs such as that of Achilles and of other classical places, continues to the present, as with the large number of tourists visiting World War I and II sites. At the same time, the respective attention paid to individual sites reflected (and reflects) a sense of particular interest and importance that involved subjective considerations.

The rivalry between the Ottomans and the Mamluks provided a continuity and a historical drama from the fifteenth century into the sixteenth, but this was subordinated to the greater dramas of the Ottoman rivalry with the heterodox Shi'ite Safavid rulers of Persia (Iran) that began in the 1500s; followed by that from the 1520s with the Habsburg rulers of Austria and Spain. In the latter, the forces of Suleiman the Magnificent (r. 1520–1566) unsuccessfully besieged Vienna in 1529. There are still contemporary historical references to these struggles that are potent, notably the neo-Ottoman strand in modern Turkish culture, one seen in the extensive celebration of the life and conquests of Suleiman, a celebration that has launched much television footage. Moreover, maps of Ottoman conquests are prominently displayed in certain Turkish cities.

Separately, the Shi'ite-Sunni rivalry of the sixteenth century is one that goes back to the first fundamental rift within Islam, that in the seventh century, and forward to a still bitter division today, one seen for example in the rivalry between Shi'ite Iran and Sunni Saudi Arabia, as well as in frequent murderous violence. This is a rivalry that is doctrinal and political, but also fought through the rival memorialization that leads to the honoring or destruction of particular shrines, such as the Imam Husayn Shrine at Karbala in Iraq. This is the mosque and burial site of Husayn ibn Ali, the third imam of Islam, a Shi'ite martyr who was killed in battle in 680. First built in 684, this shrine has been affected by successive destruction and rebuilding, a process extending to numerous explosions from 2004.

The emphasis on religion produced attitudes toward those who were members of other religions, a process that could readily be extended to different ethnicities. These attitudes and policies in part were a matter of sanctions, ranging from different levels of taxation depending on background to those provisions relating to military service, as with the Ottoman Empire. The process of identification extended to a scrutiny of ancestors. The latter was the case with ideas of racial purity and religious conformity, as in Portugal and Spain, where, building on earlier anxieties and phobias, there were strict codes, notably from the sixteenth century, based on "purity of blood." This anxiety focused on converted Jews and Muslims, and on the fear that they could impersonate and pass for "pure" Christians. Alleged crypto-Judaism was the principal target of the Inquisition and reflected, in a classic instance of blaming the victims (one to which Jews have so often been subject), a doubt of the integrity of converts, the so-called New Christians. As a consequence of the resulting oppression, there was an attempt to establish or conceal the identity of past family members.

Sixteenth-century Ottoman struggles brought together imperial ambitions, dynastic rivalries and religious competition, and, as such, may appear "traditional" in their themes. Yet, this was the historical consciousness required for the major transformation of Ottoman expansion, an expansion that directly affected the world into the early twentieth century (and indirectly thereafter), and, linked to this, the justification of this expansion. This was also the case with the historical activity associated with the Mughal rulers, who, initially thanks to conquests by Babur, dominated northern India from the 1520s, helping create or occasion a hostility to Islam that remains a factor in modern Indian politics.

In all cases, there was the classic tension frequently seen with the takeover of states, namely, the maintenance of a continuity that helped establish legitimacy and, at the same time, the honoring both of predecessors and of the providential success of conquest. Chinese historiography repeatedly saw this pattern. Indeed, the modern Communist Party offers a classic instance of the process, as it presents the past (and present) achievements of the Communist Party while also providing a selective but strongly expressed borrowing from pre-Communist history, and notably so when framing current or recent nationalist antagonism to Japan and Western powers. This antagonism extended in the COVID pandemic of 2020–2023 to a preference for traditional Chinese medicines, which were misleadingly seen as superior to Western medicines.

For the Ottomans, Mughals, and Safavids (among many dynasties in the early-modern period), there was the significance of religious identity. In the Ottoman and, eventually, Mughal cases, there were also the creation of new territorial spans and the impact on historical identities and imaginations. The Ottomans linked the Balkans, Anatolia, the Middle East, and North Africa as had not been done since the Byzantine (Eastern Roman) Empire was driven from the last two by Arab forces in the seventh century. Moreover, whereas Byzantium had not had much penetration east of Anatolia and Syria, the Ottoman Empire did, including, in particular, controlling Iraq, with only brief exceptions, from the mid-1530s to World War I.

The traditional nature of history in such contexts, that of the doings of conquerors, was amply shown in works like the anonymous *Holy Wars of Sultan Murad, Son of Mehmed Khan*, an account of the Ottoman Murad II (r. 1421–1444, 1446–1451). This work focused on his conflict with the Christians in the 1440s and notably the victory at Varna (1444), which provided an exemplary logic for Murad's reign and achievements. There was a regaining of Ottoman prestige after the total defeat of Bayezid I by Timur at Ankara in 1402. Moreover, drawing on the depiction of unnamed caliphs in the fictional epic the *Battalname* about battles against Byzantium (the Eastern Roman Empire), there was an emphasis on Murad seeking the support of God against non-Muslims and also behaving honorably.[3] The panegyric Ottoman royal histories produced by the official court historians, however, were in manuscripts, and their wider impact was limited.

Drawing, as many conquerors did, on different traditions, and enhancing his prestige accordingly, Murad's son, Mehmed II, took the sobriquet "the Conqueror" and the Byzantine title of "Caesar" when he captured Constantinople (Byzantium, Istanbul) in 1453. This was an important element of the incorporating element of expansionism, one that included fictive representation by the ruler and related titles, iconography, narratives, and ideology. The symbols of the past were readily plundered, copied, and, if necessary, remolded.[4] At the same time, the initiative was not always from the center, as the legitimation and exultation of rulership, both new and otherwise, were often the product of the particular interests of specific groups of subjects, as, for example, with the role of Muslim sects within the Ottoman Empire in the production of hagiographical literature.[5]

With the prevalence of monarchical rule, it was unsurprising that the Court (that is, the royal Court as opposed to the legal) approach to history remained important and across the relevant arts. Indeed, modern presidential systems can witness the same process. This distinction between *Court* and *court* looks toward the Italian eighteenth-century distinction between military (national, external) and civil (internal, constitutional) history. In popular history, Court history prevails to the present.

As before, empires were not the sole states, and history, accordingly, as the record of state identity and interest, covered a broader range of political activity. Moreover, thanks to printing, the milieux available for fixing and propagating historical narratives increased, as did the chance of these accounts surviving to posterity, and thus becoming history of a different type. This creates the challenge today of distinguishing the volume and type of what survived from its significance and novelty.

Indeed, in so far as it is helpful to think in terms of ages of historiography, then the scale of production and (separately) of that which survives (which, to a degree, are the historical and historiographical records, respectively) are central. In contrast, trends in assessment in, and of, specific milieux are less consequential. Quantity in the production of historical records is a key element in part because it poses the question of which records and accounts received (and receive) most attention and thus play a role in modern assessment. Furthermore, quantity itself provides an opportunity for the diffusion of historical information and analysis, and that is the crucial factor in past historiography and, thus, the building block to its present state.

Printing represented possibilities for both the volume and type of historical and historiographical material. Print cultures, notably in China but also those in Europe, could see printing by government and, separately, by those seeking profit. In the European context, there was the additional dynamic, from the early sixteenth century, of the particular religious, political, social, and cultural configurations of religious strife. Protestantism was very much a movement both that sought the authority of print and that totally had to recast the context and content of Christian history, including that of church-state relations. Protestant works on ecclesiastical history, such as the *Magdeburg Centuries* (1559–1574), and Catholic counters relied on being printed. As a result, the refusal to permit publication served as a means of control.[6]

The extent to which Christian clerics commented on political matters reflected the habitual absence of any distinction between religion and politics, and this ensured that, as was normal, the authority of the former was added to the latter. There was, therefore, a conflation of the means of authorizing the past and those of deriving lessons from it. Thus, William Stephens's *Thanksgiving Sermon . . . upon Occasion of His Majesty's Deliverance from a Villainous Assassination*, preached to the mayor and aldermen of London in 1696, when continuity was being sought under William III (r. 1689–1702) during war with France, tapped into the policy of Elizabeth I (r. 1558–1603): "That England should always make itself the head and protection of the whole Protestant interest. . . . By making all true Protestants, ie. all true Christians, her friends, she enabled England to make good her oldest maxim of State, which is to keep the balance of Europe equal and steady." This theme was to be taken up by later historians, such as Montagu Burrows in *The History of the Foreign Policy of Great Britain* (1895).

There was no large-scale affirmation through print, comparable to the Reformation and Counter-Reformation, in the case of Muslim struggles with Christianity, Hinduism, and Buddhism or within Islam, and this opened up a major divide within the world of public history. This situation looked toward the distinctiveness of the modern Anglo-American historical world, although factors other than a liberal Protestant legacy were significant. Historical identification was fully present in Islam, and not least in the religious differences between Sunnis and Shi'ites, but there was not the world of print to amplify this situation.

The situation was similar on the global scale, with societies that either lacked printing or where it was only developed to a limited extent. The role of oral history remained dominant, although visual artifacts could also be significant, the last sometimes including manuscript books. To a considerable degree, these, especially oral history, were the dominant forms of historical presentation in the Americas, sub-Saharan Africa, Oceania, and Southeast, Central, and North Asia. As such, and this was in the long precensus age, at least a third of the world's population was not part of the span of printing, and that excludes the indirect extent on the illiterate of the impact of printed works in areas where the latter circulated.

However, any understanding of historical consciousness would be unreasonably simplified by an amalgamation of these cultures and societies into one; for, in practice, they covered a great range of environments, religions, and social and political forms. Separately, there were historical imaginations and processes that reflected and commented on this variety. For example, notions of "tribalism" and of a "tribal" character to history, as a description of many, or all, of these societies, can be crude, pejorative, and misplaced. This was not least because they can underplay the extent to which an aspect of history within Christendom was that of tribalism plus printing. A similar approach can be probed for other cultures.

The European voyages of exploration (like the Chinese ones into the Indian Ocean in the early fifteenth century) brought into contact societies of very different character and with historical reference points that did not relate to each other. In part, this was a new iteration of the contact with "barbarians" seen for example in Japanese views of the indigenous Ainu people of Hokkaido. These views have continued to be influential into modern times. Such peoples were generally of a different religion and ethnicity, which thus became a character and definition of their barbarity.

Yet, from the fifteenth century, there was a more general apparent need to relate and rank distant peoples, not least for Christendom. This was a consequence of what became a lasting engagement with people who were "discovered" (a poor choice of word as these people were aware that they existed), although living at a considerable distance, as a consequence of transoceanic voyages of discovery. This process looked toward a significant transition in "universal history," as also, for Christians, did the longer-term encounter with advanced non-Christian societies from beyond the span of Islam. The latter was in large part defined by Christians as an opponent and therefore assessed accordingly, but there was not that comparable precedent for further distant societies.

Most notably, Spanish commentators faced problems in how to assess America and its native populations, problems that threw light on the use of history. The Reconquista and the Christian Mission provided a framework, but not the only one. In addition, classical literature provided pertinent models, with Roman expansion serving as a reference point for its Spanish successor, as it was later also to do for Britain. However, the Roman example was mixed. In particular, the lack of classical literary sources for the Americas encouraged a reconceptualization of the nature of intellectual authority, with the stress on eyewitness as opposed to literary accounts proving important to the process by which America was understood by the Spaniards. This issue for Christian ideas of time and space was very different from the challenge seen in China. There, after the end, in the late 1430s, of voyages of exploration, the prime contact was only with neighboring states that were assessed in the traditional Sinocentric terms of metropole as opposed to barbarism. This approach was complicated not so much by encounters with European voyagers from the 1520s, for that was contained.

The exemplary history offered in sixteenth-century Portugal, notably under Manuel I (r. 1495–1521), sought to link traditional Reconquista themes to new transoceanic opportunities and conquests. Manuel commissioned from the historian Duarte Galvăo *Cronica de El-Reid: Alfonso Henriques*, the life and deeds of Portugal's first king. Finished in 1505, this dealt with the victory at Ourique (1139) over the Moors (on which see chap. 2), which was also to be commemorated by the construction of the Royal Basilica in Castro Verde ordered in 1573 by King Sebastian. The historical role of the Portuguese crown as the protector of Christianity, a role vindicated by success, was a justification, in turn, by the Portuguese, for overseas expansionism, and in the competition for prestige in both roles with neighboring Spain. Galvăo prefigured Luís Vaz de Camões, the poet who celebrated Vasco da Gama in his epic *Os Lusíadas* (*The Lusiads*, 1572), an account of the travails and triumphs of the explorers. Both da Gama and Camões were buried in the impressive Jéronimos monastery built, following Manuel's commission, at Belém between 1502 and 1562.

There are parallels in the case of England. The late sixteenth century saw the celebration of recent English exploration, and notably so in books. At the same time, a longer-term background to the present was offered in history plays in which there were references ahead to the present, as with Shakespeare's *Macbeth* and also his (co-written) *Henry VIII*. The range of historical reference with Shakespeare extended to antiquity (*Julius Caesar, Antony and Cleopatra*), however fictional (*Troilus and Cressida, Titus Andronicus*). There was also a presentation by Shakespeare of much of English history, notably from the late fourteenth century to the early sixteenth century, in *Richard II* to *Henry VIII*, a presentation focused on monarchs and their spouses and leading ministers.

As such, the approach was not too different to that of recent historical films and novels, such as the best-selling ones by Hilary Mantel. So also with historical films and novels in other countries, for example France and Japan. The tremendously successful Mantel *Wolf Hall* trilogy (2009–2020), novels that have been turned into television and radio shows and plays, also indicates an interaction between popular literature and scholarship. Mantel followed the prominent scholar Geoffrey Elton in his somewhat uncritical praise of Thomas Cromwell, and both were critical of Henry VIII's earlier minister, Thomas Wolsey. Yet, Mantel did not follow Elton in his concern with Cromwell's administrative vocation, which would scarcely have matched popular interests. Moreover, Elton would never have claimed, as Mantel did in 2012, that Thomas Cromwell's 1536 Poor Law legislation was more enlightened in its attitudes than the then Conservative-led coalition government, which she stated was "going back to the Middle Ages." Far more people would have been aware of this poorly thought-through comparison than of any scholarly literature on the subject.

In a practice that continues to the present, it was common in historical fiction (and scholarship) to draw on more than one source without necessarily seeking to ensure coherence. Thus, for *Richard II* (1595), Shakespeare relied on chronicles that were at odds with each other. It was a shift from a reliance on the critical chronicler Thomas Walsingham, in the first part of the play, to Jean Creton and the author of the anonymous *Traison et Mort de Richard II*, both sympathetic to Richard (r. 1377–1399), later on in the work, that helped explain the development of the play into a form of Passion narrative that offers echoes of the fate of Jesus in the person of Richard. In one light, audiences were given a chance to decide on the interpretation they preferred and thus to assess right and wrong themselves. But the lack of a determination to ensure coherence was more significant.

Alongside transoceanic exploration, Christian states looked back into their past. Thus, Cervantes's well-received play *El cerco de Numancia* (ca. 1582, published 1585), presented the triumphant destiny of Spain as rising out of the ashes of the Celtic city of Numantia, which had fought to the end when besieged by the Romans in 134–133 BCE. True love is counterpointed with Roman lust in this play; most of the inhabitants committed suicide, and their collective self-sacrifice is shown as heroic.

In a historiographical constant that should not arouse surprise today, instant history was a major aspect of the propagandist purpose. Thus, for example, Titian's marvelous equestrian portrait of the Habsburg ruler Emperor Charles V at his victory at Mühlberg (1547) was a celebration of religious commitment and imperial position as the victory was won over Protestant rebels. This was also a placing of Charles within the history of both his Habsburg dynasty and the continuity of (Holy Roman) emperors. Charles was a new Charlemagne, who, in a parallel across more than seven centuries, had also defeated Saxons who were opposed to Catholicism, for the Protestant commander at Mühlberg was Elector John Frederick I of Saxony, who was thereafter condemned as a heretic and imprisoned.

There was also architectural celebration. Victor Amadeus II of Savoy-Piedmont (r. 1675–1730) began work in 1717 on a huge church at Superga to commemorate his victory at nearby Turin over the French in 1706, a redemption of an imperiled state. Outside the walls, the site was chosen because it was from there that he had ascertained the weakest point in the French position. For the Savoyard dynasty, this was an equivalent victory to that of the Christians outside Vienna in 1683, although it did not resonate as widely or as lastingly as the latter. Behind the church, consecrated in 1727, which still dominates the Turin skyline, a monastery was built that was designed to serve as the mausoleum for the dynasty, the monks offering perpetual prayers for the salvation of its dead members. This was very much a form of living history, one of active redemption. Warfare brought a celebration not only of rulership but also of the entities for which they fought. It was not necessarily nationalistic, but had a nationalist potential.

The celebration of monarchical valor was a counterpoint to *opera seria*, the world of classical mythology, serious heroism and solemn music; showing that the modern and the past were as one. So, differently, with the continuing commemoration of particular saints, for example the Umbrian saint Peter Cresci (d. 1323), for whose skull Cosimo III of Tuscany (r. 1670–1723) commissioned a reliquary.

The timescale in the celebration of rulers was generally different but not always so. For example, alongside distant saints, came more recent ones, such as Jesuit missionaries. The common theme was one of heroism. For lay figures, such as Victor Amadeus II, there was accordingly a record in statues and other forms, as there were for other rulers and across cultures. For example, in Prussia, references abounded to the Great Elector's victory over the Swedes at Fehrbellin in 1675, in practice a relatively minor victory. This victory by his grandfather Frederick William, elector of Brandenburg (r. 1640–1688), provided Frederick William I, king in (not of) Prussia (r. 1713–1740), with an example of meritorious rulership that encouraged his militarism and his reaction against the less bellicose stance of the intervening ruler Frederick I. Frederick II, in his *The History of My Own Times*, also praised the Great Elector. So also with Louis XIV of France (r. 1643–1715), looking to his grandfather Henry IV (r. 1589–1610) and rejecting the example of his less manly father, Louis XIII (r. 1610–1643). Dynastic imaging thus offered the possibility of seeking or, rather, selecting, the exemplary history required.

In contrast, city-state republics provided a very different sense of continuity and value. They looked back to often-embellished histories as well as to the historical resonance provided by republican Athens and Rome. The historians of the latter were adopted as a pattern by those of the modern republics, such as Niccolò Machiavelli (1469–1527) for Florence. This was an aspect of opposing ideas of Rome. Alongside the republican one proposed by

Machiavelli came the classic imperial one that was to be defended by the Counter-Reformation and the antityrannical ideas associated with the Roman historian Tacitus (ca. 56–ca. 120).

Within Eurasia, the most dramatic developments in terms of the scale of power in the fifteenth to eighteenth centuries again occurred in East Asia. After the Ming dynasty (r. 1368–1644) was brought to an end, its Manchu successor (r. 1644–1912) was, on the pattern last seen with the Mongols in the thirteenth and fourteenth centuries, conquerors from the north. This revived the issues posed by the Chinese presentation of "barbarism," and by the need for adaptation on the part of the latter. In terms of continuity, the Manchu dynasty both took over the position of emperor and the related "Mandate of History," and sought to make a success of a tripartite state of Manchu, Mongols and Han Chinese. In doing so, the Manchu devoted scant attention to discussion of the Ming period, many books of which were destroyed.

However, as a consequence of their important and eventually successful struggle with the Dzungars of Xinjiang from the 1690s to the 1750s, the Manchu were able to draw on earlier imperial Chinese practices of conflict with Central Asian peoples and, as with the Tang dynasty, of expansion there. In addition, this struggle was one in which contrasting views of Buddhism were in competition, as well as related questions of religious authority and legitimation.[7]

This struggle with the Dzungars provided a basis for the efforts of the talented Qianlong emperor (r. 1735–1796) to define his rulership, in terms of regulating and preserving Chinese culture, with the encyclopedic *Four*

Treasuries Project (1772–1781) and also by drawing on the Manchu heritage. In the latter case, and building on the institutionalization of government rituals by the Kangxi emperor (r. 1661–1722), notably in the *Collected Statutes of the Great Qing* (1690),[8] the emperor compiled texts setting down aspects of this heritage, including history, as well as having a Shamanic Code compiled in 1741–1747 in order to define Manchu religious practice. It was printed in 1778.[9] This was an instance of the value of printing for providing information on the past that might be useful or, alternatively or in addition, of particular antiquarian interest. Indeed, the antiquarian mindset was far from new, but the scale of possibilities for bringing forward its products changed greatly with printing.

There was no comparable Chinese engagement with the history of distant societies. This contrast with the West was seen also in greater Western interest in China (present and past), as with the 1773 Amsterdam edition of Joseph-Marie Amiot's *Rituels des Tartares Mandchous déterminés et fixés par l'Empereur*, the first published version of the Shamanic Code. Amiot (1718–1793) was a French Jesuit missionary who lived in China from 1750.

Such individuals were important cultural intermediaries, not least in providing and/or disseminating accounts of history. Whether or not they are to be referred to as transnational, a modern term, they made a major contribution to links between countries, in a fashion that has continued to the present. While much could be lost in translation, there was also often considerable perception in this process. It represented an important (and continuing) strand in historiography. This is one that is less pertinent if the prime theme in discussing historiography is one of historical method, or, linked to that, some form of progressive rationalism; but more so if the prime theme is the propagation of ideology and historical accounts, as intermediaries makes it easier to win allies and sympathizers across borders.

Alongside traditional types of culturally delimited "universal histories," the eighteenth century also saw Western efforts to incorporate the non-Western world into accounts that were designed to be of global validity. These took a number of forms, but, looking toward modern liberal patterns of historiography, the most significant for the future was the lessening of an explicitly Christian or European framework. This was seen for example in Voltaire's *Essai sur les moeurs et l'esprit des nations* (1745–1753).

This lessening was also seen in the historical sociology that became influential in the eighteenth century, and that was to affect a range of nineteenth-century intellectual developments, including liberalism and Marxism. This sociology proposed a history in stages, or "stadial history"; with particular characteristics linked to the means of economic activity, notably, in a sequence, pastoralism, arable agriculture, and industry, which therefore became both the key environmental context and the means of development. This form of history centered the West but also differentiated within it and provided a ranking of societies that was unrelated to that of response to the Christian message.

"Stadial history" was seen in such impressive works as Giambattista Vico's *Scienza Nuova* (1725), Adam Smith's *The Wealth of Nations* (1776), or William Robertson's well-regarded *The History of the Reign of Charles V* (1769), each of which offered a skilled contextualization for history.

Vico brought to this type of history the argument that rational thought had developed as a stage beyond myth. Historical understanding was affected by the Enlightenment proposition that humans live in a universe governed by natural laws. In short, a rational response to circumstances pertained, with nations defined through a mixture of geography, language, culture, physical features, and even traits of personality. In turn, the interests of nations were to be defined in terms of protecting their geographical, cultural, and defensive integrity.

Social change was seen as at issue in "stadial history," but there could be more immediate political references when such change was discussed. Thus, in 1805, William Godwin, a radical writer, claimed that money had taken over: "I saw that the public character of England . . . was gone. I perceived that we were grown a commercial and arithmetical nation. . . . Contractors, directors, and upstarts,—men fattened on the vitals of their fellow-citizens—have taken the place which was once filled by the Wentworths, the Seldens, and the Pyms."[10] The last references are to figures who had opposed monarchical authoritarianism in the seventeenth century. This was a different context than the remark about that earlier struggle that had been made by John Adam in Worcester, on which see chapter 4.

Alongside consciously modern "stadial" approaches, however varied, it would be seriously mistaken to assume that the providential approach to the continuum of past, present and future became less pronounced. Indeed, the opposite may well have been the case, not least because the strength of religious commitment in the eighteenth century, particularly in Europe, but also elsewhere, has been widely underestimated, and notably so both by generalists and by those working on historiography. Moreover, much religious commitment continued to show providential themes.

In the case of Europe, there was also the extent to which disruption led to new life, scope and scale for conspiracy theories, which helped lead to a revival of the attitudes associated with the Wars of Religion of 1524–1648 that followed the Protestant Reformation. This has very much been seen with the creation of "left" and "right" as antitheses due to the French Revolution that began in 1789. In a different, but related, process, the French Revolution also gave new force to a sense of struggle presented in terms of challenges to Christianity and the Catholic Church.[11] Presented as conspiracy theory, the latter struggle could be placed in terms of an antipathy to the Enlightenment; but also could be given an apocalyptic setting.

Moreover, the long-standing propensity for "secret history," both in formal history, as in David Jones's *The Secret History of White Hall from the Restoration of Charles II down to the Abdication of the late King James* (1697), and in fiction, contributed to the same end of sustaining the genre of conspiracy theory and encouraging specific settings for it. "Secret histories" assumed an "us" and a "them": those who conspired and those who read about it. The surviving evidence for these processes are most common for European societies. This is particularly the case for those societies that experienced civil war, a situation that naturally encouraged, alongside rational fear, conspiracy theories and paranoid historical consciousness, as in America in 1777 in which North Carolinians suspicious of the revolutionary cause believed it was a

Catholic-inspired plot to subvert Protestant political culture.[12]

Indeed, far from receding in a supposedly more rational present, the paranoid historical consciousness has become more common. This can be seen as a condition and product of modern historical awareness, as growing literacy and access to means of communication have made it easier to propagate such ideas. Thus, the Cold War (1917–1989), discussed in chapter 7, can be regarded as another iteration of the ideological clashes of the wars of religion and also those of Revolution considered in chapter 4. In that perspective, the notion of a somehow abstracted academic historiography and history of historiography organized in terms of methodological development and intellectual priorities is rather unhelpful. Chapter 10 considers what the next stage will be in terms of the dominant ideological clashes affecting historiography.

Reverting to the past, we would be mistaken to imagine that these paranoid views were only present in Western societies and/or ones with a freedom to debate the past. Instead, these views were prevalent, as the present day, or the feared future, led to anxiety that was then explained historically.

Moreover, in Western historical thought, the Enlightenment position, with its inherent optimism, was challenged by a historical placing of pessimism in terms of a threat, indeed the risk of dissolution, always being possible. This pessimism had a number of different manifestations. In his *The History of the Decline and Fall of the Roman Empire* (1776–1788), Edward Gibbon saw this and other processes of decline as both domestic and international. The former was generally presented in moralistic terms with reference to rulers and elites that fell from their purpose. This approach joined politics, history, and morality and was seen more widely across the historical imagination in the full range of cultures.[13] At the same time, Gibbon also discerned the possibility of renewed threat from outside Europe, as when he observed: "This apparent security should not tempt us to forget that new enemies and unknown dangers may possibly arise from some obscure people, scarcely visible in the map of the world. The Arabs or Saracens, who spread their conquests from India to Spain, had languished in poverty and contempt till Mahomet breathed into those savage bodies that soul of enthusiasm."[14] This was an aspect of the extent to which the past could provide both stories and hint at fears of the present, again a timeless circumstance. For Europe, in fact, there was to be no such invasion from outside. However, the situation was very different as far as other cultures were concerned in the late eighteenth and nineteenth centuries. This indicates the extent to which European developments were highly atypical in terms of the experience of history.

So also with the countries where the liberal tradition of historical scholarship has been particularly free of governmental direction over the last three-quarters of a century: America and Britain. Neither was occupied by foreign foes, as, in whole or large part, were France, Germany, Italy, Japan, China, and the Soviet Union. This highly significant atypicality of the Anglo-American experience may have a relationship with some of the particular characteristics of public history and academic historiography in the two countries. I emphasize the term *may*, as those considering the past can be overly apt to bring out relationships as causal rather than, as they should be, coincidental, partial, or possible.

On the other hand, there was no unifying experience in the prerevolutionary eighteenth century, European or otherwise. For example, alongside criticism of the churches, came the vitality of traditional belief and practice. In Brittany, there were many chapels dedicated to early Celtic saints unrecognized by the official Catholic calendar. In a popular reenactment of history that persists today, large processions take place to chapels where semi-legendary saints such as Noyale, Tréphine, and Trémeur, having been beheaded, are interred or have had their heads restored by other saints.

Moreover, as another cause of variety, the structural relationships in historical consciousness, notably between the local and the larger scale, were complicated by contingent (or chance) ones. A key instance was that of incorporation within imperial systems. Moreover, this process has left far more evidence in some cases than others. The former cases may be used to serve for the latter, but it is not clear how reasonable that analytical method necessarily is.

Thus, the seventeenth century contributed *antispagnolismo* to Italian historical consciousness. Hostility to Spain had a number of bases, historical, thematic and regional, but the shared arguments was that Spanish rule was an occupation, that this occupation was harmful, and that, in particular, it both represented and further caused a failure to achieve prosperity and, it was increasingly argued, accept modernity. Already present in the seventeenth century, notably among Neapolitan critics of Spanish rule, these arguments were to be crucial to Enlightenment thinkers opposed in the eighteenth century to the power of the Catholic Church and therefore the historical legacy of the Counter-Reformation. These arguments were also crucial, in the nineteenth century, to the Risorgimento ["rising again" movement for Italian unification] and to liberal Italy, not least by placing, for castigation, the allies of Spain, notably the Papacy, the Bourbon rulers of Naples and Sicily, and the nobility of the South. Moreover, in the twentieth century, and indicating the variety of directions from which historical criticisms could be mounted, Fascist commentators tended to oppose the Spanish link, both as a demonstration and exploitation of Italian weakness and as a cause of weakness. These arguments were also deployed post-1945 by the heirs of the liberals.[15] Far from the past simply being the plaything of authoritarian governments and their populist arguments, as is often argued today, it was more consistently used and frequently so with similar arguments.

These historical accounts were all useful for views of the Italian nation, but they underplayed the complexity of the links between Spain and Italy as well as the range and extent of local participation in this Italo-Spanish world. In short, they were an early instance of the misleading tendency to treat the fact of empire, rather than its nature, and, in particular, to prefer the rhetoric of anti-imperialism to the extent to which empire provided a basis for the "transnationalism," to use a later term, that was such an important theme in history. Furthermore, these anti-imperial accounts assumed (and, as with modern discussion of the British Empire, continue to assume) that there was a clear alternative, in this case an "Italian" one, that was not a view offered at the time. Instead, in Italy, the alternative to Spain in the seventeenth century was, frequently, that of an alignment with France, an alignment by independent rulers or by factions within states, which also had their own rivalries with each other. There was no Italian nation-state in prototype or prospect.

Within Italy in the seventeenth and eighteenth centuries, there was a shared identity that was commonly accepted, at least by those who were a bit literate. There was, however, no equivalent to the federal practices offered by the German constitution, notably the Imperial Diet, imperial courts, and the regional system of imperial circles that raised troops for the imperial army.

A difference of emphasis between Germany and Italy was apparent in public history, not least in the arts, with a greater emphasis in the former on aspects of past unity. In Italy, that was provided by Rome but that had had no recent political resonance. In the Würzburg *Residenz* of Prince Bishop Karl Philipp von Greiffenclau, the vaulting of the Imperial Hall in 1752 included *The Marriage of Emperor Frederick Barbarossa to Beatrice of Burgundy*, a wedding that took place there in 1156, and, emphasizing the legitimated original of local power, *The Investiture of Herold as Duke of Franconia by Barbarossa at the Imperial Diet in Würzburg in 1168.*

As with other cultures, the range of reference offered in the Germanic-speaking lands underlined the varied possibilities of historical examples and pointers. This can be seen in the often ambiguous relationship with Rome, one in which, on a long-established pattern, modern anti-papalism could be strengthened by a use of past opposition. Thus, in 1769, Holy Roman Emperor Joseph II, the ruler of Austria and a Catholic opponent of papal power, was the dedicatee of the play *Die Hermannsschlacht* (*Hermann's Battle*), a glorification of the struggle of the ancient Germans against imperial Rome and the victory of Arminius (German Hermann) in the Teutoburg Forest in 9 CE. Its author, Friedrich Klopstock (1724–1803), also sought, in *Oden* (1771) and other works, to replace classical myths with Germanic ones.

The contrast between Italy and Germany showed how the political circumstances of the present helped moderate the impact of structural developments in, and from, the past. Similar moderation occurred with circumstances that shaped the fixing, varying, and refixing of frontiers.

As an instance of the role of both, the anti-Spanish narrative proved easier in Portugal than in Naples. Spanish rule (1580–1640) had become increasingly unpopular in Portugal, where it lacked the longevity seen in Naples, and was overthrown in 1640, whereas a comparable attempt in Naples in 1647 had failed. In retrospect, Spanish rule was to be regarded with ambivalence, not least because of the lengthy independence struggle from 1640 to 1668. In the eighteenth-century bishop's garden in Castelo Branco, the statues of monarchs stand guard on the balustrades, but the Spanish monarchs are half-sized. Ironically, this element captured the role of respective attention in the depiction of the past.

Aside from asserting national independence, the use of history, both sacred and secular, in so far as they were separate, also served to help in debates over how best to govern, with history, whether recent or distant, deployed as the source and evidence of the right approach. This was an aspect of history as being shaped by purpose and, accordingly, shaping developments rather than being an arbitrary assemblage of events. Having purpose, moreover, helped exalt the value of commentary on the past and demonstrated the role of such commentary as part of a divinely created universe or, at least, one with meaning.

Eighteenth-century France saw debates over governance both royal and ecclesiastical, the latter including the relationship between papal and episcopal authority. In his *Histoire critique de l'éstablissement de la monarchie française dans les Gaules* (1734), the Abbé Jean-Baptiste Dubos argued that the royal authority of the Bourbons, the ruling dynasty since 1589, represented a rightful return to the situation under the Franks in the eighth and ninth centuries. Dubos presented this as a return, after a long period of usurpation in which the aristocracy had been too powerful, indeed acting as usurpers of rightful royal authority. For Dubos, the authority of Clovis (d. 511), who had united the Frankish tribes, derived from that of the Roman emperors, which was an apparently appropriate, albeit inaccurate, account of legitimacy.

On a pattern that was in part a reaction against Louis XIV (r. 1643–1715), this positive argument toward royal authority clashed with that, advanced by the Comte Henri de Boulainvilliers, of the nobility as playing a key limiting role because they were descended from freedom-loving Franks who had conquered those weakened by imperial rule, thus overthrowing the foreign control of Rome. Author of the *Histoire de l'ancien gouvernement de la France* (1727), Boulainvilliers claimed that Clovis had been elected by the other Franks, thus implying that consent was a key element in subsequent legitimacy, an attitude influential among some of the nobility. Although in

a Catholic context, this work looked to elements of Fran-
cois Hotman's *Franco-Gallia* (1573), an attack on absolutist
monarchical power as a usurpation of Gothic liberty and
thus an appeal to history in defense of liberty against the
corruption of institutions.

Such debates echoed those from, and about, the classical period, notably about governance in Athens and Rome.
This indicated how porous the boundaries between past
and present were seen to be as well as the value of using
past episodes to set the parameters for the consideration
of others.

Aside from historical debate over constitutional points,
there was the use of historical material for government
and not only in the form of law, which is a purposeful use
of the past for the present by citing precedents, or history
that was designed by some to do the same for statecraft.
On a long-standing pattern, the compiling of archive material was seen as beneficial. For example, the Russian
government archive established in 1724 was part of what
was seen as modern statehood. History as a tool of governance was not simply a matter of archival retention, but
multifaceted. It included the reflection by officials on what
in effect was collective experience. Thus, in 1791, William,
Lord Auckland, a senior British envoy, wrote to Sir Robert Murray Keith, a counterpart, criticizing proposals for
a league against Revolutionary France: "I have no great
idea of the proposed crusade against France; there exist
few examples in history of these leagues against particular
nations having produced anything like the end for which
they were instituted, and for this plain reason that the
parties concerned in such leagues are subject to every impression that can tend to disunion, and the party attacked

becomes on the other hand more united than ever."[16] This was a well-founded argument, one the ministry preferred to the more excitable pressure from Edmund Burke, but it fell foul in early 1793 of the increasing radicalization of the Revolution.

The focus on government meant a concentration on men, which was a characteristic of historical writing and probably also of most historical discussion. That, however, did not mean that women lacked prominent public historical roles. In Christendom, these went back to biblical examples such as Judith, the valiant killer of Holofenes, a killer frequently celebrated on canvas. In Britain, Boudica (Latinized as Boadicea), an opponent of Roman rule, was the first among the British female rulers whose martial virtues were emphasized. As an opponent of Spain, Elizabeth I (r. 1558–1603) was seen as a powerful woman who had changed the course of history.

Rulers were not alone. A key issue, furthermore, certainly by the eighteenth century, was the extent to which women contributed to the progress of civilization and the advance of Britain. The changing position of women was incorporated into a progressive view of national culture and destiny by being regarded as an aspect of Protestantism, and women's role in marriage was seen as an important element in the moral improvement of society and, notably, the refinement of men and the appropriate conduct of the clergy. The past was presented as transmitting to the present a powerful cultural ancestry in which women could enjoy high status and act as examples.

More generally, history as morality teaching by example provided an approach that could be variously deployed depending on cultural circumstances, and authorial interest. It drew on storytelling, but also on the role of law in confirming rights, and affirming and applying principles. Indeed, law and history were closely intertwined. Religion continued to play a major role. Historical works readily found Providence the key defender of nationhood, and history-writing thus an appropriate way to assert nationalism. In his dedication of volume two of his history of England to George I of Britain (r. 1714–1727), Laurence Echard, a clergyman, presented the Glorious Revolution of 1688–1689, the basis of George's position, as "wonderful and providential." He also wrote: "England in an especial manner has been such a mighty and distinct scene of action, in the latter ages of the world, that during the compass of this History, there appears a greater variety of changes, governments and establishments; and there seems to have been more visible and signal instances of judgements and punishments, mercies and deliverances from above, than perhaps can be paralleled in any other part of the Western world."

The text of this book was very clear that "Divine Providence" played a key role, not least due to the lapsed nature of mankind as a consequence of Adam's Fall.[17] This lapsed nature made divine support even more necessary, a point valid for nations as well as individuals and for present time as well as all time. The restoration of the Stuart monarchy in 1660 in the person of Charles II (r. 1660–1685) was described accordingly as "the most free and exalted expression of a delivered and overjoyed nation, triumphantly restored, without one drop of blood, by the All-merciful and powerful Hand of Heaven."[18]

For England/Britain, as for other states, national history and identity, the two mutually dependent, could not

be separated from Providence. The perfectability of society was not at the behest of humans. Instead, while the
emphasis on Providence could be a solution for Humanity
as a whole, as with millenarian ideas, it was generally understood in the period in terms of particular intervention
on behalf of individual nations. Although there are no
direct links, there is a comparison with the tension today
between global approaches to identity (and therefore past,
present, and future) and those that are more state specific.

Echard was a moderate Tory, and in Britain, the Whigs
added a powerful theme of human intervention in the
shape of the idea of the balance of power, a concept that
joined classical ideas of equipoise to those based on modern mechanistic understandings of science, especially as
advanced by Isaac Newton (1643–1727). The balance of
power could relate both to international relations and to
governance within states. This interpretation permitted
a representation of Britain in terms of moderation, which
was to be a standard theme in the self-presentation of
British distinctiveness. Indeed, a key source, and notably
in England, was that of the supposed middle way or *via
media* in church matters between radical Protestantism
and Catholicism. This account drew on classical ideas of
moderation. In political terms, there was a standard Aristotelian tension between royal prerogatives and popular
privileges, a tension that, at its best, produced a balance
that guaranteed liberty. Very different in time, the Saxon
witan (which was seen as a parliament) and the post-1688
Parliament were presented in England as the prime instances of this balance, and there was a ready reading,
forward and back, from one to the other.

The dedication in 1744 to Frederick, Prince of Wales, by Nicholas Tindal, another Anglican clergyman, of a translation of Paul de Rapin-Thoyras's influential Whiggish history of England, set out this theme:

> You will see here the origin and nature of our excellent constitution, where the prerogatives of the Crown, and Privileges of the subject are so heavily proportioned, that the King and the People are inseparably united in the same interests and views. You will observe that this union, though talked of by even the most arbitrary princes with respect to their subjects, is peculiar to the English monarchy, and the most solid foundation of the sovereign's glory, and the people's happiness.
>
> Accordingly, you will constantly find, that in the reigns where this union was cultivated, the kingdom flourished, and the prince was glorious, powerful, trusted, beloved. On the contrary, when, by an arbitrary disposition, of evil counsels, it was interrupted, the constitution languished, mutual confidence vanished, distrust, jealousy, discord arose; and when entirely broken ... confusion and civil wars ensued.

Similar views were also found in the writings of George Lyttelton (1709–1773), who was a Whig member of Parliament as well as an author, including of history. He saw a long-standing English identity that he traced back to the Saxon system of limited royal power. This was then presented as surviving the Norman Conquest of 1066, only for a division to open up between the "nobles" and "the people," with the former a burden on the latter. Lyttelton praised the reign of Elizabeth I (1558–1603) as coming "to an equal balance, which is the true perfection of it," only to degenerate in the seventeenth century under the Stuarts, before revival as a result of the Glorious Revolution of 1688–1689: "The government was settled on a new foundation, agreeable to the ancient Saxon principles from which it had declined."[19]

This understanding of a revolution as a return to past circumstances, and, ideally, to a past golden age that had been lost as a consequence of usurpations of some type, was a significant variant on the progressivism or improvability with which Whig thought is associated. The account of the events of 1688–1689 as the Glorious Revolution, a convenient myth as well as a constitutional necessity,[20] made it possible to reconcile both views and sets of images, and this helped Whiggism be deployed as a potent and resonant ideology. Moreover, the continuing importance of the Revolution Settlement as a later version of Magna Carta (1215), on which see the last chapter, was readily apparent. Multiple themes, interpretations, and echoes, like identities, were significant and were located in terms of a lasting struggle.

Yet, the extent to which modern history was apparently a matter not for mature academic scrutiny but rather for partisan polemic (a critical approach still seen today in many history departments in modern universities), affected the presentation of the past. In 1776, Thomas Pelham wrote to his father of "a kind of modern history which historians have not yet come down to."[21] The following year, Frederik Willem Pestel, professor of the Law of Nations and of the Public Law at the University of Leiden, told Philip Yorke that he wished to teach him what was "not to be found in any book that he knows of, which was to give a sort of system of policy and of the present Balance of Europe, drawn from the facts that have happened since the period mentioned [Peace of Westphalia, 1648], a study which he says is entirely new, and not followed in our universities."[22]

Pestel's reflection captured the need for an academic historical approach that was more explicitly open to the issues of the present. That was definitely the case with the public history of the period and was so whatever the method of expression. Inevitably, such a need was to encourage the particular explicit politicization of history seen in the last quarter millennium.

FOUR

—w—

REJECTING THE PAST

A new epoch in the annals of the world.

—*Morning Herald*, May 31, 1790

IN 1786, JOHN ADAMS, AMERICA'S first ambassador to Britain, toured England with Thomas Jefferson, who was visiting from his ambassadorial post in Paris. The men were to be the second and third presidents, respectively, and rivals. In his diary, Adams recorded: "Edgehill and Worcester were curious and interesting to us, as scenes where freemen had fought for their rights. The people in the neighbourhood appeared so ignorant and careless at Worcester, that I was provoked, and asked, 'And do Englishmen so soon forget the ground where liberty was fought for? Tell your neighbours and your children that this is holy ground; much holier than that on which your churches stand. All England should come in pilgrimage to this hill once a year.'"

To Adams, what he saw was clear. A people ignorant of their past and with a lost nationalism, one, indeed, that might be a precursor of the modern situation. Edgehill (1642) was the first battle of the English Civil War between Parliamentarians and Royalists, and Worcester (1651), Oliver Cromwell's last victory, brought to a decisive end the Stuart attempt to defeat the Parliamentarian regime in battle. However, it is worth, as so often when citing or contextualizing evidence, to extend quotations and expand consideration. Adams continued: "This animated them, and they seemed much pleased with it. Perhaps their awkwardness before might arise from their uncertainty of our sentiments concerning the civil wars."[1] Conversely, in Worcester, there was a more Royalist culture, as revealed by the contents of Valentine Green's *History and Antiquities of the City and Suburbs of Worcester* (1764) and the highly positive response to George III's visit in 1788, and those who held these views would not have sympathized with Adams. The Parliamentarian troops had inflicted serious damage in Worcester in 1651, and that remained part of the historical memory.

Adams offered a prime instance of the extent to which the new revolution in America meant not simply a rejection of the past, but also a search for a different one. This search built on the British (and thus British American) case with the Glorious Revolution of 1688–1689 but took it in a new direction. Radical Whiggism developed outside Britain but within the British world. From the 1770s, such radicalism, accompanied by rejection of both present and past, were to be an important aspect of the history of a number of countries, notably the Thirteen Colonies that became the basis of the United States, Revolutionary France, Haiti, and then the states

of Latin America. This process involved a search for a
newly useful and different past history, both domestic
and international.[2]

This search, the subject of this chapter, entailed a rejection of the colonial past, one that required new origin
myths, as did the history-making linked to the course and
consequences of the politicization that stemmed from the
civil wars that were important causes of eventual success
for independence movements. In practice, as with other
revolutionary movements, there was, due to the timescale
of revolution, a rapid history of the present that, in retrospect, became the basis for different new histories. The
Declaration of Independence (1776) offered an account
of recent history and current circumstances that, in turn,
offered a new history for America: "The history of the
present King of Great Britain is a history of unremitting
injuries and usurpations, all having in direct object the
establishment of an absolute tyranny over these States." A
draft added the appeal to the historical view that would be
taken in the future: "Future ages will scarcely believe that
the hardiness of one man adventured, within the short
compass of twelve years only, to lay a foundation so broad
and undisguised for tyranny over a people fostered and
fixed in principles of freedom."

The nonsense about George that was to be offered with
great success in the musical *Hamilton* (2015) revealed the
aptness of this accusation as polemic. In an instructive
limitation of any sense of modernity, some of the language
in the Declaration was biblical, making George akin to an
Old Testament plague.[3] This was to be the precursor of a
process that continued into the twentieth century, with
the new histories of states that followed the collapse of

other empires. Doubtless, this practice will continue into the future.

Jefferson, who was responsible for the Declaration of Independence, was very historically minded. He looked to Gothic liberty and suggested Hengist and Horsa, Jutish invaders of Roman Britain (who were in practice fictional), for the design of the Seal of the United States. British, more especially English, precedent weighed heavily with his generation and later in America, and lawyers reinforced that tendency. This was an instance of a tension between such historical appeals, for example attacks on the Norman Yoke and historically grounded claims in favor of natural rights.

The historical landscape of newly independent states changed greatly. Stalin referred to the Soviet Union as a country with an unstable past. Some processes and ideologies were more immediate and destructive than others. There was the removal of statues and royal coats of arms and the changing of place names, all part of breaks with monarchy and foreign empire, a modern version of the Roman *damnatio memoriae*. States were created as independent territories and named for their liberators, as with Bolivia. Others were renamed, as with Haiti.

Separately, the extent to which independence was not a single act but, instead, a process in which contributions and milieux were varied and goals differing helped ensure that credit for victory was claimed in a multifarious and generally clashing fashion.[4] This process became part of the new histories of independent states. Moreover, the political partisanship that followed independence in turn affected the use of history, leading to partisan accounts and commemoration, as in America with the death of

George Washington in 1799. The use of the recent past overlapped with the journalism of the present, with both employed as evidence in political contention. The War of 1812–1815 with Britain was similarly recorded in very different fashions by the governing Democratic Republicans and the opposition Federalists, and the dominance of the account offered by the former helped discredit the latter. This contributed to the Federalist defeats in the elections of 1816 and 1820, defeats that led to the demise of the party. In part, this was a matter of the historical weighting as inevitable of what had in practice been more contingent. This was the case with the memorialization of a war in terms of American successes in repelling British attacks at Baltimore (1814) and New Orleans (1815) rather than of American failures to conquer Canada.

Nation-building was linked to public memorialization and also to political advantage, as with the number of former generals who rose to government office in many of the new states. Haiti, America, France, and Mexico had this fact in common. As a result, military history was in part a matter of current politics and the celebration of rulers and would-be rulers. This included the history offered on canvas, in statuary, and in other artistic forms. The statue of George III was torn down in New York.

More generally, the present served as a stage for a different historical imagery and particularly so in looking to past republics, as with the case of republican Rome and the painters of revolutionary France, notably Jacques Louis David (1748–1825). Aspirationally relevant episodes and iconography were deployed, as in David's *The Intervention of the Sabine Women* (1799), and used in the naming of institutions, whether the American Senate or the

French Consuls. Before rejecting monarchy, the Revolutionary speakers in France had already called on Greek and Roman examples, as in January 1792, when the Girondin Pierre Vergniaud, in a bellicose speech to the National Assembly, drew attention to Demosthenes stirring up the Athenians against the threat from Philip of Macedon.[5]

Change was most abrupt, although differently so, in France and Haiti. Initially, the revolutionaries in France were committed to the new and to modernity, notably in opposition to both feudalism (a strand linking them to earlier Enlightenment writers) and to heredity as a justification for rank, hierarchy, and subordination. After debates reflecting very different ideas about the relationship between crown and nation, the National Assembly on May 22, 1790, decided that the king could not declare war without its approval. This was not only seen in France as historic and as reflecting knowledge derived from history. The *Times* on May 26 argued that it was clear from history that the most harmful conflicts "originated in the injustice, the animosity, or the capricious passion of individuals," while the radical *Morning Herald* on May 31 saw the decree as "the very essence of true philosophy! a death's wound to despotism, arbitrary power, and false prerogative of ambitious, cruel, bloodthirsty tyrants . . . and the total extirpation of that radical disease of the French Cabinet aspiring to universal dominion! . . . may be said to form a new epoch in the annals of the world, tending to spread universal amity . . . this great and beatific revolution!"

More specifically, if there was alliance with Spain, a "national" treaty was to replace a family compact between the two ruling houses, a decision made by the National

Assembly on August 26. Again, this was praised by liberals elsewhere, with John Sommers Cocks, a Foxite Whig member of Parliament, telling the House of Commons in London in 1791, again with a sense of historical development: "There was one principle in the French revolution which could not be doubted, and that was that war should not be entered into unless for the purpose of self-defence. This was not an age when ministers, or king's favourites, or king's mistresses, or the mistresses of ministers . . . could make war merely for their own will and pleasure: that age was past, and he trusted that this country would never engage in a war, from blind confidence in any minister."[6]

On all sides, the language employed reflected and reflected on differing historiographies, worldviews in which past practices were to be the basis for action or for rejection. This was true of specifics, as in 1792 when France rejected the Peace of Westphalia of 1648 with its closure of the navigation of the River Scheldt, and of the very tone employed. William, Lord Auckland, British envoy in The Hague, reported of his French counterpart in 1792: "M. de Maude made a long visit yesterday to the Grand Pensionary, and uttered nothing but classical phrases, natural philosophy, and belles lettres."[7]

Moreover, republicanism, from 1792, and de-Christianization, ensured the appropriation and destruction of previous sites of legitimacy and continuity. The rejection of Christianity entailed a new understanding of the purpose of time, new providentialism, and the introduction, in 1793, of a new, non-Christian, calendar. The last, in this case a radically different one, was a classic instance of a revolutionary reach for newness, although it was to be abandoned as radicalism was contained. There was much iconic destructiveness. For example, the bronze equestrian statue of Henry IV erected in 1618 on the Pont Neuf in Paris was destroyed in 1792, only to be rebuilt in 1818. Ironically, Henry had been cited earlier in the National Assembly as an apparently suitable counterpoint of regal energy and anti-Habsburg activity to the enervated and suspect current holder of the throne, Louis XVI, who was linked to an Austrian alliance bitterly denounced by the Revolutionaries in the winter of 1791–1792. The royal corpses from Saint-Denis were exhumed and reburied in a common grave in 1793, while the urn containing Louis XIV's heart, preserved in the Parisian church of Saint-Paul-Saint-Louis, was melted down and the heart destroyed.

Another aspect of a new historical consciousness was seen in the determination to present a public, national history, as part of a rejection of ancien régime practices. This was to be a characteristic, at least officially, of the state history that became prominent in what was self-consciously depicted as a modern age of historicism. Thus, the state archives were opened to the public, the Archives Nationales being established in Paris in 1790. In 1794, furthermore, prerevolutionary archives were centralized. Moreover, the quest for openness in government, seen with the Revolutionaries' at least public commitment to open diplomacy, as well as the publication of information on state finances, was a very different form of accountability to the earlier situation. In 1794, the National Assembly opened the archives to the public.

In contrast to France, and more particularly to Haiti, there was a greater degree of conservatism and continuity in the historical consciousness, and racial history, of the new American state. Far from rejecting the legacy of the slave trade and slavery, the new state enunciated a doctrine of human rights and then hedged it with the caveats of continuity. In France, the rejection of slavery seen with the Revolution was rescinded by Napoleon, an issue that has recently become much more significant in the evaluation of his reputation than was hitherto the case.

In contrast, the overthrow of French imperial rule in Saint-Dominque (from 1804 Haiti) involved the end of slavery and the total destruction of white colonial control by blacks, the majority of whom were former slaves. The scale of the change, including the great harshness of colonial conditions and the extent of revolutionary disruption, with brutality and devastation by all sides, was such that the past, prerevolutionary, history of the territory was not usable by the new independent state. This situation was furthered by the weakness of the prerevolutionary cultural infrastructure. Moreover, there was no link between the people and the indigenous population that had been destroyed by disease and brutality following Spanish conquest. At the same time, due to enslavement, there was no strong link with Africa. Instead, it was the struggle for freedom that provided the new history. The recovered memory of Africa in Haiti was very indirect and also influenced by the extent to which African polities did not have a trans-Atlantic political or economic reach. In contrast, the major Haitian historian, Thomas Madiou (1815–84), produced a *Histoire d'Haiti* that drew on French sources as well as oral accounts, providing an account that emphasized the rebellion against slavery. Madiou was an officeholder, not least a diplomat, journalist, and director of the National High School.

Haiti broke from the rule of France and much more definitively than former French colonies in Africa after 1960 (with the prominent exception of Guinea). Moreover, the new history offered as a consequence of the French and Haitian revolutions differed. Initial possible parallels between the Glorious Revolution (British) and then American revolutions on the one hand and the French and then Haitian on the other did not survive the contrasting contexts and the pressure of events. In part, the difference between France and Haiti was a matter of respective wealth and cultural infrastructure. Political factors were also important. Both France and Haiti saw close to a century of often acute political instability follow their revolutions as well as similar outcomes, including the establishment in both of imperial rulers. Nevertheless, in France, it was easier to employ governmental structures and economic wealth in order to introduce new histories. This was notably the case of the recent past because such history was important to the assertion of legitimacy.

In the case of France, after the strong reaction, from 1794, against the Revolutionary Terror of 1793–1794, this legitimacy also entailed the presentation of links with previous regimes that were judged appropriate. The theme of renewal through restoration was present also from 1814 in France with, successively, new Bourbon, republican, Napoleonic, and republican regimes. The very term *restoration*, however, was value-laden, and this was the case whether the term was employed by supporters (as a form of legitimation) or opponents (as a form of rejection).

The reaction in France from 1794 represented a clear rejection of the logic of revolutionary newness seen in the earlier assault on history. However, the counterrevolution led, from 1799, in a very different direction. It could be presented as a new synthesis only if dictatorial military rule is seen as latent in the original intentions of the Revolutionaries, which was certainly not the case. Napoleon did, however, continue the Revolutionaries' replacement of historical criteria, those of jurisdictional-territorial units, in the radical redrawing of frontiers within and outside France.

In practice, Napoleon was not somehow a triumphant will outside history or a great innovator, as he liked to imagine. One of the many generals across the world who came to power by force in the period from 1780 to 1830 (and more generally), he sought to use the historical structures and culture of the French state, notably monarchy, Christianity, and aristocracy. Yet, Napoleon also wished to present a new history, one that made sense of his position. In Napoleon's case, culturally, this was a neoclassical history. In part as a consequence of the destruction of earlier models and practices, with the overthrow of the ancien régime, which could be seen as a feudal accretion on the classical past, neoclassicism became newly potent in France as a historical and cultural idiom and setting. Indeed, rather as Benito Mussolini was to do more understandably (although similarly ridiculously) in Italy, where he was dictator from 1922 to 1943, Napoleon looked back to Rome.

As with all appeals to the past, antiquity offered much variety, and, not least, could be seen as providing a range of contexts and purposes. Napoleon as "historian" had also looked to ancient Egypt when he campaigned there in 1798–1799, inaugurating a major and unprecedented study that, as it were, bypassed Rome. Once, however, he

had seized power in France (1799) and promoted himself
from first consul to emperor (1804), it was ancient Rome
that appeared more relevant as well as easier of access. In
part, this was a reflection of the significance of his establishment of a personal position in Italy as the king of the
new kingdom of Italy he had founded in 1805, using, in a
borrowing of historical legitimation, the Iron Crown of
Lombardy to that end.

Napoleon fashioned, in his own iconography and that
of the regime, a self-image in terms of the achievements,
glamour, and status of antiquity, all of which had come to
the fore with neoclassicism. The boldness of Napoleon's
ambition included his drive to reset the basis for history
by seizing archives across Europe. He constructed a large
new building in Paris where this material could be used
to justify his civilizational role as well as for more specific
intentions of French power and profit. In 1809, defeated
Austria was made to hand over the records of the Holy
Roman Empire, and thereafter, Napoleon's gaze extended
to other holdings, notably those of the Papacy and those
of Spanish America. The Congress of Vienna of 1814–1815
stipulated a return of such holdings. Yet, their destination
was affected by what states were now independent, and
their new post-Napoleonic territorial span.

There was a degree of energy in the fashioning of the
past under Napoleon, as in the use of lists to fix and trian-
gulate data. This was seen in the employment of genealogical tables and time charts, as akin to geographical maps,
in the location of information in the *Atlas historique, généa-
logique, chronologique et géographique* (1802–1804) by "Le
Sage," Marie-Joseph-Emmanuel-Auguste-Dieudonné de
Las Cases, Marquis de la Caussade (1766–1842). A French

émigré who had settled in London, Las Cases returned to Paris in 1802, and his work was officially adopted by the Ministry of the Interior for use in French schools and by the Foreign Ministry for the use of legations. Greatly successful, the work, which had originally appeared in London in English in 1801, went through many French editions as well as appearing in German and Italian translations before being reprinted in English in Philadelphia in 1820. The plan of the work, printed in the 1801 edition, brought sight very much into historical comprehension: "If it were possible, in studying history, to see the personage of which it is spoken, constantly in its chronological place, without having recourse to chronology, and always surrounded by its ancestors and descendants, without being constrained to study genealogy . . . it is certain it would then be engraved on the memory, attended by all the advantages that would assist the recollection, and rectify the judgment; for while the ear listened to the history of any one, the eye would see at the same time the precise epocha of their existence, their contemporaries, parentage, relations, etc." Time, like space, became a matter of distance, "the change of events and successions" being followed as "the turnings of roads." This was an approach that had only limited success, which serves as a reminder of directions not followed in historiography.

Napoleon's fashioning of the past included the writing out of unwelcome episodes, such as failure in Saint-Domingue/Haiti in 1803,[8] and large-scale misrepresentation, as with the defeat of the French fleet by the British at Trafalgar in 1805. "To lie like the *Moniteur*," the leading French newspaper, became a regular phrase. With Napoleon, the instrumentalism of history was clear to see, not

least in the large-scale pillage of artistic treasures at his behest. His patronage of congratulatory art was continued
by his nephew, Napoleon III, who, in 1865, commissioned
a large equestrian statue of his uncle in his birthplace,
Ajaccio.

The contentiousness of Napoleon I's policies, however,
became more apparent with time and helped make the attempt to celebrate 2021 as the "Year of Napoleon" difficult.
It was not clear how best to commemorate Napoleon, not
least in terms of his reintroduction of slavery. A French
state characteristically confident in its deployment of its
past was unusually lacking in confidence in this case, a
lack seen in President Macron's low-key response to the
bicentenary of Napoleon's death.

In Latin America, although Spain remained in control
of Cuba and Puerto Rico until 1898, and briefly regained
power in the Dominican Republic in the 1860s, a series of
newly independent states replaced Portuguese and Spanish rule of the mainland from the 1810s and 1820s. This was
important to the history of history, for in this case, there
was a large number of new states, each having to construct a history. Moreover, with the significant exceptions
of Brazil, Chile, Argentina, and Paraguay, these states divided, creating more governments having to engage with
a new history. In addition, none was regained by the colonial ruler, except, and then only briefly, the Dominican
Republic by Spain. Nor was there a conqueror and over-
seer to influence, if not determine, the new history, as
happened for the states established in Europe from 1792
by Revolutionary and Napoleonic France.

Brazil had a war of independence from Portugal but
also marked political continuity with its former colonial

ruler. Indeed, a member of the ruling family of the latter was the emperor of Brazil until, in 1889, Pedro II was deposed and a republic declared. In contrast, and again as a reminder of the dependence of historical accounts on the contingencies of the present, there was no such continuity in the case of the former Spanish colonies. Nor, however, could there be a reaching back to pre-Spanish history. It had been glorious in the sense in particular of Aztec and Inca imperial power in the early sixteenth century. Yet, this legacy was unacceptable. First, a pre-Christian identity was not possible for Latin American societies that very much asserted their Catholicism as a civilizational context and proof. Secondly, there was continuity in the often harsh racial dynamics of the newly independent states. The descendants of Spanish conquerors remained dominant, while those inhabitants, the majority in most cases, who were of native or (because of past migration as slaves) African descent were kept from power and, indeed, recognition. Indeed, in Argentina and Chile, there was major expansion at the expense of native peoples. The situation continued until recent years, when such descent, and related demands for power and redistribution, became important to the politics of a number of states, including Bolivia.

Nation-building in newly independent Spanish America focused on the often bitter struggle for independence. For Venezuela and Colombia, the emphasis has been on the legacy of Simón Bolívar, the central figure in the difficult struggle and one whose historical resonance has continued to the present in Venezuela, being much used by Hugo Chávez, president from 1999 until 2013. However, this legacy, like that of other figures of the independence period, proved divisive in the period when Bolívar was known, as opposed to becoming a later symbol. This was so for two particular reasons. First, several liberators, such as Bolívar, were associated with attempts to create states different to those that had eventually emerged. Secondly, their domestic position proved contentious. In some states, such as Argentina and Mexico (and, separately, the United States), the struggle was between centralists and regionalists, and, in others, sometimes linked to the former and sometimes separate, it was between secular liberals and clerical conservatives.

These tensions—often pursued through civil wars, as also in Central America where an earlier, larger independent state collapsed—made the historical component of nation-building difficult. In addition, there could be a failure to incorporate other, often different accounts, not least those of communities, especially "marginal" rural ones, and those whose religious commitment was unwelcome or difficult to incorporate. These elements could combine, as in Mexico in the Yucatán and in Haiti with voodoo.[9] Yucatán was independent from Mexico in 1823 and 1841–1848, and from 1847 to 1901 was involved in a lengthy war, the Caste War, in which native Maya opposed the Hispanic population. Hostilities continued in the twentieth century, with the last fighting in 1933.

At the same time, and notably after the pattern of France, a republic from 1871, history was regarded by Latin American national governments as important to this process of nation-building. Thus, in 1884, Argentine history became part of the curriculum when compulsory, free primary education was introduced, and school ceremonies celebrating national anniversaries were also encouraged. The same process was seen elsewhere.

A populist patriotic historiography not limited to dynasticism, in order to support and mold a new nation was not the same as such a history to affirm a renewed nation. Yet, there was a common purpose. Indeed, the process, begun in the late eighteenth century, was to become the norm. The use of history became more insistent in Europe in the conflicts that began in 1792, in part because French imperialism, whether or not presented in a universalist (by the Revolutionaries) or imperial (as by Napoleonic) guise, led to a reaction that drew on different currents. There were notably, as in Spain, those of Christian commitment and anti-French nationalism. In Germany, previous nationalist images were reworked to a new purpose against France and a deep history drawn on to that end. Thus, the defeat of the Romans in the Teutoburg Forest in 9 CE, on which see the previous chapter, was deployed anew in Heinrich von Kleist's play *Die Hermannsschlackt* (1809) and in Caspar David Friedrich's painting *Old Heroes' Graves* (1812) in which Arminius is named.

In 1793, giving the annual Martyrdom Day sermon in Westminster Abbey before the House of Lords, marking the anniversary of the execution of Charles I in 1649, Samuel Horsley, bishop of St. David's and a supporter of William Pitt the Younger, contributed with his weight of history, rejecting the notion of an original compact arising from the abandonment of a state of nature and stressing, instead, royal authority. According to Horsley, the existing constitution was the product and safeguard of a "legal contract" between the Crown and the people, while the obedience of the latter was a religious duty. Horsley's forceful peroration linked the executions of Charles I and Louis XVI: "This foul murder and these barbarities, have filled the measure of the guilt and infamy of France. O my country! Read the horror of thy own deed in this recent heightened imitation! Lament and weep, that this black French treason should have found its example, in the crime of thy unnatural sons!"[10]

The protracted warfare from 1792 to 1815, the reliance on large conscript forces, and the search for a popular legitimacy, in part in order to reject French imperialism, combined to ensure that historical nationalism and nationalist history became more urgent and apparent in Europe. Whether continued French success would have led in a different direction is unclear, as is how far a very contrasting context for European historiographies would have thereby arisen. As Britain and Russia were not subjugated, there is no reason to assume that they would have lost a sense of national historical autonomy and required for their historical account some lasting compromise with defeat. The situation was very different in the German and Italian lands, all of which had been subjugated by 1809. This opens up the question of how far cooperation with the French would have led to a history of recent years, on the part of those who cooperated, that resulted in a different approach to "deeper" or more long-term history." This might have created a rift with the bulk of the population that did not have to reach such an overt accommodation. How far this serves as an instance of the wider patterning by political response of histories in societies affected by foreign imperialism is open to discussion. Yet again, particular conjunctures, political and otherwise, complicate the issue.

Linked to the overthrow of empires from 1775 to 1825, ideas of the nation were greatly affected by nationalism in the West. In contrast, this was not the case across most of the world, including China, the Ottoman Empire, and the Indian principalities. However, there was to be an eventual convergence with the Western model in the twentieth century, as non-Western states came to take this nationalist position, in part in reaction to Western imperialism and in part due to republicanism. Yet, the intervening difference, during the nineteenth century, between models and practices of history across the world, one that carried forward the previous situation of variety, was striking. We turn to it in the following chapter.

FIVE

—〰—

NEW PASTS

Thy shores are empires, changed in all save thee;
Assyria, Greece, Rome, Carthage, what are they?

> —Lord Byron, *Childe Harold's Pilgrimage* (1812)
> of the Mediterranean

IN THE NINETEENTH CENTURY, THE establishment
of new states, new governmental units within which history was to be presented, was matched by that of new institutions, practices, or bases for the discussion and study
of the subject. This was in a process that was to become
a more common aspect of the world of historical awareness. The most significant match was that of the use of the
vernacular and the creation of public educational and archival systems. All were features that gathered pace in the
nineteenth century. This was particularly so of its closing
decades, because it was then that these educational systems became more prominent. Indeed, they were to have
a central role for governmental domestic policy in many
(but not all) states.[1]

As ever, the balance of emphasis in the discussion
reflects inherent prejudices of consequence. Academic

historians tend to place the emphasis on their predecessors and, in particular, on the establishment of universities and the development of "scientific" history, in the sense of objective, nonpartisan historical work explicitly based on an exhaustive and critical use of archival sources, which was the definition that attracted support in the nineteenth century, a period in which the concept of science enjoyed increasing prestige and definition. This process was notably identified with the Prussian historian Leopold von Ranke (1795–1886), professor of history at Berlin from 1825.[2] The subsequent diffusion of this practice, for example from Berlin to America—not least at the University of Chicago, founded in 1890—then attracts attention.

Science in this period went beyond today's preoccupation with natural science, especially where expressed mathematically. Science was understood as reason applied to evidence, as with Adam Smith's *Wealth of Nations*. Ranke's method drew on philology, which made the method scientific, in contrast to belles lettres and philosophical histories. "Scientific" history also drew on the prestige and precision of the natural sciences, but it was apt to downplay the role of "agency" on the part of the historian, notably the extent to which subjectivity played a role in which topics and sources were chosen, the particular questions posed, and the methods employed. With the use of the term *science* and the commitment to objectivity as a possibility and a goal, it was as if there was a clear-cut teleology within the historical profession, one that matched the teleology its members discerned, a guiding purpose providing a meaning that could and should be unlocked. The apparently obvious and predictable methods of depositing, organizing, and using materials in archives represented a linked and supportive teleology, as was similarly the case with the shaping of archaeological time and substance.

At the same time, as if to indicate that subjectivity might occur due to a lack of rigor, scientific history repeatedly drew attention to issues in the sources and in source-analysis, not least in order to establish the relative value of particular accounts. This was not a new practice, but it was insistent. Thus, William Smith's *Ancient Atlas* (1874) provided extensive notes on the sources for each map, with that on Hispania observing: "It is extremely difficult to construct an accurate and tolerably complete map of ancient Spain, for the topographical statements of Strabo and Mela are generally confined to the coast districts. Pliny gives statistical surveys and in part alphabetical lists of towns rather than topographically arranged materials. Ptolemy's map, on the other hand, is evidently full of great errors, so that those places which are based on its authority must always be very uncertain. We are, therefore, here more than elsewhere dependent upon the itineraries, the ruins, and the inscriptions."[3]

There was also considerable interest in other forms of historical narrative and explanation that, while operating at a very different scale, provided ideas and metaphors for human history. This was the case with geological history and then with its evolutionary counterpart associated with Charles Darwin. Both posed challenges for conventional religious accounts of the Creation as well as leaving a past in the present.[4] This was recorded in geological maps and also, very differently, in fiction. In Ann Radcliffe's very popular novel *The Italian* (1797), there is a journey above a chasm "which some strong convulsion of the earth seemed to have formed."

There was also the merging of geology and history in order to advance particular viewpoints, as in variants of pseudo-history. Atlantis, a fictional island from the period of antiquity, provided a good instance. The extent to which tsunamis and geological events caused land to be flooded led to the idea of lost places. Plato presented Atlantis in an allegory on hubris as an opponent of Athens, but it was also employed in utopian accounts, as in Thomas More's *Utopia* (1516) and Francis Bacon's *The New Atlantis* (1627). Ignatius Donnelly's *Atlantis: The Antediluvian World* (1882) presented it as a continent destroyed by the biblical flood, while Helena Blavatsky's *The Secret Doctrine* (1888) offered a positive account of a pre-Aryan civilization in Atlantis.

In geology and evolution as scholarly subjects, there was, as with history, the concern to offer a narrative orderliness and therefore patterns to shape and gloss the contingent confusion of the past. Past attempts to reconcile geology with theology failed. More recently, there has been little attempt to integrate history with geology in conceptual or empirical terms, in contrast to the rise of environmental history as a discipline, more particularly in the form of climate change.

Geology, a span of difference largely outside human life, was complemented by archaeology. This did not offer the dramatic setting and narrative of geology but similarly proposed a world that could not be so automatically reduced to a progressivism culminating in the modern. Yet, the romantic appeal of the past was complemented by an awareness of difference that include the greater knowledge enjoyed in the present. Thus, in *The Hound of the Baskervilles* (1902), Dr. Watson reports to Sherlock Holmes:

> The longer one stays here the more does the spirit of the moor sink one's soul, its vastness, and also its grim charm. When you are once out upon its bosom you have left all traces of modern England behind you, but on the other hand you are conscious everywhere of the homes and the work of the prehistoric people. On all sides of you as you walk are the houses of these forgotten folk, with their graves and the huge monoliths which are supposed to have marked their temples. As you look at their grey stone huts against the scarred hillsides you leave your own age behind you, and if you were to see a skin-clad, hairy man crawl out from the low door, fitting a flint-tipped arrow on to the string of his bow, you would feel that his presence there was more natural than your own. The strange thing is that they should have lived so thickly on what must always have been most unfruitful soil. I am no antiquarian, but I could imagine that they were some unwarlike and harried race who were forced to accept that which none other would occupy.

Archaeological research was bound up in ideas of historical layering. Thus, in 1890, Flinders Petrie applied to the Tell el-Hesi site his theory of the stratified formation of an ancient city mound, the first time this had been done in biblical archaeology.

The Hound of the Baskervilles reflected a theme Doyle developed elsewhere, that of the historical character of the *pays* or locality. This character was important to the regional or civic culture that was repurposed within nation-states, as well as being a reflection of specific identity and purpose within these states. Archaeological discussion emphasized continuities in settlement and identity. Local archaeological research was valuable in this context, not least as it did not stress political division. The British equivalent of *Heimat* was expressed by Emil Reich, an anglicized German, in his *New Student's Atlas of British History* (1903), when he wrote the "influence of the locality . . . is both spiritual, through its historical traditions, and physiological, through its climatic and other physical factors."

The role of evolution was understood in the extent to which environmental influence allegedly explained the differing political trajectories of various ethnic groups and the processes by which they had become nations and states with particular characteristics, interests, and boundaries. Nationalism was therefore an aspect of environmentalism, helping make it appear natural and necessary. William Hughes, professor of geography in the College for Civil Engineers in London, argued in 1840:

> Not only does the narrative of past events require in the student a knowledge of the localities which have been the scenes of their occurrence but the influence which physical characteristics have exercised over the formation of the national character—the modes of thought and feeling—the customary associations—the manners and institutions—of the inhabitants of a country, form elements in its condition which must be understood and appreciated before its political and religious history can be read with advantage. The different circumstances under which an inland or a maritime country is placed, and the various influences of the lofty chain of mountains or the widespread plain—the parched and arid desert or the fertile valley—the navigable river or the rapid mountain torrent—have exercised a large share in directing the progress of civilisation.[5]

In part a version of Heinrich Berghaus's *Physikalischer Atlas* (1845–1848), Alexander Keith Johnston's *The Physical Atlas* (1848) offered what appeared to be another science of history: "As there are natural laws for the organisation of individual man, so there must be natural laws for the growth and decline of nations." Physical geography was seen by Johnston as crucial to an understanding of past and present. Ethnicity was presented as crucial: "The history of mankind exhibits nothing but the development of the different races, varieties, etc. of the human family, partly apart, and for the last three thousand years as mutually influencing each other; so that a progress in the history of mankind is always indicated either by the appearance of a new stock of people on the stage of the world, or by the produce of a crossing of two races." And racism was clearly present: "Among the nations belonging to the different varieties of the so-called Caucasian species, there is an evident tendency towards improvement, on an increasingly scale. This is fully borne out by the history of the last three thousand years."

Ethnic accounts generally left little room for multiethnicity. Darwinian ideas were repeatedly deployed when discussing ethnic groups, as in the *Historical Atlas of Modern Europe* (1902), in which, for the map of Europe from 527 to 750, J. B. Bury, Regius Professor of Greek at Trinity College, Dublin, wrote: "The sixth century determined which of the Teutonic peoples, settled within the borders of the Roman Empire, were the fittest to survive and play a part in mediaeval and modern history."

A sense of the inevitable consequences of the ranking of races was presented in *Relations of Geography and*

History (1901) by the Oxford academic Hereford George.
He wrote of the Americans and Canadians having:

> before them the prospect of indefinite expansion, at the
> cost of getting rid of the aborgines, thinly scattered over
> the whole area, whom they were neither able nor desirous
> to convert into slaves. Before both alike the red men disap-
> peared: they were incapable of assimilating civilisation, and
> have in great measure died out, there having been practi-
> cally no admixture of races. The analogy is very close with
> many of the movements of prehistoric man, when newcom-
> ers expropriated the old inhabitants, driving them out or
> destroying them, but enslaving or otherwise absorbing only
> a few. Civilised man works by different means, and with less
> definite intention to destroy; but the result is the same.[6]

Thus, in a pattern repeatedly seen with archaeology, distant history was used to argue for the inevitability of the
recent processes that contributed to the present day.

These "deep histories" also could give credibility to
ideas of societal adaptation and development based on
materialism. These ideas left their most prominent legacy
with Karl Marx's theory of historical development. Marx
argued that the motor of history, and the related definition
of social groups and their antagonistic relationships, were
set by their respective linkages to the means of economic
production. The flavor of Marxist historicist prediction
can be gauged from *The Communist Manifesto* (1848):

> In Germany, the petite bourgeois class, a relic of the six-
> teenth century, and since then constantly cropping up again
> under various forms, is the real social basis of the existing
> state of things. To preserve this class is to preserve the exist-
> ing state of things in Germany. The industrial and politi-
> cal supremacy of the bourgeoisie threatens it with certain

destruction; on the one hand, from the concentration of capital; on the other, from the rise of a revolutionary pro-letariat. . . . The communists turn their attention chiefly to Germany, because that country is on the eve of a bourgeois revolution that is bound to be carried out under more advanced conditions of European civilisation, and with a much more developed proletariat, than that of England in the seventeenth and of France in the eighteenth century and because the bourgeois revolution in Germany will be but the prelude to an immediately following proletarian revolution.

The assessment was wrong.

While lacking in any substantial originality, Marx's thesis repurposed the stadial theories of the eighteenth century to the world of industrialization, and also sought to shape the understanding of the latter for political pur-poses, so that the future could be both understood and directed. His developmental schema was different to those of others who saw shape in the past, but there was a progressivism that was common to their philosophers and therefore their use of time. This was seen for example with the French philosopher Auguste Comte (1794–1857) and (not that they always agreed) his British counterpart John Stuart Mill (1806–1873). The idea of progressivism in human society was given a national direction in many influential works, for example Henry Buckle's *History of Civilization in England* (1857–1861). A sense of progress was very much seen in the last plate of *J. H. Colton's Historical Atlas* (1860), an American work: "The discoveries of the nineteenth century surpassing all that the human mind ever imagined in any former age. . . . The human intel-lect, enlightened by the experience of every past century, and inspired by the wisdom of every former dispensation, advances now to new triumphs over the physical and mental universe, with a power that is rapidly accumulating."

Developments in religious thought and scholarship could also be of significance, although there were generally crosscurrents. In nineteenth-century Protestantism, liberal biblical scholarship challenged the literal inspiration of scripture and sought to explain faith in what was presented as a rational fashion, although that was scarcely a new project. David Friedrich Strauss (1808–1874) contradicted the historicity of supernatural elements, as well as Christology in the Gospels, in his *Das Leben Jesu* (*The Life of Jesus*, 1835–1836). This did not happen without challenge: *Essays and Reviews* (1860), which brought German biblical criticism to a wide audience, was prosecuted for heresy. As a reminder of the varied reaches of history, Strauss also wrote a major biography of Ulrich von Hutten, a key figure in the early Reformation.

Historical atlases of the Bible were found in the Protestant more than the Catholic world, let alone the Orthodox, while the textual understanding of scripture served as a major encouragement to the detailed historical understanding of the Holy Land. Criticism of past scholarship was often excessive but also helped establish current norms for historical work. Thus, William Hughes wrote in his *Illuminated Atlas of Scripture Geography* (1840):

> The absence of a strictly chronological arrangement in the delineation of boundaries and localities has been felt as an important defect in the maps generally prepared for the illustration of ancient geography: ancient and modern, classical and scriptural, appellations have been mixed together, without regard to the period of history to which they relate in such a manner as to leave on the mind of the student no

distinct impression of the actual condition of a country at
any one period. Yet this synchronism of geography . . . constitutes, when presented to view the most important guide
in tracing the progress of a nation's civilisation.[7]

Such synchronism was also seen as necessary for historical work. The choice of a mechanical term was apt given
the dominant attitude of the time. With its emphasis on
Mariology and papal infallibility, Catholic thought in the
late nineteenth century went in a different direction.

In accounts of nineteenth-century Western teleology, it
is all too easy to neglect the continued role of religious history as both subject and explanation. That downplays the
history offered weekly or more regularly from the pulpit
and in devotional readings and also the extent to which
providence was held to play a role in history. This was seen
in the largest conflict of the century, the Taiping Rebellion
of 1850–1864, in which the Taiping Heavenly Kingdom
sought to overthrow the existing system and replace it by
a theocratic Christianity led by Hong Xiuquan, who declared himself the younger son of Jesus and thus offered a
rebirth of the Christian mission in modern China. Hong
also claimed that he provided a revival of classical Chinese
traditions, notably of Shangdi, the God of Shang theology.

Elsewhere, Christian expansion could provide a purpose and narrative for history. Thus, Edmund McClure,
in his *Historical Church Atlas* (1897), declared

> the heathen millions of the East are brought ever more and
> more within touch of a power which shall at length win
> their allegiance, when the vision of Isaiah should be fully
> realized. How has all this come about? The annals of the
> civilized world for the last eighteen centuries will furnish an
> answer. The history of the spread of the Christian faith . . .

may be regarded as furnishing a striking evidence of God's ruling Providence in the world—an evidence which, while it strengthens our faith, must invigorate at the same time our hope of the ultimate and universal triumph of the Gospel predicted by prophecy.[8]

Somewhat differently, the Social Gospel movement promoted by Charles Finney aligned providential thinking and reform movements, with important consequences for the American Civil War (1861–1865) and later. Millennialism and providentialism were embedded in the modernizing accounts of the past and remain so in the present. Both factors played a role for each side in the Civil War. Many Northerners believed the end of slavery necessary in order to achieve divine purpose.[9] Similar arguments were advanced elsewhere. In America, this process continued with the Progressive movement and the American commitment to World War I. Achieving progress became the new millennium. Biblical language and arguments could sell positions that left scripture behind. The development of these counterfeit or bastardized forms of Christianity paralleled later political religions of the twentieth century.[10]

Alongside an emphasis on history as an inherent process of betterment could come that on improvement through rational inquiry and reform. This was a process and ideology that gave intellectuals a necessarily central role as public figures. The establishment of a larger educational system provided opportunities to propagate such an ideology but also a need for status and employment on the part of those linked to it, status and employment both to differentiate their position within the system and with reference to outside agencies and potential competitors.

Indeed, a sociology of "history" would show how a profession with specific rules and hierarchies developed in
the late nineteenth century and set in motion a particular
institutional culture for the definition and presentation
of the subject. This approach to improvement and public
education was also linked to a more diffused Whiggism
or progressivism, a confidence, ethos, and method with
a variety of political and religious standpoints but with a
common tendency to liberalism. As with most ideologies,
Whiggism was more influential precisely because it was
not formulaic and thereby constrained by an ideological
program and political program.

Whiggism provided a way for Western commentators to look at global history, for their influence could be
presented, by themselves, as necessary in order to allow
other peoples to fulfill what was presented in Western
terms as their potential. That was an aspect of the reading
of Darwinism that saw human intervention as making
it purposeful and teleological, whereas it had not previously been so. The spread of Christian civilization could
be regarded as part of the process, and if not all Whiggish
commentators did so, there was a proselytism that was
common to both. Moreover, although Darwin did not in-
tend his ideas to serve as a basis for a programmatic racist
imperial mentality, his arguments were not as cautiously
expressed as they could have been.

From the perspective of non-Western societies seeking security, this was an unattractive and dangerous presentation of history and its purpose. Nevertheless, the
challenge of the historical vision of Western imperialism
helped lead non-Western states to emulate much of this vision. Thus, Japan, China, Thailand, the Ottoman Empire

(Turkey), and Egypt, all adopted specific methods of Western national consciousness and state identity. For example, in Japan, state Shinto developed as an amalgam of a long-standing religion with a new authoritarian form of government after the Meiji Restoration of 1868. This restoration of imperial rule was a product of the overthrow of the Tokuygawa shogunate, or hereditary first ministry, that had prevailed from 1603. Now denounced in terms of "evil customs," the shogunate was overcome conceptually, both in order to look at alleged earlier models and so as to further a rapid modernization, the two being linked. Militarism and the creation of a new past played a significant role in this new order, with the foundation, in 1869, of Yasukuni as a preeminent shrine that was a symbol of nationalism and where the war dead were commemorated as part of an obvious and necessary form of public honor.

The legacy of the Meiji Restoration was to appear problematic to democratic critics as imperialist militarism gathered pace in the 1930s. Yet, in the shorter term, its verdict was more widely welcomed, although the new order entailed the suppression of opposition in the shape of the Satsuma Rebellion of 1877 and therefore initially of any positive memory of that resistance. Moreover, the two previous sentences very much reflect a presentist view of this militarism, which was widely grounded in the 1930s and, however undesirable in the light of what was to happen in terms of Japanese expansionism and with reference to modern values, was a historically grounded and coherent ideology of the period. This was not all militaristic but in part a matter, as in building in Kyoto, for example the Heian Shrine in the 1890s, of providing an exemplary national history for the revived dynasty.[11] The social, cultural, and political contexts of Japanese militarism were reconceptualized with a restaging of past and present. The samurai warriors that had, in the Satsuma Rebellion, resisted the Meiji transformation, in which they were seen as anachronistic, were removed as a status group, before being seen, from the 1890s, as a positive instance of national character, and notably of a self-sacrifice that could now influence a mass army.[12]

Across the world, the public honor on display in Japan at Yasukuni was more generally seen in the presentation of the past, whether in the arts or in education. Indeed, public honor became the national curriculum, thus helping ensure that history focused on differences and rivalry between peoples rather than commonalities linking them. The latter were certainly offered in some forms, notably in religions, most obviously Christianity, that were not restricted, as Shinto was, to particular peoples. Moreover, liberalism, at least in theory, was a global project or, at least, was advanced in that light, as in the cult of free trade.

That approach could pose problems for the assessment of non-Western cultures, as was seen with the *Historical Atlas of the Chinese Empire* (1888) by E. L. Oxenham. Working in the British Foreign Service in China and a cultural intermediary, Oxenham presented China as dynamic rather than decadent and found value in China's past—"against Plato and Aristotle place Confucius and Mencius." Furthermore, he dismissed what he termed the

prevailing cant as to the immobility of China. From the times of Yu the Great,[13] a stream of change can be noticed from a number of feudal autonomous states to a single democratic centralised autocracy. The progressive element in Chinese history has been, and is today, the monarchical element.

Gradually, and step by step, Emperor after Emperor has whit-
tled away one individual privilege after another. Hereditary
nobility, primogeniture, large estates, parks, religious
establishments, and game preserves, have all disappeared
and fallen before the resistless pressure of that multitude of
China, of which the Son of Heaven is the Representative
and the Incarnation. . . . Railways will abolish religious superstition and some cruel customs, and will purify the lower
official ranks, but it is not probable they will change one atom
the fundamental institution of China.[14]

This discussion of a fundamental continuity in Chinese
history is one that is still pertinent today; although the
contents and context of the discussion have changed, and
greatly so.

At the same time as continuities in the usage of history, the theme of the last chapter was more insistent,
for most states were new or, like Japan or China with the
Self-Strengthening Movement, sought to be newly vigorous. However much they might call on internationalist
movements, vocabularies, and idioms, from Catholicism
to liberalism, neoclassicism to anti-Western sentiment,
there was a grounding of these in terms of a historical
patriotism. The governmental basis of this provision varied greatly, most particularly between states and would-
be states. Moreover, the former were divided between
de facto empires and others, between nation-states and
others, between monarchies and republics, and between
societies with a degree of democratic representation and
others. These categories overlapped.

Yet, in all cases, history was seen as an expression
of state, group, and personal identity and as a means
to strengthen it. The role of the state did not preclude

a continued part for a wide range of other mediums for history, from individuals and families to communities, whether geographical, ethnic, religious, economic, or social. However, there was no stable basis for this role or for the understanding of the past. This was because mass literacy, comprehensive educational systems, and the struggles for primacy of newly powerful states, separately and in combination, created an inherent volatility.

In the case of major states, this volatility over identity, and the attempt to overcome that volatility by asserting clarity, included an imperial dimension. Their governments devoted attention to the public aspects of a relevant history, from educational curricula to street naming, but there was also private historical enterprise. In empires, this was a matter not only of historical initiatives from the colonies and from a range of constituencies there—not least white settlers, such as Bryan Edwards, the author of a history of the British Caribbean (1793)—but also in the metropole.

Whereas, by the late-twentieth century, the attitude was usually far more critical, the imperial dimension presented in the nineteenth was very different. For example, the novel *Westward Ho!* (1855) by the Victorian clergyman and novelist Charles Kingsley was based on the life of the Elizabethan privateer Amyas Preston (Amyas Leigh in the novel), who follows Francis Drake, a fellow Devonian, to sea. The novel focuses on a real expedition of 1595, the Preston-Somers raid on Caracas, and provides a strongly hostile account of the Inquisition and the Spaniards. It was codedicated to Sir James Brooke, rajah of Sarawak (r. 1841–1868), whom Kingsley regarded as a modern representative of the heroic character traits of the sixteenth-century English buccaneers in the Caribbean, and to George Selwyn, a missionary chaplain and the first bishop of New Zealand (which included Melanesia). The story became a film in 1919 and, in 1925, was the first novel to be adapted for radio by the BBC.

Kingsley became chaplain to Queen Victoria and regius professor of modern history at Cambridge, writing, while professor, *Hereward the Wake* (1866), a novel of heroic English nationalistic resistance to William the Conqueror (r. 1066–1085), which as a child I borrowed from the public library and read, and a novel replicated in Paul Kingsnorth's *The Wake* (2014). Kingsley's success as an Anglican intellectual captured the broader historicism of the progressive unity that church leaders and historians sought to foster and celebrate in the British Empire, an ambition that included the idea of the apostolic origins of the Church of England. They were not alone in this, but it was a combination that proved more problematic in British Catholic circles.[15]

Kingsley was not alone in offering the adventure story approach to history that is one of its most persistent strands. George Alfred Henty (1832–1902) covered both recent conflicts and earlier wars in his stories, which included *Under Drake's Flag* (1883); *With Clive in India; or, The Beginning of an Empire* (1884); *St. George for England: A Tale of Cressy* [Crécy] *and Poitiers* (1885); *With Wolfe in Canada* (1887); *Held Fast for England: A Tale of the Siege of Gibraltar* (1779–83) (1891); and *Under Wellington's Command* (1889). This theme was to be taken forward in popular historical works such as Henrietta (H. E.) Marshall's *Our Island Story* (1905), a bestseller for children that was widely read into the 1960s. It was followed by *Our Empire*

Story (1908). In turn, Robert (R. J.) Unstead, a teacher, produced many illustrated books for young readers, which again sold very well, including *Looking at History* (1955), *People in History* (1959), and *From Caractacus to Alfred* (1966). Fiction and popular histories have a reach that shapes attitudes, especially at formative ages, more than is recognized. They also spark an interest.

History was very much presented in Britain in terms of a British imperial narrative. In 1853, Edward Gover referred, in *The Historic Geographical Atlas of the Middle and Modern Ages*, to the "indomitable perseverance and skill of the Anglo-Saxon race," while the preface to the *New School Atlas of Modern History* (1911) by Ramsay Muir, professor of modern history at Liverpool University, noted: "As the Atlas is intended to be used by young people of the greatest colonising nation in history, special attention has been devoted to Indian, American and Colonial history." The text for the plate "The British Settlement of Australasia" declared: "Happy is the nation that has no history. Apart from the Maori wars in New Zealand, the only noteworthy features of the history of Australasia are the dates of the successive settlements, and the chief stages in the exploration of the region, both of which are shown." Thus, the indigenous population was written out of history.

A sense of progress through a troubled, but noble, past to a necessary present was not only seen with the British. Alongside the discussion of domestic constitutional history in this light came that of imperial expansion. Both in, and also concerning, their conquests in North Africa from 1830, French writers presented a civilizational argument in which Christianity played a role. New churches reclaimed former Christian sites, as at Hippo in Algeria, where the Basilica of St. Augustine was built in 1883 to house a fragment of Augustine's arm bones. As so often, a variety of historical models and images was offered. Thus, the French both drew on Christian and Orientalist themes and saw France as the successor to the Roman Empire. North Africa became part of the French imagination, as with the impact of the Roman amphitheater at El Djem on the protagonist in *L'Immoraliste* (*The Immoralist*, 1902), a novel by André Gide who had traveled in North Africa from 1893. Russia also looked back via Byzantium to Rome.[16] America looked to republican rather than imperial Rome. The translation of empire had competing claimants as well as Rome offering very differing models. Both republic and empire equaled Rome for many in the West, and the combination of classical literature and the scriptures ensured a frame of references that went beyond the elite.

More generally, past empires were presented as versions of present-day ones, thus justifying both. For example, the Hellenistic world was identified with that of modern Europe in the age of its colonial empires.[17]

The element of historical authority became differently important in the nineteenth century as the older view of the transfer of imperial rule keeping the dream of Rome alive was increasingly presented in terms of modern empires as the apogee of a developmental historical process. This was very much the case in Britain, with comparisons made to the benefit of the latter, as by Charles Pearson in 1869: our "troops have repeatedly fought in India against greater odds than the Romans ever encountered in the conquest of Britain."[18] The Roman chrysalis for modern imperialism also influenced a wider Western historical consciousness. It was the case, for example, with colonial societies, such as Australia, Canada, and New Zealand, and with independent former colonies, notably America, Argentina, and Brazil. Indeed, the ready reading of concepts, idioms, and examples from one imperial system to another was important to their vitality as a historical model.

Those who experienced their rule understandably could have different views. Not only was their history ignored or downplayed, but so were the names of their territories and places. Moreover, the opposition to Western civilization, not least in its Roman manifestation, or indeed simply the absence of this civilization, was frequently presented in terms of barbarism. Thus, Edward Quin, in his *Historical Atlas* (1830), a work, drawing on the methods of Friedrich Wilhelm Benicken, that was reprinted or the basis of other works until 1859, "enveloped" in clouds what was "unknown" by Europeans, while Quin explained in addition in the introduction: "There have always been, in every age of the world, parts of the earth, not unknown to the geographer or the historian, but classed, by their want of civilisation, of regular government, and of known and recognised limits, under the general description of *barbarous countries*." The teleology was clear. From 1100 to 1294, progress was associated by Quin with the rise of the middle class: "During our present period, notwithstanding the gross superstition which prevailed, the undefined state of regal power and popular rights, and the many atrocious acts which were perpetrated, Europe was fast emerging from the state of barbarism in which it had been sunk for several centuries. In England, France,

Germany and Italy, the Commons or third estate, began to be recognized and respected; industry and commerce were acquiring their due weight and estimation, and through the study of jurisprudence, the rights of persons and of property were better understood."

The following period, 1294 to 1498, was described as follows: "The darkness of the middle ages was dispelled and the way cleared for the progress of the Protestant religion by the light of science, literature, and commerce." And the period from 1558 to 1660 was described as one where "nations in general began to regard industry and commerce, rather than mere conquest, as the true sources of wealth and grandeur."

Yet again, contrasts in the role and application of history as an understood process were readily apparent. Alongside this Whiggism, for example, came different accounts of the past that were more sympathetic, including in Britain, to a politico-cultural Catholicism. More generally, history was significant as a guide to politics, because it helped describe how institutions worked or should work and helped explain political culture that set the boundaries of acceptable action. This function helped give historical contention a purpose.

Separately, by modern standards, anachronism was a major problem with nineteenth-century historical accounts, both of Western countries and by Western commentators on the rest of the world, and discussion of a scientific basis for history scarcely addresses this issue. Moreover, Ranke, and others, were not without clear political views, in the case of Ranke support for the development of a strong Germany under Prussian leadership. To Ranke, realism was conservative, while God's will was at work in history. Again, there is a parallel with those modern commentators who claim some sort of Olympian detachment when discussing historiography while decrying what is presented as governmental and/or populist folly. This claim is an aspect of what can be variously regarded as nostalgia, fantasy, false consciousness, and professional interest and, in practice, draws on each.

SIX

—ᴫ—

CONTESTING THE NATIONS

THE HISTORY OF THE NEGRO RACE IN AMERICA, 1619–1880
(1882) by George Washington Williams (1849–91) remains an demonstration of the extent to which the nineteenth century saw a variety of different voices. It did
so alongside subsequent broad-brush historiographical
patterning, such as the century as an age of nationalism.
Moreover, this was not only so in Williams's offering contrasting accounts of nationalism. Justifying E. H. Carr's
later remark "first know your historian," an important
idea, Williams himself exemplified the extent to which
historians came from many backgrounds, and many had
little to do with the formal process of historical education. Indeed, Williams was the first African American
to graduate from Newton Theological Institution near
Boston, a bastion of the liberal biblical criticism mentioned in the previous chapter. Born to poor free-black
parents, Williams fought in the American and Mexican
Civil Wars, was a Baptist minister and then lawyer, became the first African American elected to the Ohio state
legislature, strongly criticized both slavery in America

and the treatment of native people in the Congo, and also published *A History of Negro Troops in the War of Rebellion* (1887).[1] Williams scarcely matched Ranke in historical method but, in many respects, was more impressive as both individual and writer. The full-title of his first book also provides a sense of his ambition, as it continues: *Negroes as slaves, as soldiers, and as citizens; together with a preliminary consideration of the unity of the human family, an historical sketch of Africa, and an account of the negro governments of Sierra Leone and Liberia.*

It is a mistake to think that nationalism was only a condition of the modern age. As already discussed in chapter 2, nationalism is not a definition of modernity or vice versa. To refer then to the first age of modern nationalism captures the degree to which there were earlier nationalisms. The phrase also invites consideration of how far the modern, as discussed in chapter 3, is regarded as beginning in the fifteenth and sixteenth centuries. If so, nationalism might be seen in the unification of Japan in the 1580s–1620s, in Chinese resistance to the Manchu, or in the Protestant establishment of in effect state churches, notably in England but, also, in practice, elsewhere in Protestant Europe. The eventual success of Dutch and Portuguese opposition to Spanish rule can also be seen in this light, alongside the failure of the Bohemian counterpart against Austrian control.

That these episodes are considered in chapter 3, and, in contrast, a different and later age of nationalism in this chapter, does not establish some sort of development or progress. At any rate, the overthrows of imperial rule in 1775–1814, discussed in chapter 4, began another age of nationalism that is our subject now. This age ended with the internationalism thrown to the fore with the Bolshe-vik Revolution of 1917 and the reaction to it. The political volatility of this age understandably centered for many contemporaries on military history. That was the key form of historical commemoration, one that joined the classroom to the public square, the family to the nation. There were other types of history that were significant in the nineteenth century, notably high political and diplo-matic history, but it was to be military history that was emphasized. It provided narratives, explanations, and ex-emplary tales and linked the individual to the nation, the specific to the general, and the present to the past.

In addition, military history sold, as it continues to do. That is a dimension that tends to be underplayed in historiography, and the reasons are instructive. First, an emphasis on book sales gives agency to consumers—both readers and the implementing entrepreneurs in the shape of publishers, bookshops, and reviewers—rather than fo-cusing on authors. The logic of book sales has rarely ap-pealed to those who write about historiography, a logic that is commercial as well as relating to the public au-dience. Secondly, there has been a consistent tendency in the academic profession, and notably so in recent de-cades, to write down the significance of military history in the past or its consequence in the historical world of the present.

In the late nineteenth century, however, military his-tory appeared the most urgent for states and societies in competition, a competition enforced on individuals and families through comprehensive conscription systems. Historical education was the counterpart to these sys-tems, and this linkage helped explain why there could be scant tolerance of differing accounts about national development. Indeed, in the West, such differing accounts were present most in states that did not have conscription, notably America (with a brief exception during the Civil War) and Britain. The Protestantism of these states was also a factor.

Differing historical accounts were present in states with bitterly divided politics, such as France. Yet, not least as an aspect of this division and of how history "recovered" (represented) the experience of previous divisions, the general assumptions in these was that such difference, and indeed division, was wrong and weakening. Indeed, whatever the academic norms about the value of debate, there was a far more limited or, at least, restricted in its span public sympathy for its context, course, or consequences; a situation that has remained the case to the present.

History was profitable as well as apparently necessary. Profit, personal and otherwise, came from its role in the educational system, and from the possibilities for publishing created by rapidly increasingly populations, mass literacy, more disposable income, interest in a relevant past, and the ability to commodify this interest. Writers of both fact and fiction sought to engage readers and to socialize them in an exemplary account of the past. These accounts provided excitement but were also seen as able to counter the disorientating experience of rapid change in the present, if that view is not too instrumental and academic. Similarly, paintings, statuary, drama, and opera, like historical novels, sought to bridge fact and fiction.

Thus, Giacomo Meyerbeer's spectacular opera *Les Huguenots* (1836), a fictional (and lengthy) work that culminated in a real event, the St. Bartholomew's Day Massacre (1572), premiered with great success and was the first opera to be performed at the Paris Opéra more than a thousand times. This powerful attack on Catholic religious fanaticism was very much intended to relate to contemporary French politics. A similar attack occurs in Fromental Halévy's highly successful *La Juive* (1835), which was set in the Council of Constance of 1414, in which Cardinal de Brogni is the villain.

A heroic reading of Italy's past was more consistently offered in opera, which repeatedly provided an imaginative history that offered powerful images. Deeply committed to the Risorgimento but mindful of the problems posed by Austrian censorship, as Austria ruled much of Italy until 1866,[2] Giuseppi Verdi (1813–1901) used often distant and indirect references, rather as Gioachino Rossini (1792–1868) had done with *William Tell* (1829). In Verdi's *Nabucco* (1842), the exiled Hebrew slaves in Mesopotamia (Iraq) offered an allegory for oppressed Italians, while *La battaglia di Legnano* (1849) employed the defeat of the (German) Emperor Barbarossa by the Lombard League in 1176 as a rallying call for the present. Set in Mantua, *Rigoletto* (1851) depicted a villainous duke, presumably one of the Gonzaga who had ruled from 1328 to 1708. In *La Forza del Destino* (1861), Verdi showed the defeat at Velletri in 1744 of the Austrians by the Neapolitans. Verdi supported Giuseppe Garibaldi's expedition, a key episode in the Risorgimento, in 1860 and served in the Italian parliament.

In *Tosca* (which had its premiere in Rome in 1900 and was based on Victorien Sardou's 1887 play *La Tosca*), Giacomo Puccini (1858–1924) presented papal Rome in

1800 in the grip of counterrevolutionary forces who had suppressed the Roman Republic the previous year, as indeed happened. The heroes, Cavaradossi and Angelotti, are stalwarts of liberty, while the sadistic villain, Baron Scarpia, the head of the Secret Police, is out to suppress all those seeking change. Napoleon's failure or success echoes through the action, as his initial failure in the early stages of the battle of Marengo is greeted by the Papal authorities with a *Te Deum*, but his eventual success both inspires the captured Cavaradossi, a freethinker living in sin, to sing triumphantly of liberty and dismays Scarpia. Modern settings of the opera in Fascist Italy (1922–1943) do violence to the intensity of the moment it re-creates and reflect a glib and, often misleading, reading from one episode and cultural impulse to another. Yet, that is part of the more general bridging of history and also of the malleability of the past.

In the nineteenth century, as in other periods, the bridging of fact and fiction was part of the search for a workable or useable past. This was one that had to be defined and explained as the demands of a literate population appeared more pressing. This was notably so in the face of democratization and class consciousness, but the agenda also included new political units as well as responses to changes in religious observance.

As an aspect of an exemplary past, there was also an engagement with archaeology, ethnography, and philology as means to assert continuity and to propose a prehistory that linked place and people and provided authentication accordingly. This was an aspect of the essentialism of nationalism, one in which earlier peoples and periods were appropriated or overlooked.

The same processes of asserting identity through history and culture, and of linking people and place, were pushed hard by would-be countries seeking to assert their independent identity and autonomy, even independence. This was the case, for example, with the Confederacy in America and, eventually more successfully, with Finland, Poland, Ireland, and Norway in Europe. Locating the Confederacy with this list may well surprise some commentators, but it serves to underline the degree to which historical analysis is unfixed as so much depends on what is grouped together and on why this grouping occurs. The early 1860s saw failed rebellions in both America and Poland. They were dissimilar in many respects but so also are many instances that are put together for analysis.

Failure could lend particular energy to presenting history, as the losers had more of a reason to challenge outcomes. Thus, émigrés were an important part of the presentation of history, one in which a sense of cultural and political distinction was important. Histories were a key instance of such distinction. In 1762, Paisij Xilendarski's Slavo-Bulgarian history was completed. A glorious and united past could be part of this process of national assertion, although, prior to 1900, there were few successes, other than Belgium breaking away from the Netherlands in 1830. The staging of a historical opera, commemorating the 1647 Neapolitan rising against Spanish rule, Daniel Auber's dramatic *La Muette de Portici* (1828), helped provoke the initial rising in Brussels in 1830.

The creation of Germany and Italy, although asserted as nationalism, was in part a matter of state-building on the part of Prussia and Piedmont, just as expansion by Wessex had been a key element in the establishment of the

Old English state in the tenth century and that of Castile and Aragon in the Reconquista from the Moors in Spain. Moreover, underlining the questionable nature of developmental ideas, the extent to which each of these episodes of nation-building was due to unification, or a cause of it, can be debated. German institutions and patriotism (and Italian patriotism, but not institutions) long preceded this conjuncture in the mid-nineteenth century and could lead, and have continued to lead, in different directions. Monumental assertion was part of the process. In 1879, Wilhelm I lent strong support to the reconstruction of the Goslar imperial palace built by Henry III (r. 1017–1056). The large-scale historical paintings in the great hall depicted the glorious past when Salian emperors lived in the town. Large bronze statues of Emperor Frederick I "Barbarossa" (r. 1152–1190) were part of the equation. The entire project reflected a yearning for historical significance, as the Second Reich, in fact a Prussian enterprise, sought, like other new states before and since, to accumulate suitable antecedents. In 1874, Wilhelm erected a monument over the grave of Emperor Lothair I (r. 817–855) in Prüm.

The German search for medieval antecedents was more widespread than simply a case of Prussia-Germany. Thus, Ludwig II of Bavaria (r. 1864–1886) provided a Gothic revival character for Bavarian monarchy, one that underlined its own historical roots and prestige, especially with reference to Emperor Louis IV, the Bavarian (r. 1328–1347). These roots were also seen with the castle building of Ludwig, notably at Neuschwanstein. Neo-Gothic building was a dominant theme of the period.

These processes were not simply stylistic but in practice intensely political, not least as the identities of states were contested past, present, and future. This was not only the case of would-be nations, such as Poland, but also of imperial powers. Napoleon III, in his attempt to demonstrate a pre-Roman origin for France, commemorated the Gauls' resistance to Roman conquest, notably at the site of Alesia in 52 BCE, the last stand of resistance, erecting there a bronze statue of Vercingétorix of the Arverni tribe, its leader. A divided tribal opposition was presented as the valorous resistance of a Gaulish nation. The defeat had been bad, but France was given a hero, and France entered civilization—in the form of Roman civilization—which, for Napoleon III, looking in retrospect, was an excellent thing. Moreover, linkage with Rome was a means to underline Catholic identity, for France had become Catholic under the Roman Empire. Divisions within France—for example, over relations with the Habsburgs in the early seventeenth century—were downplayed or ignored, in this case the dévots, who sought an anti-Protestant alliance with the Habsburgs, clashing in the 1620s and 1630s with the policy of Cardinal Richelieu.

Recent history was also at issue. Thus, Napoleon III criticized earlier regimes for failing to modify the terms of the Congress of Vienna (1814–1815), terms that he alleged humiliated France. In turn, Napoleon III's defeat at the hands of Germany in 1870 served to castigate him and was highlighted by discussion of more successful rulers, such as Philip Augustus (r. 1180–1223), Henry IV (r. 1589–1610), and Louis XIV (r. 1643–1715). Under the Third Republic (1870–1940), there was a tension between tracing origins to the pre-Roman Gauls, the approach favored by supporters of the republic, or to the Franks, the approach supported by conservative opponents as the latter, who favored a Catholic identity for France, looked to the baptism of Clovis, France's first Christian monarch in 508: he had converted to Catholicism in 496. Republicans had scant sympathy with the medieval period, which was presented as dominated by an anarchic nobility and, in part, by English intervention. In contrast to conservatives, it was an age of devotion and social stability.

Heroic but failed resistance to Roman conquest was also commemorated in a dramatic statue near Parliament, *Boadicea and her Daughters* by Thomas Thornycroft. Erected in 1902, it was ironic in its location in that the Iceni under Boadicea (Boudicca) had burned down London. Earlier, William Hutchinson, in his *History of the County of Cumberland* (1794), in the case of the Brigantes and Druids, and Edward Gibbon in that of the Caledonians saw primitive virtue as opposed to vice-ridden Romans. In this, Gibbon in part drew on the Roman historian Tacitus, for the contrast was also seen with Roman writers.

In contrast, Italian nationalists had nothing positive to say about those who had overthrown the Western Roman Empire in the fifth century. Indeed, the Risorgimento of Italian nationalism was strongly grounded in the idea of a Roman revival, and Roman glory and heritage were always mentioned in its speeches, letters, and works. As first a republic and then an empire, Italy offered a range of references. Due to the unwillingness to incorporate conquerors, the Goths and, more briefly, Huns who dominated fifth century Italy, were excluded from the codependency of history and geography that was so important to the historical nationalism of the nineteenth century.

In Germany, this codependency led to the focus on *Heimat*, a local identity that was expressed within the context of a Germanness that was at once national and about ideas of home. This was an effective strand of nationalism that built on earlier practices of identity, including of religion, dialect, family, and occupation. A *Heimat* movement came to be significant from the 1890s, with its institutionalization in museums of local history and in other forms of localist heritage, not least the evolution of "peasant costumes." At a time of urbanization and industrialization, this was very much a small-town and rural Germany, one that prefigured similar trends in twentieth-century America and Japan.

The stress on particular ethnicities and landscapes was part of the process by which the nation was both expressed and created. Expression and creation were two sides of the same coin, as nationhood entailed prioritizing among multiple and potentially competing identities.

This tension was repeatedly present. In Portugal, the long resistance in 208–17 BCE, to eventual Roman conquest, a resistance that had impressed Roman commentators as well as providing a way to praise their own successes, attracted interest in the nineteenth century from nationalist commentators and artists engaged with the idea of an exemplary pre-Roman national origin and concerned to trace difference from Spain to pre-Roman tribes. However, there was a marked preference in Portugal, instead, for claiming a Roman legacy and for focusing not on the resistance to the Romans but, instead, on the eventually successful medieval resistance to the Muslims. The latter resistance could be presented as having an exemplary Christian character.

Whereas, in Italy, there was an understandable focus on a glorious Roman past, in Portugal the Roman legacy was less significant and also far less present, indeed less present than in Spain, which was more integrated into the Roman Empire. Like Britain, Portugal was to use the Roman legacy in the nineteenth century to justify its transoceanic colonial rule, but it shrugged off the administrative legacy of Roman rule of the peninsula focusing instead on the centuries of state formation in the medieval period. This stress was encouraged because it was only then that Portugal became a separate state. Moreover, the emphasis on Christianity was not on its origins under Roman rule but rather as the product of the driving back of the Moors.

The Roman legacy was not the sole one from antiquity open to Westerners in this period. Indeed, an intensification of links with other cultures offered variety. Greece could be accessed within the Roman tradition, but far less so Egypt, let alone Mesopotamia. This linkage was an element in Napoleonic interest in Egypt but also with the acquisition by modern empires of references to those of the past, for example, Paris acquiring a pharaonic obelisk in 1833 and London, another, Cleopatra's Needle, which was erected atop the recently completed Victoria Embankment in 1876, where it remains. The naming indicated a ready process of location historically, but this obelisk otherwise had nothing whatever to do with Cleopatra. Museums provided a sense of cultural progression culminating in the present institution. This was a potent historiography.

At the same time, the selectivity involved was readily apparent. Some past cultures appeared of greater interest or relevance, in part because of the stories and ancestry that could be told about and through them. There was also the issue of the drama of the past, as with the Assyrian remains shown in the British Museum. There was a re-contextualization of such remains that argued to present interests. The remains that failed to engage comparable engagement were decontextualised in the abrupt form of being held in reserve collections and never shown. This was a parallel with aspects of the metropolitan culture that no longer appeared of particular interest.

More generally, the process of national expression was supported by historians and para-historians, such as archivists, many of whom benefited greatly from state-supported educational systems and in a very different fashion from earlier ecclesiastical systems. Unsurprisingly, these individuals were keen backers of the official national approach to history. This differs from the liberal, at times radical, Western academic culture of the present day, but, today, far from this critique being typical, the role of the state is more accepted in some Western and most non-Western societies.

Nationalism was also seen as necessary when discussing foreign states. Thus, Ramsay Muir, writing in 1911, instructed his readers to consider the map of Europe in 1815 in the following light:

> Note especially the features of the settlement, which by disregarding national sentiment produced the principal troubles of the 19th century: (1) The forced union of Sweden and Norway; (2) the similar union of Holland and Belgium; (3) the restoration of the old disunion in Italy and the controlling power exercised by Austria there in the possession of Lombardy and Venetia; the one favourable feature being the expansion of the kingdom of Sardinia by the addition of Liguria and other lands; (4) the revival, in the German Confederation, of a ghost of the old Holy Roman Empire,

powerless to achieve anything and useful only as an aid to
Austria in checking any movement towards unity or liberty.

This is a reminder that works on historiography should
include not just academic tomes but also the wide range
of aligned works, which, in dictionaries and encyclope-
dias can be highly directive, not least in deliberately being designed to lack ambiguity. Any implication that an
academic who produces such a work is somehow part of
an ethereal priesthood of quality, while those who are
nonacademics lack that capability, is ridiculous.

Returning to the nineteenth century, the linkage of
self-consciously scientific history in Prussia/Germany
(with its emphasis on the detailed study of sources), with
support for German nationalism, was more generally programmatic. Yet, this link was particularly the case with
German academic culture and its influence elsewhere.
Although the German empire created in 1871, very much
was formed as a counterpoint to the other German (and
Habsburg-ruled) empire based in Vienna, its identity was
given a would-be legitimating longevity by having a medieval forbear in the shape of the first empire, that from 800
to 1806. In practice, the latter was, more properly, linked
with the Austrian empire through having had Habsburg
rule from 1438, with only one brief exception, in the early
1740s. In practice, indeed, the Prusso-German account
was convenient rather than accurate, but that was very
much a pattern in the deployment of the past. The notion
of potent medieval forbears proved particularly attractive
in nineteenth-century Europe, as well as in Japan, for it
provided not only longevity and legitimacy but also an
apparent counterpointing to an alleged loss of value in

modern industrial society. The latter greatly worried rural elites, not least due to the extent to which this society appeared to place value on everything bar lineage. There was no equivalent medievalism in the Americas, but there could be a ruralism and small-town identity opposed to such industrial society. Moreover, this ruralism/small-town identity could be linked to racist concepts of cultural identity and to particular hostility to immigration.

In the case of Germany, there was also the lesson that the first empire had been undermined by particularism, especially weakened against foreign threats, and that care needed to be taken to guard against a return of this weakness. The protonationalism made possible by the long identity of individual German territories such as Bavaria and Saxony combined with the closely intertwined history of bitter religious difference within Germany since the Reformation were to be subsumed by the successful use by Prussia's Hohenzollern dynasty of German nationalism. Ignoring or underplaying past cooperation with non-German powers, such as France in the late 1670s, this agenda very much focused on past conflict with others, especially France. This approach was taken forward by memorialization, as with the monument erected in Leipzig to commemorate the centenary of the crushing defeat of Napoleon in 1813.[3] This process was to be continued in the cauldron of world war. In turn, rival German powers were criticized for being allied with non-German counterparts. Thus, Gustav Droysen, in his influential *Geschichte der Preussischen Politik* (1855–1886), argued that the Austrians were overly beholden in the seventeenth century to Spain, which was presented as Jesuitical.

This process was similar in other new states. In general, there was a zero-sum approach to the past, with historical nationalism basing its success on the defeats of rivals, whether internationalisms, such as the Papacy, other nationalisms, would-be nationalisms, or domestic opposition and limitations. This was seen, for example, in Italy with the shunning of separate consciousnesses, notably that offered by Naples. Yet, in many states, such "antiseparatism" was relatively unproblematic compared to the extent to which constructions of national identity could interact strongly with political contention at the national level. At the same time, the combination could pose serious issues of political identity, as did the Irish Question for Britain.

This interaction was, differently, seen repeatedly in France with the reworking and presentation of history in order to provide acceptable versions for the present, notably so for the ancien régime, the French Revolution, and Napoleon. These versions could be directed at political rivals but also at what were presented as negative social, ethnic, or cultural groups, notably Jews, Freemasons, Protestants, and, on the other political flank, Catholic zealots and the Papacy. With such paranoid typecasting, the pattern for the more recent age of nationalism that stemmed from the end of the Cold War was clearly set.

In Italy, the papal role in opposing the Risorgimento ensured that liberal nationalism was directed against it, and history was developed and deployed accordingly. The rationalism and astronomical ideas of Galileo Galilei (1564–1642), a prominent mathematician, had led to condemnation by the Inquisition in 1633 and to Pope Clement XIII (r. 1730–1740) trying to prevent the erection of a mausoleum for him in Florence. Instead, Galilei became a hero for the newly created nation. In 1887, a marble column to him, a public sign of approval, was inaugurated in Rome, the event applauded by the anticlerical press and sharply criticized by the official Vatican newspaper. Bologna, another city from which papal power had been driven, gained a Piazza Galileo.

As a result of the harsh treatment of the Papacy as well as the intransigence of the latter toward the new Italian state, the ability of the Risorgimento to act as a unifying national myth was compromised. Yet, linked to the belief in struggle and war, the Risorgimento was the central narrative in the history of the new state. Many prominent individuals had a particular history. Francesco Crispi, Liberal prime minister in 1887–1890 and 1893–1896, had taken part in the revolutions of 1848 and had joined Garibaldi in invading Sicily in 1860, the totemic episode in the Risorgimento.

Success was inscribed in street names and statues across Italy, with streets and squares named after the rulers of the House of Savoy, now, thanks to unification, kings of Italy, and after the politicians, ministers and military leaders who had furthered the Risorgimento, notably Mazzini, Cavour, and Garibaldi. Thus, formerly a papal town, Ancona has a Corso Garibaldi and a Corso Mazzini. Urbino, another former papal town, gained a Corso Garibaldi. In Siena, the Museo Civico includes a Sala del Risorgimento offering the standard frescoes of the period that depicted the narrative of the Risorgimento. In Massa Marittima, the Piazza Duomo became the Piazza Garibaldi. The difference between the leaders meant that it was possible to strike contrasting political resonances.

Deeper history was also deployed in order to provide accounts and images of an exemplary past. Thus, the restoration of Portuguese independence from Spain in

1640–1668 was commemorated in central Lisbon with the obelisk erected in 1886 in the Praça dos Restauradores. The obelisk records the names and dates of the battles in the War of Restoration, the name itself programmatic for public history, while the bronze figures on the pedestal show Victory and Freedom. Individual families also maintained their relevant heritage. For example, the title of Marquês de Fronteira had been granted to Dom João de Mascarenhas, Second Count of Torre, to reward his participation in the war, and his palace, built in 1671, included a "Battle Room."

Very differently, the liberals of nineteenth-century Portugal and Spain seized monastic lands, which was presented as a move toward modernity. This seizure disrupted the institutional fabric and continuity of many communities. Thus, Oporto's São Bento railway station, finished in 1916, was built on the site of a monastery. Many monasteries became barracks.

So even more with the republican revolution in Portugal in 1910. This led to changes in symbolism, from the national anthem to place names, as well as action against popular religious festivals. In Lisbon, the royal palace was turned into government offices, while the name of the Rua das Trinas was changed to Rua Sara de Matos, whom it was alleged had been murdered by nuns, and a large monument was built to this "martyr" at the Prazeres Cemetery. Across the country, the main town square became the Praça da República. As part of the new history, the anarchists who had murdered Charles I and his heir in Lisbon in 1908 were rehabilitated. This was a narrative that linked the contexts for history presentation in the nineteenth century with those in the twentieth.

The role of violence, in fact or by means of intimidation, was to be common in many, if not most, nondemocratic changes of governance, "history" thus receiving a helping hand. However, there was a degree to which many revolutions were unhappy with this legacy, or preferred to present change as emerging from the popular will as part of an inevitability of transformation. This element represented a newly vigorous idiom for a process that can be readily traced to antiquity.

At the same time, whatever the discontinuities linked to violence, there was an emphasis on themes of continuity, with national identity providing a theme against which present rulers or governments could be seen and presented as inadequate. This was a means of historical argument both in democracies and in revolutionary situations, but not in autocracies unless at the expense of rival states or supposedly challenging international forces. Thus, in 1904, Winston Churchill, breaking with the Conservatives and declaring his candidacy as a "Free Trade" supporter backed by the Liberals, as opposed to the protectionism of the Conservative government, asked the voters of northwest Manchester "Whether we are to model ourselves upon the clanking military empires of the Continent of Europe, with their gorgeous Imperial hierarchy fed by enormous tariffs, defended by mighty armies, and propped by every influence of caste privilege and commercial monopoly, or whether our development is to proceed by well-tried English methods towards the ancient and lofty ideals of English citizenship." The following April, Churchill referred in a speech to the "regular, settled lines of English democratic development" underpinning the "free British Empire."[4] Alongside such themes of development came the use of episodes from the past in order to provide comments for the present, not least symbolic and mythic supports in times of praise or solace.[5] At the same time, the past could be criticized, and from a variety of directions, as well as praised,[6] and this contestation was probably more common than the currently available studies indicate, as the latter are apt to focus on the creation of a useful historical myth, a process referred to as the invention of tradition.

Environmentalism as an apparently determining factor in historical development became less significant in the early twentieth century than in discussion in the late nineteenth century, when environmentalism was to the fore both in the shadow of evolutionary ideas and with reference to the specific characteristics of individual countries. In part, this reflected a greater primacy for ideological programs that sought a global scope unrelated to nationalism, notably Communism. However, there were also important intellectual developments, particularly, but not only, in France and America. As with so much that relates to historiography, this was not a case of developments narrowly defined in terms of the work of historians. In France, the key figure, Paul Vidal de la Blache (1843–1918), professor of geography at the Sorbonne from 1899, argued that the environment created a context for human development rather than determining it.

The emphasis on causation was therefore shifted back to humanity and to the varieties of human activity. Vidal de la Blache sought to bridge fact and fiction. František Palacký (1798–1876), himself very much part of the great national awakening, observed, "One Czech Sir Walter Scott would be a bigger boost for Czech interests than five Zizkas," the last a reference to a Czech military leader of the fifteenth century.[7]

Vidal de la Blache's work was taken up by Lucien Febvre (1878–1956), who preferred the idea of an interaction between environment and humanity to that of influences and also directed attention to the problematic nature of the sources of environmental determinism that were all-too-often presented in simplistic terms, for example, climate. An advocate of "possibilisme," Febvre was to be prominent among the *Annales* school of French historians, who were to be the most significant group of the twentieth-century, a school named after its journal, *Annales d'histoire économique et social*, which was established in 1929 by Febvre and Marc Bloch. The emphasis was on long-term trends and on socioeconomic history.

Criticism of environmental determinism was also voiced in America, notably by Frederick Jackson Turner (1861–1932), professor at Harvard from 1910 to 1922, who emphasized the role of the frontier in American history. Turner stressed human dynamism, social factors, and interaction with the environment and proved very influential, not least within the American Historical Association, as well as helped his students into important jobs and ensuring that frontier topics became influential in the teaching of American history. The thesis also affected popular histories, including novels and films, although these were scarcely dependent on Turner's work. Yet, although the latter eventually attracted scholarly criticism, that had scant influence on the public presentation of the West.[8] This contrast is more generally the case, and should direct attention to the popular histories and formats.

SEVEN

HISTORY IN THE LONG COLD WAR, 1917–1989

HISTORY IN THE TWENTIETH CENTURY was not a limp accompaniment to an age rushing to make the future. This chapter will show that that was not the case, but shaping the period in terms of a clear context and obvious narrative is far from easy.

The lack of a uniform background is one element that makes this task difficult. An age of nationalism might seem an ironic or ridiculous title for a period of spreading empires in the nineteenth and very early twentieth centuries, empires—such as the British in Egypt, the Japanese in Korea and the American in the Philippines—that suppressed nationalism. Yet, it is a reasonable assessment. There was the rise of new nations in Latin America and, later, the nationalistic unification of Italy and Germany, as well as the expression of nationalistic sentiment more generally in Europe. The description also carries the extent to which the apparently global civilizational message of Western liberalism, certainly a self-regarding message, was in practice expressed in terms of national empires and related commercial and fiscal patterns.

A different situation, however, was to pertain from 1917. Western nation-empires continued until the mid-1970s, when the last major one, that of Portugal, collapsed in 1974–1975 following the Carnation Revolution. Moreover, these empires, individually and in aggregate, grew to unprecedented size (for them) after World War I (1914–1918), as Britain and France gained much of the Ottoman Empire, while the transoceanic German Empire went to them or their allies. Yet, separately, there was also the need and narrative for new nonimperial nation-states, or pseudo-nation-states, that emerged from the chaos of the war. This was the case in eastern Europe, from Finland southward to the new federal state of a Yugoslavia based on a Greater Serbia, on the pattern of earlier Piedmontese or Prussian expansion. The Serbian king became Peter of Yugoslavia in 1918. As a result of internal strife, notably in the 1910s, there were also non-Western states with a post-imperial ideology: China, Turkey, and, very differently, Iran and Saudi Arabia, a group that was to be joined by Egypt and Iraq, albeit both being under the shadow of continued British power.

Monarchy was a theme in some, although not all (for example, not in Czechoslovakia, Finland, the Baltic Republics, China, or Turkey), of these new states. Thus, the role of the ruler was central to the historical message in Iran prior to the overthrow of the monarchy in 1978–1979. In the *Historical Atlas of Iran* (1971), which celebrated the background to the Pahlevi dynasty and, more particularly, the shah's regime, the monarchs of the early tenth to the mid-eleventh century "put great effort into reviving national traditions, preserving the customs of their ancestors and providing for the welfare of their subjects.

This is true to such an extent that it can be said that the era of the greatest attainment of Iranian civilisation and of the Islamic sciences and literature is the period of these same noble and magnanimous men." Subsequent problems were blamed on barbarians in the shape of the Mongols—"domination by savage yellow-skinned tribes from Central Asia," who created a dark age lasting to the start of the sixteenth century. Rebirth then was associated with a dynasty, that of the Safavids, who were described in terms of a prospectus for the necessary government of Iran as seen by the ruling Pahlevi dynasty: "a strong and independent central government," and the extension of Iran to its "natural frontiers." Moreover, "the archaeological evidence . . . shows that the people of Iran possessed an extremely advanced civilisation as long ago as 7000 years," which was a standard form of assertion through longevity.

However, as with Western empires, others could experience these non-Western states as empires. Indeed, the process by which rule was consolidated and boundaries were affirmed saw this situation. So also did the recasting, as with the creation of Turkey from the Ottoman Empire, of once "multiple" empires as ethnically more unitary in their identity. This recasting involved the suppression of other voices, such as Greeks and Armenians. An imperial nationalism was also the experience of tribes and other minority groups repressed in Iran, Iraq, Saudi Arabia, and elsewhere, for example, Iraqi Christians.

Yet, alongside continued Western nation-empires and new non-Western ones, there was also a state that claimed to propound a universal ideology, valid across time and space, and one that it both sought to foster and found

supporters for elsewhere. Russia, violently reconceptualized as the Soviet Union, was in practice a totalitarian empire that enforced its control in areas that sought to resist
but were conquered in 1919–1921, notably Central Asia, the
Caucasus, and Ukraine. This empire drew on a range of
historical backgrounds, including Russian expansionism
and the worker internationalism that offered a different
form of expansionism as well as the nineteenth-century
tension between Slavophils and Westernizers, the Marxist theory that provided a sense of historical inevitability,
and the element of fatalism, which has always been an
underrated aspect of the historical psyche.

Had Russia remained the power limited by opposition in 1918–1921, then its significance would have been
restricted. Then, with the support in particular of Britain
and France, its forces were repelled from Poland, Finland,
and the Baltic republics (Estonia, Latvia, Lithuania), a
development that the Soviet Union sought to ignore and,
indeed, largely reversed in 1939–1941 and with greater success, but eventual failure, in 1944–1991. In turn, under Putin there has been a major attempt to expand anew both
power and influence.

In 1918–1921, Russia's allies totally failed to gain lasting traction in Hungary, Germany, and elsewhere. And
even more so, the Kuomintang (Chinese nationalists)
moving on from overcoming the warlords, defeated
or largely contained Chinese Communism in a series of struggles from 1927 until the late 1930s—struggles
that are largely left out of the narrative of the modern
Chinese state, apart from as part of a laudatory account
of Mao Zedong's career. Ironically, the failure of modern
China to come to grips with the relative success of the

Kuomintang prior to World War II leads to an underrating of the later Communist success in the Chinese Civil War of 1946–1949. So also does the Communist emphasis on Kuomintang deficiencies, which, by making the outcome inevitable in terms of some supposed Marxist/Maoist teleology, leads to an underplaying of the military achievement of imposing defeat on it.

Yet, however limited territorially by opposition, the Soviet approach in the early stages of the Cold War, those prior to World War II, was of broader significance because it won a degree of support then in both the West and the non-West and, thus, became part of the historical debate. At the same time, there were cross-currents in the Soviet historical consciousness. As with the French Revolution, the early Communists broke with the past. In part, this break reflected the Marxist idea of revolutionary progress, but there was also the very significant opposition to the Russian Orthodox Church, which had been highly important to the ideology of the Romanov dynasty. Indeed, in this and other instances, it is impossible adequately to consider the history of history without devoting due attention to the roles of religion and antireligion. This situation very much remains the case. As a result, nationalist or Communist accounts that underplay the role of religion, or treat it as only an expression of "underlying realities," are flawed. The role of religion was an aspect of the degree to which there was in Russia, alongside changes in regime direction, a continuity in social practice. This was an aspect of the "upward-facing" as well as "downward-directing" aspect of public history.

Joseph Stalin, the Communist dictator of the Soviet Union from 1928 to 1953, was personally greatly interested in Russian and Communist history, on which he published. Under his rule, there was a broadening out of the official historical consciousness to include a Russian imperialism judged acceptable. Yet, Leninist internationalism and Soviet Marxism both remained in the Soviet historical quiver under Stalin, and each helped ensure a measure of support across the world.

Communist historical works had strengths as well as weaknesses. The concern to highlight social and economic history was the key instance of the former. There was a parallel with the interest elsewhere in such topics, notably in the case of the *Annales* school in France, but whereas the latter saw open intellectual enquiry, this was not the case with the Soviet Union. Instead, limitations were imposed by the narrow and rigid official ideology. This led to ahistorical perceptions and often to exaggeration of what were taken to be developments in the "forces of production" and manifestations of "class struggle." Capitalism was presented as internally divided and dependent on suppressing widespread popular opposition, the latter, including anti-imperial struggles, understood in Marxist terms. In general, the extent and importance of popular risings were exaggerated in order to substantiate the theme of class war. In contrast, Communist works emphasized external but not internal opposition and threats in Communist states. The impact of such works was increased by the very rigid nature of the national curriculum in Communist states, with every school supposed to teach the same thing, to the same class, at the same time, which was also the case in France.

Aside from Communism, there was also in the early twentieth century a more general modernism that had scant interest in the past or that could castigate it as a cause of pathology, as in the cruder public use of psychiatric ideas and language. As with Darwin and evolution, Freud and psychiatry were to be applied in a fashion that was not intended by the progenitor, but that was scarcely surprising. Indeed, this process reflected the extent to which history, both as subject and as practice, drew heavily on other subjects, and sought to use them as convenient. This is a consistent theme in historiography. In part, it is a product of the make-do nature of a subject necessarily driven to expedients in order to understand and explain phenomena arranged in a past that cannot be readily recovered through an equivalent to experimentation. The repetition under recordable circumstances of the latter, the essence of research in the physical sciences, is alien to the academic study of history, although not to how it is frequently experienced and discussed, namely as a repeated phenomenon. Indeed, individual and collective fear can be an aspect of this experience and discussion of the past.

Among the other cultural movements of the early twentieth century, modernism challenged established methods of representation, searching for different forms of reality and unreality, and in a fashion that included variants that challenged the notion of history. Thus, launched in Italy in 1909, and self-consciously dynamic, Futurism wanted to destroy the old, and in 1910 its founder, Filippo Tommaso Marinetti, called for the asphalting or paving of the Grand Canal in Venice because it was allegedly a symbol of the past and of past values. While correct, this was not terribly helpful as a response. More generally, the role of young males in revolutionary movements was another aspect of modernism, and was linked to revolutionary ideology providing a substitute providentialism in its own arms and/or framing ideologies as prophets or seers with their own eschatology.

Meanwhile, there were more immediate problems. The collapse of empires created the need for workable histories on the part of new states, such as Ireland and Iraq, in part as an aspect of stabilization. Thus in Ireland, where independence was followed by civil war and the defeats of antigovernmental forces opposed to the partition of the island, "history," and notably recent history, had a correct tinge, if not more. In some cases, part of this workable character for history was expounded in light of how the new histories would accord with that of the Cold War, because states adopted a position in this international confrontation that was at once geopolitical, socioeconomic, and cultural. More generally, there was the need to make success appear correct. As many conflicts involved ethnic rivalry, and notably so in eastern Europe, there was an ethnographic character to the relevant history.

Soviet ideology and policy also fired up an anti-Soviet historical consciousness that added the issues of the post-1917 present to longer-term identities and views. These ranged to include, prominently, Catholic antisecularism, Polish and Japanese nationalism, and British imperialism but also much else. Indeed, the Cold War, both the first and the second one that followed World War II, helped provide a call to action, both ideological and more pragmatic, for and against Communism.

Differently, the Soviet Union was also more widely significant in that it provided a model for the authoritarian direction of all aspects of society including the use and presentation of history. That does not imply that non-Communist states copied from the Soviet Union, as the Communist ones were to do; but, rather, that this direction posed a challenge to those seeking to confront the Soviet Union.

The attention devoted by historians and other commentators to the ideological struggle of the 1930s focuses in particular on the rival case of Nazi Germany (1933–1945). Its regime drew, for its use of history, on the attitudes of relevant leaders, notably Adolf Hitler; on German traditions, especially far-right ones but also those of the government system; and on the example of Fascist Italy under Mussolini. Yet, although Hitler was to ally with Stalin in 1939–1941, hostility to Communism was insistent and second in his obsessive and brutal drives, being surpassed only by his genocidal hatred of Judaism, which to Hitler was a historic struggle capable of defining history. The Nazis established a totalitarian regime but were not consistent in their approach to history. Historians had to be non-Jewish as well as very, very pro-German (as many Jews were), but there was eclecticism, not just in responding to circumstances but also in continuing writing as before but with only a few routine phrases added. While anti-Habsburg, Hitler was not consistently opposed to Austrian traditions. In one of his *Tischgespräche,* Hitler railed against sycophants who tried to prove that medieval emperors, like Hitler, should have turned east rather than south toward Italy. He complained in 1942 that a few centuries on, he did not want a professor to accuse him of having chosen the wrong path. Instead, he argued that things had to be judged by their context. Hitler went on to defend Charlemagne, whom Himmler had attacked, with reason, as a Saxon slayer.[1]

The depiction of the regime as the Third Reich was a clear departure from the democratic Weimar Republic (1919–1933), a depiction that linked the Nazi regime to the First (800–1806) and Second (1871–1918) Reichs, and, in the latter case, took forward the Prussian unification of Germany. This process downgraded regional historical narratives, such as that of Bavaria, which had retained an independent monarchy until 1918.

Nazi history saw an intertwining of ideology, ethnicity, and geopolitics. The history of the Germans was presented in a dramatic fashion, and the contemporary struggle against Communism as a necessary continuation of resisting past threats. Launched in 1941, the major offensive designed to lead to the overthrow of the Soviet Union was named after the Emperor Barbarossa.

Under the Nazis, past themes of German national history were linked to a determination to assert Aryan superiority, and there was a persistent meshing of national and racial themes. For the Nazis, race not the state was the central theme in nation and country, and this provided a link with the remote past, including through archaeology. This reach back to the power of the past offered an account different to the Soviet focus on the future. The emphasis on race was used to substantiate Nazi antisemitism, but did not itself explain the separate millenarian fervor, one imposed on the Jews with apocalyptic violence.[2] Hitler's sense that he understood this dimension to German and world history helped ensure that, to him, history was a lived process that he encapsulated. From this narrative, flowed the particular manifestations of Nazi history, from the purging and appointment of academics and teachers, to such spheres as film and archaeology. Nazi racism meant a particular focus on past family members, in a perverted search for a non-Jewish "purity" that could only be proven from the past.

There was a rapid recasting of the present to demonstrate an exemplary past. Thus, in 1933, on Hitler's birthday, there was a performance of Hanns Johst's play *Schlageter*, which included the line "When I hear 'culture' . . . I release the safety catch on my Browning." The hero, Albert Schlageter, a Freikorps member executed by the French in 1923 for sabotaging a railway, was also referred to in Hitler's *Mein Kampf* and commemorated in memorials. Johst (1890–1978), an SS officer as well as a dramatist of Nazi themes, remained unrepentant to the end. Nazi memorialization included temples of honor in Munich for those killed in 1923 in Hitler's unsuccessful coup attempt. Academics who came to the fore, or further to the fore, might be competent historians, but they were often antisemites. Thus, Heinrich Ritter von Srbik, a member of the Reichstag and president of the Academy of Sciences from 1938 to 1945, a German nationalist, had been a member of the Bärenhöhle (bear cave) prewar antisemitic group of academics who kept Jewish academics from the University of Vienna.[3] His wartime *Wien und Versailles 1692–1697* (1944) is a scholarly study, but in 1942 in the last volume of his *Deutsche Einheit* (German Unity), he praised Hitler's achievement and referred to Germany's thousand-year mission.

The emphasis on national strength was to be continued in the post-Hitler world by historians who had been members of the Nazi Party either from conviction or as opportunistic men for all seasons. Thus, in his *Friedrich der Grosse* (1983), Theodor Schieder (1908–1984), a major historian from a Third Reich background, described the First Reich as anachronistic and the Habsburg monarchy as "an hermaphrodite." Instead, he presented Prussia as having a necessary sense of mission. Aside from Schieder's worship of military success in the case of Frederick the Great (r. 1740–1786), such a study was an unintended commentary on the extent to which 1806 saw not only the end of the First Reich but also Prussia's heavy defeat by Napoleon. Nazis were apt to see Frederick as a worthy predecessor for Hitler, who also liked to present himself as a military genius and thus as able to impose his skill and will on circumstances, no matter the weight of resources deployed against him.

Conversely, the flight of Jewish historians helped provide an important burst to transnationalism in terms of historical knowledge, interests, and ideas. Indeed, this was possibly the most significant moment of academic historians ever, partly because of the scale but also because the Germanic lands were the leading centers of historical scholarship. In contrast to such scholarship, there was much about the American and British traditions of appointment and promotion that was reliant on the ability offered by background, lineage, and connections rather than the irritations posed by having to produce scholarly research. I noted this culture when, after appointment to the University of Durham, a leading British department, in 1980, I was advised by the second-ranking modernist that a doctorate was unnecessary. I, however, chose not to follow his example. This flight proved particularly significant in America and Britain. As a student in Cambridge in the 1970s, I was taught by Jewish (Geoffrey Elton) and part-Jewish (Walter Ullmann) historians who had fled the Nazis, the first an expert on Tudor England and the second on the medieval Papacy.

The role of diaspora historians, in this case refugees from Communism (and, in some cases, anti-Communism), was also prominent during the Cold War. This role was to be made more significant by the extent to which the end of the latter saw the emergence of a fresh series of nation-states, providing opportunities to reintegrate diaspora perspectives. During the Cold War, relevant works in the diaspora contested the views offered in the Communist world. *Ukraine: A Historical Atlas* (1985) was published by Paul Magocsi, professor of Ukrainian studies at the University of Toronto, and owed much in its publication there to the support of Peter Jacyk, a Canadian Ukrainian. Following on from the eminent Ukrainian historian Mykhailo Hrushevsky, Magocsi's emphasis was on the continuity of Ukraine and it was treated both as a country and as the area occupied by Ukrainians rather than the Ukrainian Soviet Socialist Republic. In the preface, Magocsi wrote, "Like most other countries, Ukraine has experienced varying periods of political discontinuity. This means that, like Belgium, Poland, Italy, or Germany, for instance, Ukraine might not have existed in its present form, or even as a concept during long periods in the past. Yet, the histories of those countries from earliest times according to their present-day boundaries—and Ukraine is no exception— are legitimate subjects of study." Thus, Ukraine was compared to other countries that were independent.

Other conservative authoritarian states, from Italy to Slovakia, Brazil to Spain, saw aspects of the tendencies present in Nazi Germany, but, in each case, with an emphasis in accord with the circumstances and ideology of

the regime, notably its leader, as well as of potential opponents. History as presented was to reflect an ideology that
was actively pursued. There was a common anti-Communism, an ethnic consciousness, an authoritarianism,
and a Catholic politics, without, however, implying any
papal role. History was deployed to present these values
and to annex the past accordingly, sometimes in a highly
misleading fashion.

In 1934, under António de Oliveira Salazar, the Portuguese prime minister from 1932 to 1968, a monument to
the Marquis of Pombal, chief minister from 1756 to 1777,
was unveiled in Lisbon, the base of the monument referring to Pombal's reforms. Salazar built the statue to honor
Pombal's political strength and concern to revive state
and empire, and depicted himself as similar. Both men
were certainly authoritarians and political economists,
but, totally unlike the pious Salazar, Pombal was anticlerical, and the Republicans, who had conceived of the idea
for the monument, wanted to pay tribute to his hostility
to the Jesuits. The Republicans were displaced in a coup
in 1926, but Salazar, who came to power under the new
regime, turned the comparison to his own purposes. The
history of more recent years was used in an attempt to
vindicate the regime, with Salazar reflecting in 1933 on
the situation prior to his regime: "Our revolutions, our
apparent incapacity to govern ourselves, the rottenness
of our administration, our general backwardness, all were
held up to our national discredit." Such arguments were
employed by Salazar, and others, to justify hostility to
democracy, liberalism, and freemasonry.

In Portugal, there was also a physical celebration of a
designated national past in the shape of the restoration of

medieval buildings. Thus, the twelfth-century tower of the castle at Lamego was restored as part of the celebrations for the eight hundredth anniversary of Portuguese independence in 1139, the castles of Bragança, Guimarães, Almourol, and Monsanto also being heavily restored from the 1930s. Held in 1940, to commemorate, both that anniversary and three hundred years from the restoration of independence, the Portuguese World Exhibition staged at Belém had over two million visitors and a replica of a seventeenth-century galleon was a major sight, as was a monument to Portugal's explorers.

A similar process continued during World War II with regimes that allied with Germany, notably, in 1940–1944, Vichy France, the collaborationist regime that replaced the defeated Third Republic. The past, however, could be differently deployed, Vichy being happier to use Catholicism than was Mussolini. The latter, in contrast, made much of references to imperial Rome. For example, a youth movement, covering boys from six to twenty-one and girls from nine to seventeen that sought to direct the young, was called Gioventú Italiana del Littorio (Italian Youth of the Lictor), the lictor being a Roman magisterial bodyguard that held the *fasces*, a bound bundle of rods symbolizing authority and power.

Frontier changes were an aspect of the use of history. Thus, 1940 saw Germany's ally Hungary gain much of Transylvania from Romania. The wartime Hungarian regime took forward prewar themes of ethnic nationalism, not least through the work of the newly founded Institute of Central and Eastern European History in Budapest University. Supporting Hungarian claims, scholars there, such as Imre Lukinich, argued that far from being the original population, Romanians appeared in Transylvania relatively late and in small numbers, arriving en masse only in the fourteenth century.

In turn, the Nazi defeat led to the fall of most of the European (but not Latin American) conservative authoritarian regimes. However, as an instance of the durability of Iberophone dictatorships also seen in Latin America, Franco's Spain and Salazar's Portugal continued into the 1970s. These offered instances of the widespread type of the public history of a totalitarian regime, as well as the, by then, more unusual content, for Europe, of an authoritarian, conservative, Catholic one. Thus, in 1949, Franco had restored the monastery of Yuste, where the Emperor Charles V had lived in retirement: the image of devout Catholicism was appropriate to Franco's regime. That Charles V appeared in chapter 2 in another light, as the triumphant ruler as general celebrated on canvas by Titian, is a reminder of how frequently that situation of multiple use and complex identity can be seen. This should serve against the simplistic use of historical figures and episodes to make easy criticisms or, more generally, to substantiate simplistic accounts of circumstances and disturbances.

However, Francoist history appeared a curiosity. Instead, the dominant theme from 1945 was the new salience and complexity of the Cold War historical consciousness. The challenge of Soviet Communism was made more prominent not only by a major increase in the span of Soviet power but also by the total collapse of Nazism. That provided the Soviet Union with an opportunity to suppress popular opposition in eastern Europe. In addition, misleading accounts of the war were propagated, for example, of cooperation between civilians and Communist partisans,[4] as were misrepresentations of the contributions of the Western Allies to the defeat of the Axis and Japan through both direct military action and vital material aid to the Soviet Union. These were also pronounced strands in accounts of the war produced by left-wing historians and commentators in western Europe.

Moreover, the Communist triumph in China in 1949 greatly expanded the Cold War narrative. At the same time, this triumph ultimately complicated this narrative as Communist histories became seriously involved in competing nationalist interests and ideological differences, a process clearly seen from what became the irreconcilable division and bitter polemics between Yugoslavia and the Soviet Union from 1948, and China and the Soviet Union from 1960. So separately with the degree to which a disillusionment with Soviet Communism opened opportunities for other voices on the radical left, and notably so after the brutal Soviet suppression of Hungarian reform Communism in 1956, and the appearance of the generationally driven New Left from the mid-1960s.

Communist history, in turn, encouraged anew anti-Communist narratives. These were both external—stemming from other, non-Communist, countries—and internal. The latter can be the hardest to disinter because totalitarian ideologies both seek to overcome other views and also to define them as social pathologies and thus criminal. This approach was totally misleading (albeit instructive), but government repression can be the source that survives most readily. In the case of Soviet and eastern European Communism (although not their far more

successful Chinese counterpart), the events of their total collapse in 1989–1991, and the sequel, however, have
cast instructive light on the nature of this totalitarian
ideology and have invited attention to the true situation
during Communist primacy. It is very clear that anti-
and non-Communist themes were strong during this
primacy and, ironically, underrated by many academic
subject-specialists, some of whom were sympathetic to
the regimes and/or lulled by the world of conferences
and official links. These themes reflected the strength of
family and community as both the expression of values
and the means through which historical awareness was
created and conveyed. Thus, in Poland, nationalism and
Catholicism proved much more vital than Communism.
This provides the perspective of comparative history, and
therefore counterfactualism, or "what if?" history, on the
more limited extent of opposition to the Nazi regime in
Germany in 1933–1945.

In turn, this ideology in Poland and other former Communist states has framed a history of the recovered experience and present memory of the Communist years.
This history has enshrined earlier beliefs and events to
a particular purpose. This situation invites a consideration of the marginality of the official historical account
of Communist states, or indeed, others. The latter was a
matter not only of the state, but also of its manifestations
including its direct control of education. Thus, the formal teaching of history, in both schools and universities
(and academics were a central part of the project), was an
aspect of state-enforced ideology. Much historiographical work focuses on such systems without inviting due

attention to their effectiveness or, more commonly, limited effectiveness.

Separately, a similar point can be raised about practice in the liberal West. It lacks comparable totalitarianism, but there can be an imprisonment by approved opinion and/or timidity and, linked to this, a focus on the formal processes and content of academic-endorsed pedagogy rather than on its impact and the idea of developing the potential of students for independent thought. Indeed, the notion of "false consciousness" can be deployed to assess those who do not accept what is the officially endorsed view.

Only in part due to differences between Communist states, Communist history was no monolith, for as the present changed, so the past that supposedly led to it had to alter and often abruptly so. Indeed, that was part of the problem for the custodians of the system. This situation offers a way to approach the likely future development of Chinese public history. However, in that case, there are also the important contextual changes presented, for example, by the scale of social media in China and the state effort involved in its regulation.

The changes in the Soviet case were most common in response to new regimes, and notably so after the death in 1953 of Stalin and the abandonment of his habitual murderous brutality. The criticisms of Stalin by Nikita Khrushchev and, encouraged by him, others after 1956, and notably in the aftermath of the 1956 and 1961 Party Congresses, encouraged an abrupt rethinking of Stalin's role but also one that revealed contrasting views among the public. There was public change, in the renaming of streets and the movement of Stalin's body but also the need to define a stance in the textbooks that would be different to that under Stalin but would not disgrace the Communist Party.[5]

Yet, there were also changes as a result of events in the Communist bloc, notably the Sino-Soviet split from the 1960s. These developments related most clearly to very recent history, but there was also an impact on earlier history, in large part because it was framed in a Marxist-Leninist context, or rather straitjacket, one that was decreed in a fashion allowing for insufficient flexibility. In between these two timetables, came that of the history of the previous century, and notably of the establishment of Communist rule, and then of World War II. The tensions within Communism played through these and related episodes.

As with Nazism, there was, with Communism, a zeal for perfection that linked past, present, and future. Whereas the Nazis had sought to purge society by a racial classification based on the past, notably Jewish antecedents, so the Communists did the same by stigmatizing those of bourgeois background. Their children were denied educational opportunities.

There were other comparisons. As in the case of the Nazi use of archaeology, so Communist regimes employed archaeology in order to support Marxist accounts of development and to substantiate views on ethnic territoriality, for example to demonstrate how the Novgorod digs supposedly showed a Slavic presence in the Russian Northwest by the mid-800s. There was a determination to reject historical origin accounts that were judged disparaging. One such instance—which, moreover, had a prehistory dating to the eighteenth century of the Viking versus anti-Viking controversy—was the rejection of the thesis that Vikings had played a major role in the development of Rus. Unacceptable to Slavophiles, who, like the Soviet Communists, instead supported a Slavo-Rus culture, this rejection was given renewed energy after World War II in part because the thesis had been advanced anew by Germans. Stalin's career and death were important to the chronology of these debates, as he interfered, often with murderous disfavor. The debate subsequently continued, with academic cross-currents matched by political tensions, while there has been public support in the media for the rejectionists. They represent an aspect of a Russian nationalism that was present in the debates over archaeological findings and was matched by those over literary finds.[6]

Communist regimes also sought to shape an acceptable pre-Communist history, not least in terms both of international links and in the account of social and cultural developments. For example, in 1983, when East Germany celebrated the hundredth anniversary of the death of Karl Marx, it also marked the five hundredth anniversary of the birth of Martin Luther. For the East German Communists, he could be seen as a progressive German and thus a figure worthy of memorialization. The Reformation and, thereby, Protestantism were annexed to the Communist state, which was a way to root the latter in the German past. Wittenberg, where Luther denounced papal authority, was preserved as a historic site. The emphasis was not on the Reformation as a religious movement. In part, illustrated broadsheets fueled the Reformation agitation, which was somewhat parallel to the effects of social media over the last decade.

Attempting also to establish a pedigree for social revolution, the Communist authorities in East Germany described the Peasants' War (1524–1525) as a proto-Communist revolution, playing down other interpretations. In doing so, the German past was presented as progressive and East Germany as its heir, with Thomas Müntzer, a radical cleric, celebrated and seen as an early exponent of the working class. He appeared on the five-mark bill, was the subject of a biographic film in 1956, and many factories and streets were named after him. The year 1989 saw not only a conference on Müntzer attended by Erich Honecker, the East German leader, but also the opening in Bad Frankenhausen of the *Bauernkriegspanorama* (*Peasants' War Panorama*), a massive, pseudo-realist painting by Werner Tübke. In practice, there was no simple class conflict in the early sixteenth century.

The politicized writing of the past was wide-ranging and assertive. The 1974 Party Congress of the Romanian Communist Party required historians to describe Dacia, the opponent of Rome, as both a state and a progenitor of modern Romania. President Nicolae Ceauşescu, dictator from 1965 to 1989, used Dacian and Roman names for cities, and associated himself with prominent former Romanians, notably Mircea the Elder; Voivode (ruler) of Wallachia 1386–1418, under whom Wallachia expanded and who was the subject of a 1989 biopic; and Michael the Brave, in 1600 the first unifier of Romania and a national hero, the subject of a biopic in 1970.

Other left-wing states similarly adopted a history that combined ideology and nationalism. Thus, in the 1980s, Ethiopia presented its long-standing rivalry with the Somali Republic in terms of earlier support for coastal

Muslims by foreign foes, the Turks in the sixteenth century and the British in the nineteenth.[7] Whatever its
political significance, the comparison was of scant analytical value. Traditional themes were also seen in the case
of Cuba, with nationalist defiance of America combined
with the Communist portrayal of that state as an imperial
power seeking economic domination.

While it is appropriate to note common themes in
Communist and left-wing history, there were also important shifts. For example, during World War II, Russian
nationalism, which had been downplayed in the earlier
Communist era, was rehabilitated in order to rally popular
support. The resulting National Bolshevik undercurrent
continued into the postwar world, with consequences for
the Russian nationalism that played a role in the breakup
of the Soviet Union. Even aside from the need for official
history to validate present positions, historical messages
varied more than a Marxist position would suggest.

If a key element of Communism was a drive for improvability, so this was the case for its anti-Communist
rivals, although, generally, in a far less authoritarian and
lethal fashion. Alongside ideologies, and the attendant
historical imagination that put an emphasis on conservatism, came non-Communist reform accounts. In particular, American modernism drew on a strong note of
exceptionalist national confidence in which economic
development sat alongside constitutional progress. This
was much to the fore from the early twentieth century,
not least in the confident, economically booming 1920s.
The section on American history that appeared in *Putnam's Historical Atlas* (1927) by Robert McElroy, professor of American history in Oxford, included an essay on

American economic history that, although making reference to "the scandals of an age of progress," closed with a
paean of praise:

> The building of railroads toward the setting sun, the expan-
> sion of highways, canals, tram lines, automobile routes to
> meet migrations unrivalled in all history; the enormous
> expansion of factories and of trade, internal and external;
> the interpretation of laws meant for an age of small things to
> meet an age of great things; the growth of credit, perfecting
> of banking systems, stabilisation of currency by the educa-
> tion of public opinion against the heresies of the ages; the
> building of schools enough to educate not a class, but every
> class, regardless of wealth, race, creed, or place of birth; the
> assimilation of millions of immigrants from almost every
> stock on earth; the harmonising of religions so that the bells
> of one village church will not sound discordant as the rest
> chime in.
>
> With all its faults, American economic expansion is an
> epic of glory; and as we see its steady acceleration there is
> an added sense of satisfaction in the thought that the end
> is not yet.[8]

An instructive element was the treatment of ethnicity.
The roles of African Americans, Asians, and Hispanics
was underplayed and those of Native Americans scandal-
ously neglected, but within the confines of an essentially
white and male-dominated society, race was not used to
define American identity to the extent seen in Europe.
At the same time, and the point remains relative, white
(like black) is a monolith, an abstraction for a wide range
of circumstances and for an internally divided reality.
Thus, "white" in America tended to mean a homogeneity
of white, Anglo-Saxon, and Protestant, with Jews, Irish,
Italians, and Poles all excluded.

American notions of modernism became more significant in the post-1945 Cold War because, in place of the
earlier dominant role of Britain, came that of America
with its (then) cult of progress and very different global
message. The anti-Communist democratic liberalism of
America was directed at home at what was presented as
selfish and narrow-minded conservatism, the two depicted in terms of antiprogressive economic interests and
Southern racists. American history was deployed with
reference to this liberalism, as in Arthur Schlesinger's
very favorable biographies of Andrew Jackson, Franklin
Roosevelt, and John Kennedy, with scant attempt to consider the extent to which clashing tendencies also contributed to an American identity or indeed to probe the racist
dimension of Jackson's populism.[9]

American liberal progressivism, was highly influential
in academe and notably so in the more powerful institutions of what was (and remains) a very hierarchical
system. This progressivism was very much presented
in terms of a modernism defined in terms of rationality
and standardization, and motivation was considered as
a matter of instrumental behavior as opposed to traditional action. Capitalism and Protestantism were parts
of the equation of modernism and were contrasted to
what was seen as irrational. The modernist approach was
more generally seen in the counterpointing of civilization
and barbarism as both distinct and crucial. Thus, in *The
World: Its History in Maps* (1963), an influential American
work, the authors used color to represent a clear sense of
progress: "Spots of colour are set against vast expanses of
neutral tint, representing the portions of the globe where
barbarism and savage forms of society prevailed . . . the

use of solid colours to define the limits of high civilisation give visual focus to the maps."[10]

The clearly repeated assumption was that there was no overlap between civilization and barbarism, a view that very much reflected a problematic set of values. Thus, "by AD 100 . . . an unbroken zone of civilised life from the Atlantic to the Pacific. . . . The area of civilisation was still narrow and exposed to unrelenting barbarian pressures, and development in the different regions was still largely autonomous; but with the expansion of the major civilisations and the elimination of the geographical gaps between them, the way was open for inter-regional contacts."[11]

Modernization theory became a key tool in the social sciences, a theory emphasizing rational abstract principles as well as an abandonment of past practice in a reshaped social Darwinism. Political science originated as a progressive effort to make politics and public administration a science and that shaped the discipline. Defending liberal progressivism and heavily criticizing conservatism, not least as "without history," however became a problem when the next progressive generation rejected the liberal part, which can be seen as the situation today.[12]

Key American texts included Walt Rostow's *Politics and the Stages of Growth* (1971) and Francis Fukuyama's *The End of History and the Last Man* (1992). Rational choice was seen as at play, from biological preference to economic and political practice, and these were also read back into the past. There was an assumption that optimum accounts were possible, could be readily defined, and should be implemented. Rational choice led to an essentially secularist account of decision-making. Moreover, in contrast, social cohesion in terms of what was presented as anachronistic, notably notions of honor and lineage, was treated as mistaken. Experts displaced the clergy as authorities, and notably from the 1950s. The modernism of liberal progressives rejected the allegedly backward past for a supposedly scientific future. Consumerism reinforced some of the trend with its stress on the new and the latest. Particularly, but not only, in the 1960s, and again in the 1990s, modernization was regarded as a form of global New Deal, able to create a new world order.[13]

This was very different to conservative Western practices, such as the Salazarist attempt to justify the continuation of Portugal's overseas empire, which gave Salazar an impression of national mission and strength. This left the *Monument to the Discoveries* constructed at Belém in 1960 for the five hundredth anniversary of the death of Henry the Navigator, who was seen as an exemplary figure, exploration then being presented in this light. In contrast, by the 2010s, exploration was to be presented by critics as an aspect of Western expansionism that had genocidal consequences.

The cult of reason was understood by twentieth-century Western intellectuals as inherently secular, with faith banished to the private sphere. With rational choice supposedly dominant, the present apparently necessarily understood the past better than its present had done. Historians, indeed, could be seen as a universal corrective explaining past mistakes in a counterfactual purging based on the "what should have been" principle. Reason therefore could reveal the prospectus, to a better-understood past, an improved past and present, and a better future. Yet a circularity in thought, and a selectivity in evidence, were repeatedly inherent to this process of discussing rational choice and, more generally, reason. Functions were presented in a quasi-automatic fashion, with needs and drives readily ascribed to individuals, groups, states, and civilizations, and effects ascribed to functions, while those functions were defined by the effects they produced. This is a flawed approach.

In America, unlike the Soviet Union, there was no single, officially approved, exposition of history. That situation helped ensure that what would later be termed "history wars" were active in America throughout the period. These "history wars" were linked to conventional politics and yet also could enjoy considerable autonomy from them. So also, although often with very different contexts, elsewhere in the West and, indeed, often to a surreptitious extent, the Communist bloc. This situation provided a background for the situation discussed in the following chapter.

As a reminder of the far from static context during the post-1945 Cold War, an unprecedented number of states saw part or all of independence (for example, India from 1947), new constitutions (for example, Japan in 1947), and radically different political systems (for example, Iraq from 1958). These each entailed new presentations of the past, from education to statuary. Thus, any shift to republicanism was accompanied by a displacement of the monarchical theme, from textbooks and town centers to national anthems and flags, alike.

In the new histories, in turn, there was an intertwining between political change, the justification of the position of the new governing regime, and the propagation of a different public history. The commitment to all three was closely linked, such that a liberalism of opinion, at least in terms of attacking the new national history, was generally lacking. This was even more the case as public intellectuals benefited directly from their links to the regime and to a more consistent and insistent degree than in liberal states, where the process, however, was also seen and was sometimes more present than tends to be appreciated.

In population terms, the largest state that gained independence in the twentieth century was India, and history there was heavily politicized in terms of the turn from colonial rule by Britain. The role of Indians in enabling and cooperating in this rule was downplayed; as were the achievements of India as part of empire. Unsurprisingly, this was an aspect of a situation in which the regional imperialism of the British government in India, a policy continued once independence was achieved, attracted scant domestic criticism. The history of India as part of the British empire remains highly contentious in India, Britain, and elsewhere, leading in particular to accounts in which India as presented as failing to sustain economic performance and to achieve growth due to baleful British policies. There is also a presentation of British rule as inherently violent. The question of whether these arguments have been pushed too far is not one welcomed in Indian public debate. India had an anticolonial legitimacy.

But, more specifically, there is a partisan political dimension. Attacking Britain for its imperial role and, specifically, for being allegedly unsympathetic to Hindus (for which there is no evidence) provides the BJP (Bharatiya Janata Party, the Hindu nationalist party) with a way to locate Muslims as also non-Indian. Much is now invested, politically and culturally, in anti-Muslim sentiment, and that stance leads to pressure to remove the Mughals from textbooks. In this approach, British imperial rule is apparently part of a hostile sequence.

The Indian pattern was seen in many former colonies, for example Indonesia, which, until 1949, was the Dutch East Indies: indeed (as with India and the British), the identity of Indonesia as a single state was created by the Dutch. At the same time, the criticism of former imperial rulers varied in its intensity. Thus, in former French Africa, it was strong in Guinea but not in Ivory Coast or Senegal. The particular politics of the winning of independence and the new regime were crucial differences rather than any inherent history. In Guinea, the attitude of Ahmed Sékou Touré was central. The great-grandson of a pre-French ruler, he was the founding president from 1958 to 1984. That he ran an authoritarian state added an ironic note to the criticism of France.

There was also the question of which past to reject. Thus, in the Philippines, there was criticism of Spain, the imperial ruler from 1565 to 1898, rather than of America and Japan, separately the rulers in 1898–1946. In terms of public perception, such points were to the fore, rather than the conceptual and methodological debates that attracted many scholars in the West.

Moreover, the public perception of the past owed much to media that had little to do with scholars or scholarship. That was very much the case with cinema, for which directors and scriptwriters paid scant attention to formal processes of scholarship, however much this scholarship was mediated into more accessible forms. Instead, filmmakers sought to give the past a clear contextual depiction in order to provide a setting for character-based drama.

Film repeatedly provided very clear accounts of the past, and the selection of plots and images both reflected and sustained particular interpretations. Thus, the Spartacus slave revolt of 73–71 BCE against Roman rule—the basis of *Spartacus* (1951), a successful novel by the American Communist Howard Fast, turned into Stanley Kubrick's film *Spartacus* (1960)—served as the basis for a depiction of the wrongness of a political system that also crucified Jesus. This attitude matched a Christian ecclesiology about Rome before its conversion to Christianity, as well as an American commitment to the exemplary "common man." Similar assumptions and values were advanced in other films, such as *Ben-Hur* (1925 and 1959), *Demetrius and the Gladiators* (1954), *Gladiator* (2000), *Spartacus* (2004), and the American television series *Spartacus: Blood and Sand* (2010).

Differently, the Spanish film *Even the Rain* (2010) ahistorically transposes into the social tensions in modern-day Bolivia Hatuey, a chief of the Taíno who was captured and burned at the stake in 1512 by the conquering Spaniards. Now he is acclaimed as Cuba's first national hero and there are monuments to him in the towns of Baracoa and Yara. Furthermore, the Taíno heritage has attracted more attention in the Caribbean from the 1990s, and it is now more widely appreciated that far from becoming extinct, many Taíno women raised families headed by European men and passed on genes and cultural practices that remained parts of Caribbean society. This heritage, however, can cut across the focus on African slaves, although there have been attempts to link the two groups as common victims of Western exploitation.

Identity and historical authenticity meant accounts of the past in which there was a stress on "real" independence whatever the nature of "foreign" rule. Thus, Hindu nationalists emphasized successful Maratha resistance to the rule of the Muslim Mughal dynasty in the late seventeenth century. Similarly, gaining independence in World War II was ascribed in whole or part to resistance activity, as in Ethiopia (1941), France (1944), and Yugoslavia (1944) rather than to invading Allied forces. The emphasis on new nationhood frequently entailed an opposition to certain forms of internationalism, although, in this emphasis, anticolonialism attracted a lot of popular attention. So also, depending on circumstances, could other aspects of internationalism, such as that of the Catholic Church, that are unpopular in self-defined progressive cultures.[14] More generally, and on a long-standing pattern, internationalism does not generally accord with national historical perspectives unless on the terms of the latter.

This combination of national and international narratives helped frame the history that was presented, including for violence and oppression that was deliberately ignored or misrepresented—as with suppression of apparent opposition in Indonesia (for 1965–1966), Thailand (1976), and China (1989)—despite the large number of perpetrators and victims that could be involved. Depending on political circumstances, however, systematic atrocities could attract attention. It could also serve as a reason why there was an emphasis on a "pact of forgiving" or process of forgetting. These became an explicit form of history but also one that was highly contentious and, as in Spain, entwined with political division. Forgiving could be stigmatized as amnesia. The topic, moreover, became one of academic study and also of legal consideration, both domestic and international. Understandably, it usually proved impossible to move away from a firmly grounded sense of division and anger. Moreover, for recent decades, this can be fostered by fresh uncovering of the brutality of the past, for example in Yugoslavia with the large-scale slaughter of their opponents by the victorious Communists in 1944–1945. Indeed, the uncovering of graves, as for example from the Spanish Civil War (1936–1939), provides a means to fight out "history wars" anew, literally offering new battlegrounds for memorialization.

The long period covered in this chapter reflects the prominence given to a particular theme: that of the challenge posed by a major state, the Soviet Union, endorsing a global historical ideology, Communism. Yet, every historical work is itself a contribution to historiography and should be seen in this light. Thus, at the same time as adopting the theme taken in this chapter, there is the danger in taking that as the obvious, indeed only, way to organize the past. That is mistaken. Aside from downplaying other issues, by omission or simplification, that is the danger of a deceptive simultaneity, one of presenting and analyzing together events, issues, and works, that, in practice, it is misleading to juxtapose and that can only be understood in their own chronological context. More generally, consideration of this point raises a particular problem, one in which historiography matches other aspects of history, namely, that any ordering automatically suggests a hierarchy of concern and interest, a sense of progression and a degree of causation and these cannot be readily separated or countered.

The chronological factor is also significant. The habit of treating all or part of the Cold War as a unit can be misleading unless due care is taken to underline this point. Thus, to take only the Cold War from 1945 to 1991, it is not simply that there were major shifts, notably in the mid-1950s, the early 1960s, the early 1970s, and the mid-1980s. There was also the impact of the oil crisis of 1973. Moreover, key social contexts included the cult of youth and consumerism that gathered pace from the 1960s.

All of these raise the habitual questions involved in discussion of past, namely, the relative significance implied by choice of topic and by organizational approach, for example the use of textual continuity or not, let alone the degree of explicit or implied causation. The answers given to these questions vary greatly by commentator and through time. For example, answers involving issues of cultural identity are more common now than would have been the case a half century ago when social, political and national identities were more to the fore. These questions and answers are important to any discussion of historiography, and more so than is often appreciated. Rather than presenting our accounts of the past in terms of some clear progression, it is necessary to hardwire in a variety in circumstance and diversity in approach.

EIGHT

—w—

METHODS FOR A
MODERN AGE

The *AHR* Forum, "Historiographic 'Turns' in Critical
Perspective," looks at what several of the contributors
call "turn talk"—a preoccupation with dramatic or
decisive changes in historical understanding in the last
thirty years. The best-known of these are the cultural
and linguistic turns proclaimed at the end of the 1980s,
transformations in the theorising and practice of history
that both grew out of and critiqued the prevailing mode of
social history. But subsequent turns have been announced
with increasing alacrity—the transnational turn, the
spatial turn, the moral turn, the emotional turn, and the
digital turn, among others—suggesting that perhaps the
concept itself has lost some of its heuristic value.[1]

THERE IS IN FACT MUCH of interest in this 2012 forum in the *American Historical Review* and some valuable
reflections, but it seems safe to this academic to say that
there is also much that has only limited public appeal or
interest. Moreover, although there is a necessary, albeit
somewhat self-conscious, critique of Western-centricity,
in the forum, much of the content is very self-absorbed
and narrow in its approach. The forum also provided little

of direct value to the current understanding of histories across the world. Indeed, despite talking repeatedly about being global in scope, much of the modish Western academic history was absorbed in very limited theoretical concerns expressed in often opaque language and clearly not designed to reach out to the public. Indeed, this branch of the bourgeoisie ignored the workers and everyone else bar themselves.

This remains the case with the forum and also, indeed, more generally. When many Western historical theorists were absorbed in the 2000s with postmodernist assertions of the lack of objective and authoritative truth, much of the conventional account of historiography thus developed appeared of only limited interest or significance, and it was certainly so outside academe. This criticism could be sharpened for the 2010s as, in a marked cross-current to past postmodernist arguments, public debates over fake news (a proposition that itself inherently testified to true news and history) came to encompass such objectively clear phenomena as the existence of sustained climate change. Demonstrating the latter proved an important aspect of the development of historical methods and of the propagation of the resulting information. Indeed, this was the most significant conceptual, methodological, and empirical work of recent decades.

In addition, postmodernism, the "cultural turn," many other "turns," and much else in the smorgasbord of modish modern Western academic historiography and theory, appeared to have little, indeed very little, to offer when considering such political events as the Russian invasion of Ukraine in 2022 and the more general crises of political and food security it pushed forward. Far from being

inconsequential "epiphenomena," beside such fundamen-
tals of modern social history as changing gender identities
and relations, the political developments of the present
time threaten economic crisis, if not nuclear hostilities
that would engulf much else. The ruminations of postmodernism, best characterized as a mood or a direction,
offer minimal, indeed nugatory, insight as to how historical scholarship can be tapped for transnational crisis
management. It is worth considering what Syrians, Ethio-
pians, or Ukrainians would make of being told about "safe
spaces" on Western university campuses.

Furthermore, the revival of great power confrontation
from the 2000s, one that gathered pace in the 2020s, suggested the erstwhile, serious folly of the overpowering
shift of emphasis in much of the teaching and publication
of history, funding of research, and direction of appointment, from the war/international relations/politics nexus
to those of social and cultural history. This long-term shift
was more consequential than such academic debates as
that over the desirable chronological scale of individual
works of scholarship.[2]

It would be foolish and feckless to move from such reflections to argue for the value of showing little attention
to academe itself. The great and important ability of historical scholarship to test ideas, advance judgments, and
encourage debate and developments is highly necessary,
not least in encouraging good governance and informed
public politics. Yet, alongside this ability, it is important to
consider the historical opportunities and activity present
outside academe. There is no simple list of relevant factors
but, instead, an interactive, but also divided, mélange of
new information, methods, mediums, and audiences.

New information includes the potential of new sources of data, notably but not only digital data, and the extent to which, thanks to technological developments, methods are available for scrutinizing and analyzing this data. One particularly exciting aspect is that of the access through computers to information that would hitherto have required distant and expensive research and library trips or interlibrary loan systems. The long-standing radical sense that history could be (and therefore should be) "open source," a method in part earlier and differently offered by photojournalism, was revived in the 2000s in response to digital potential.[3] America has seen particular activity in this field, with open-access projects providing a mass of material.[4] Material that is not covered by copyright can be freely downloaded without subscription or institutional means. However, there now is concern about the environmental implications of the modern range and scale of digital material, in terms of the electrical drain caused by numerous, large interconnected computer banks, which encourages discussion about new pedagogic and intellectual developments.[5]

New mediums of historical investigation and presentation cover the full range of aural and visual media. Again, there is no clear hierarchy in the importance of developments, but a chronological boost toward new mediums was provided by the congruence of the lockdowns in 2020–2022 linked to the COVID pandemic and, on the other hand, the rise of the popularity of podcasts. That the last is an aspect of the democratization of history is, in part, linked to the ease of access of podcasts and their low cost of production, but the lack of any established hierarchy of access to them or control by educational or other institutions of the content of podcasts underlines this democratization. Moreover, there is a more active subversive process in that students and others within a formal structure of regulated information provision can find a degree of freedom in making their own choices among the material that is readily available. They can also turn to sources other than those of their teachers. This is an aspect of the frequent, subversive forces, technical, doctrinal, social, and/or political, that challenge the existing provision of historical opinion.

Cost is not the sole factor. There is also the immersive character of history, one offered by a number of approaches. These include the "face of history" aspect of reading about the past by means of first-person narratives. There is also the adoption of immersive characters through playing games, notably on computers but also by means of reenactments. The overlap of these and other means is mutually supportive and helps lessen, or even, for some, marginalize other means of looking at the past.

The democratization of access to history, however understood, is possibly the most obvious feature at present. To some of its critics, this is a matter of populism, a term more used than defined and one that can be best understood as the application of what democracy can mean. In practice, however, democratization is a method, not a program or a goal. Separately, what, to one critic, is populism is democracy to another. This democratization of history is of very inconsistent quality, but the same is true of the academic version. Furthermore, present-mindedness is seen in much of this democratized history. Again there is much of the same in the choice and funding of topics and methods. This can be seen, for example, with the current and recent increase in interest in work on the slave trade. This is certainly a case of present-mindedness, whether academic or popular in its background, one encouraged by, but not determined by, the Black Lives Matter movement that came to prominence in 2020 in the West but not at all comparably so in Asia.

History's place at the fore of culture wars is no surprise. A criticism, if not attempted destruction, of alternative sensibilities or values, of the sense of continuity, of an appreciation of complexities, and of anything short of a self-righteous presentist internationalism is decried by critics of what is termed "wokeishness." More helpfully, there is a tension arising from a firm rejection of what others celebrate, such as what is presented as patriotism or family values. Moreover, in a variety of forms, including cultural Marxism and Critical Race Theory, such a "reset" can appear part of a total assault on the complexity and nuances of the past, one that seems explicitly designed to lead the present and determine the future.

The extent of coherence in this supposed movement of wokeishness is open for discussion, but there is interest in trying to suggest a history for this modern situation. In part, it is the case of a long-term process that owed much to the Marxist side in the Cold War. In turn, this process has been revived and given new direction in recent years. There is a relentlessness of admonition and criticism, sometimes styled "struggle." This is the Leninist approach—namely, that the core true believers and committed will lead the rest; that there is to be no compromise, no genuine debate; and that the end result must be power for its own sake. Moreover, looking to the Marxist denunciation of people by category, there is a prejudging of groups as inherently racist. This approach attacks the notion of every human as having intrinsic judgment and value.

In part, this revival reflects the extent to which in many countries those who were young radicals are now very much in the driving seats of intellectual and cultural would-be direction and thereby able to move from protest to proscription. Thus, the "long march through the institutions" that some have discerned has apparently succeeded. This was the case, for example, with Departments of English or with the activism of museums. The strong engagement of past, present, and future can be seen with the People's History Museum in Manchester. Its focus on protest stretches from the 1819 Peterloo Massacre to the Campaign for Nuclear Disarmament and Black Lives Matter. In 2021, the museum engaged in what it described as activities that were challenging and uncomfortable. They were certainly hostile to the then government.

That was not the same, however, as the criticism of the Enlightenment and of allegedly Western notions of rationality. Indeed, in a resumption of the postmodernist hash, objectivity for some has become a term of abuse and objection. Historical understanding is affected by any adoption of the social constructivist position that facts are irrelevant or disposable. Traditionally, history has been related to formal logic and a search for truth, as in historical statements being either true or false: statements either corresponded to what happened or they did not, which is the classical way of understanding what we mean by truth, as in these words corresponded in some way to a past state of affairs. There has always been an awareness of

selection and interpretation in the resulting history. However, such selection and interpretation does not mean a
failure to correspond to historical reality. Instead, there is
no reason to believe that a historian is making something
up, but there is every reason to think that the historian
believed they were telling the truth, in other words saying
things that corresponded to some actual state of affairs.

In contrast, a coherent picture is one in which an individual truth coheres with other beliefs so that facts are
less influential than emotion and personal belief, truth
being perspectival and a cultural construct. "Alternative
facts" then make complete sense due to the individual-
ity of perspective, however much it may appear to clash
with facts, which, indeed, are dismissed as priority is
given to individual subjectivity. Ironically, this separa-
tion of history from the correspondence theories of truth
discussed in the previous paragraph clashes with recent
and current attempts to rewrite history in order to offer a
new-style progressivist orthodoxy, for example in terms
of the protagonists of groups allegedly formerly ignored
or misrepresented. Yet, the basic historical questions
remain—Who is responsible for the accounts? How are
the events recorded? Which data is selected? Whose interests are represented? Whose interests are promoted in
this reconstruction?—and should still be asked, even of
current orthodoxies?

Moreover, adopting orthodoxies ensures a downplaying of the specificity of individual circumstances. The
adoption in other countries of the analysis of the history
of race recently advanced in America is a classic example. In part, this adoption elsewhere is the result of an
increasingly ahistorical society. Using empire to make

some sort of bridge, equating imperialism with racism, is problematic not least due to the transracial alliances involved in empire. For Britain, this was prominent in the case of African slave traders, while the British Empire in Asia was essentially an Anglo-Indian enterprise and Sudan, an Anglo-Egyptian one. The multiple complexities of former imperial links and their continual links should be addressed in an unpolemical fashion.[6] Instead, the theory and practice of empire are often misconstrued and ossified, the critics falling into the ethnic-blame fallacy trap in its focus on retroactive, collective, ethnic guilt on the part allegedly of "whites" or "white privilege."

There is a tendency among the combatants in "history wars," for example critics of empire, to write in terms of undifferentiated blocs of supposed alignment as well as to move freely back and forth across the centuries and readily ascribe causes in a somewhat reductionist fashion. Thus, the popular historian William Dalrymple, writing in *The Guardian* on June 11, 2020, linked the continued presence in Central London of a statue of Robert Clive, a key military figure in the acquisition of the Indian empire, to the Brexit vote: "a vicious asset-stripper. His statue has no place on Whitehall . . . a testament to British ignorance of our imperial past. . . . Its presence outside the Foreign Office encourages dangerous neo-imperial fantasies among the descendants of the colonisers . . . Removing the statue of Clive from the back of Downing Street would give us an opportunity finally to begin the process of education and atonement."

This idea, that education has to lead to atonement, did not suggest a commitment to informed critical debate or, differently, that the previous mantra of "reconciliation" could be anything other than as serving the guilt.

As part of a polemic against the past, there is the standard claim that it has been misrepresented hitherto. This is a highly doctrinaire approach, as with the usual attacks on Brexit being apparently a consequence of an imperial mentality that has never been confronted as well as other similar claims: "The Brexit cause relied not only upon an ideal of heroic failure, but also upon a mythologized past of going it alone."[7] Or take for example *Legacy of Violence: A History of the British Empire* (2022) by Caroline Elkins, professor of history and African American studies at Harvard: "The British government's configuration of white power clearly jettisons prospects for a federation of Western states. With the 2016 Brexit vote, the Conservatives, preferring to go it alone, prevailed by holding up Britain's mythologised past . . . the dog whistles of populist racialised power."[8]

Another example comes from *The Crimean War and Its Afterlife: Making Modern Britain* (2022) by Lara Kriegel, associate professor of history and English at Indiana University: "The Brexit case relied not only upon an idea of heroic failure, but also upon a mythological past of going it alone. . . . The inequalities laid bare by the coronavirus stoked the fires of the protests against white supremacy and in favor of Black Lives Matter during the summer of 2020."[9]

Much of the commentary was strong here on assertion rather than evidence. Moreover, as far as Brexit was concerned, "Little Englanders" who were, as it were, opting out of a wider identity were possibly more significant than neo-imperialists. That certainly requires consideration if evidence and analysis are at issue rather than the statement of opinion. Specific issues of the moment, such as Prime Minister David Cameron's lack of popularity and widespread concerns about immigration, were probably of far more consequence in the 2016 referendum than any supposed hankering after empire.

What, however, one gets in the new historical orthodoxy is a running together of past and present. The modern British are supposedly trapped by the past so that every white Briton, and certainly white males today, apparently have the same values that motivated slave traders and perpetrators of massacres unless there is atonement. Therefore, in this approach, the statues have to fall, and presumably the reading lists and libraries must be reordered and, indeed, renamed. "Decolonization" becomes a catchall that can be employed to castigate whatever is disliked and then to demand support for a purging. In part, there was the normative repetition of slogans about inherent white privilege, many linked to reductive analyses on the part of some academics keen to reduce individuals to categories and to explain people in terms of supposedly inherent thought. This is a new "cultural revolution": a narrative imposed by currently dominant interests frames history in entirely negative terms in order to delegitimize aspects of institutions and society that are disliked. The tone increasingly brings to mind religious enthusiasm.

Moreover, Western academic historians, the majority of whom ironically are clearly on the left, themselves can find they are subject, as part of "History Wars," not to the rational and empirical conventions and constraints of intellectual debate many regard as axiomatic but to an increasingly more intrusive and even controlling attitude on the part of colleagues as well as the broader world, not least some, or many, university authorities. Those who set policy in the latter do so by the finger-in-air method, one that senses what is fashionable among those who will affirm their prejudices. Given the bullying approach, tone, and stance adopted by some universities, not least in the form of anonymous denunciations, those thus attacked will be anxious. With some universities apparently endorsing the idea that the workplace is the mission field, there is, in an echo of the nonconformist tradition, the language of impatient revivalism and a modern "manifest destiny," as in concepts such as needing to grasp the moment, condemnation, and the endlessly reiterated language and idea of decolonization, one in which present-day values are very clear.

For example, *History Workshop* published a blog in 2019 in its learning and teaching section: Radhika Natarajan's "Imperial History Now," which claims that "calls to decolonise curricula are more than a matter of addition, subtraction, or replacement of authors and texts. Instead, they are calls to address the relationship between the forms of knowledge we value in the classroom and the inequities and violence that exist on our campuses and in the world. . . . Decolonising the curriculum is not an end, but the beginning of a longer process of transformation." In 2020, the Department of History at Exeter (UK) put out the following:

> As a department, we are working to decolonise the way we teach, research, and work with one another. . . . Our collective engagement with such a broad swathe of human experience encourages us to reflect on how the study of history can promote empathy and respect for everyone and the ability to recognise and challenge injustice where it exists.

... We recognise that History—and the legacies of its colonial foundations—constitutes one of the ways in which some groups of people have been, and continue to be, oppressed, ignored, or abused in our societies today. In solidarity with Black Lives Matter and other decolonial and postcolonial movements around the world, we also recognise that History can be an important tool for positive social change.

We acknowledge that much writing and teaching in History departments today, even when purporting to have a "global" focus, remains Eurocentric and thus skewed in its coverage, perspectives, and sympathies. Meanwhile, work focusing on Europe often ignores or downplays the importance of non-white actors in our shared past. We also recognise and abhor that racial prejudice continues to mar our discipline, from the under-representation of BME scholars on our reading lists and in our faculties to the day-to-day experiences of our colleagues. We recognise that the way we "do" History, at Exeter as elsewhere, needs to change if we are to remain relevant, and help to address chronic and systemic injustices, in our increasingly connected and interdependent global society.

... We believe these changes need to go beyond simply diversifying our reading lists and footnotes. As a group, we are working to re-think our pedagogical and research methodologies to more fully avail ourselves of the tools developed by postcolonial, anticolonial, and decolonial scholarship, thus enabling a stronger and broader appreciation of the complexities of past societies and cultures.

To describe this approach as tendentious is polite, not least because using the study and teaching of history to advance any sort of social change is itself problematic. Such aspiration to action clearly merits description in terms of culture wars.

History as a subject proves especially important, as the past is used as a necessary basis for the decolonizing mantra. Ludicrous claims, and old ideas, such as World Systems Theory, are taken out of storage; given a "racist," or rather antiracist, dimension; and deployed without care or context. The latter is particularly regrettable as world or global history was a valuable qualification of earlier Eurocentric models and one on which much effort was expended. It proved especially useful in demonstrating links between civilizations and in undermining any zero-sum game of cultures. Instead, empires were presented as collective undertakings in which those who were subjects had a significant role and, indeed, to a considerable extent agency or semi-independent action. Similar points were made about the slave trade.

More generally, rather than a process of stark condemnation, there is a continuing need to explain and contextualize, for example by comparing empires. Indeed, if there is no attempt to understand the values of the past, there can be scant rational discussion of it. In America, the critique of its past domestic history is also an assault on its international status and past. This is particularly the case with the attack on the "Founding Fathers" and early republican history and the misleading argument that slavery was central to the American Revolution, an argument repeated by Simon Schama in the *Financial Times* of July 10, 2021. In terms of the "world history" of the time, this approach underplays the example America offered for republicanism elsewhere, notably in Latin America. The presentation of postindependence and post–Civil War America inherently as racist extends to the argument that the civil rights movement did not go far enough. Thus, a critique of the past becomes a demand for action in the present.

In practical terms, we are seeing in such arguments a bringing to fruition of the attack on positivism that has been so insistent since the 1960s, an attack that is bridging from academic circles to a wider public and with the active encouragement of some of the former. In particular, there was, and continues to be, a critique of the practice of subordinating scholarship and the scholar to the evidence and a preference, instead, for an assertion of convenient evidence that was derived essentially from theory. Empiricism, which of course could contradict assertion, from then was discarded, or at least downplayed, as both method and value, and there was a cult of faddish intellectualism heavily based on postmodernist concepts, despite the weakness of the latter, a weakness that is conceptual, methodological, empirical, and historiographical, liberating the present from the past.

That situation raises, of course, the bigger question of how best, in the context of modern history, to discuss and teach history in general and imperialism in particular. Personal commitment does not excuse any fondness for argument by assertion and, also, without adequate qualification or sufficient caveats. This is a one-dimensional history, a unidirectional account of heroes and villains. Consider, for example, the Schama piece already mentioned. We find the use of partisan language: "Britain liquidated the institution of slavery itself in 1834 but on condition that obscene sums of British taxpayers' money would go to compensate former owners of the enslaved." Maybe so from the perspective of 2021, but the payment helped bring consent without struggle, which was somewhat different to America in the Civil War once the Union moved to abolition. Schama goes on: "Come the Civil

War across the Atlantic, the great majority of the British political elite, including Liberal Party leaders like Gladstone, whose family fortune was in cotton, cheered on the Confederacy." This is misleading at best. Leaving aside the decision by the British government not to intervene, a decision that was of great importance to the course of the war, sympathy for the Confederacy, in so far as it existed, was despite slavery and not because of it. Simplification can serve to distort.

More generally, there is the repeated failure to appreciate that people in the past believed that they were right for reasons that were perfectly legitimate in terms of their own times, experience, and general view of the world. Is it surprising that leaders and intellectuals, whether or not presented as apologists, offered a view of the world in which they associated their values and interests with progress and civilization? This is not exactly news, and ironically but all too predictably, those today imposing their views on the past display very much the same tendency in their work, identifying values with their own concept of progress. This is a characteristic of modernism. Yet, imposing anachronistic value judgments is obviously illegitimate if historical understanding is being sought. Significantly, religion is scarcely ever mentioned. The belief of missionaries that they were saving souls cannot just be ignored: What could be more important to them? They thought they were as right in undertaking their work as those do who now want to impose their views. Saving modern souls appears to be the agenda.

The conventional academic "spaces," the geopolitics of academic hierarchy and method, from the lecture hall to the curriculum, are all being repurposed to this political end and very deliberately so, as are public spaces, notably museums. Moreover, the statues that are unwelcome are treated not as isolated residues of allegedly outdated and nefarious glories, but a quasi-living reproach to the new order in a "culture wars" of the present. In the latter, there seems to be no space for neutrality or noncommitment or, indeed, tolerance and understanding.

In part, possibly, and as an aspect of decolonization, the legitimacy of opposing views is dismissed, indeed discredited, as allegedly racist and anti-intellectual, because there is an unwillingness to ask awkward questions and to ignore evidence that does not fit into the answer wanted and already asserted. Examples of the latter might include the extent of slavery and the slave trade prior to the European arrival in Africa or the major role of European powers and America in eventually ending both slavery and the slave trade, at sea as well as on land. Indeed, the extension of British imperialism was frequently linked, as in Nigeria and Sudan between 1860 and 1905, with the ending of slavery. In contrast, some of the resistance to imperialism in these areas was related to slaving interests. This does not make imperialism or resistance "good" or "bad," but should ensure that complexity is offered when explaining the past. Complexity does not prevent the opportunity to offer judgment, but the latter requires a degree of contextualization that is too often absent.

It is possible, and necessary, to debate these and other points, but debate frequently is not accepted if it involves questioning assumptions. However, questioning these assumptions is crucial to understanding the past, which is the key aspect of history as an intellectual pursuit rather than as the sphere for political engagement or a means for the propagation of governmental views. As this book argues, the latter two, however, are generally far more significant, the second very much so in authoritarian societies.

Yet, from an intellectual perspective, historians, in the sense of those interested in the past, should seek to understand why practices we now believe to be wrong and have made illegal, such as slavery or (differently) making children work or marrying them, were legitimate in the past. It is not enough, in doing so, to present only one side of, and on, the past simply because that is allegedly useful for present reasons. The way in which the future will view us ought to encourage reflection and caution on this point, but it never does. Nor is it pertinent to refuse to recognize debate in earlier, plural societies. People in the past believed that they were right for reasons that were legitimate in terms of their own times, experience, and general view of the world. These elements deserve consideration as part of the inherently pluralist conception of values in a democratic society.

Somewhat curiously, that conception is more present today for religious faith than for political opinion and notably so in the West: there is more of a willingness to accept religious diversity than political opinions judged unwelcome. This willingness is not seen across the world however. Thus, freedom of religious practice in the Middle East is most clearly present in Israel, as is also the case with democracy and care for minority rights. It is interesting to consider the one-sided anti-Israeli sources of the present "debate" that will probably be applied by posterity to conceal these points.

Returning to the broader observation, all religions in the past had views that presentists would now find reprehensible and would wish to criminalize or, indeed, are already illegal. This raises questions about the possible logic of historicizing the present politics of ambitious grievance, in terms eventually of an assault on religions. Alternatively, Critical Race Theory can be seen not only as the product of the theories developed by the Institute for Social Research at Frankfurt, notably the use of critical theory to ensure sociological change, but also particularly in America, as a form of cult or religion, with a strong notion of original sin for others and no salvation for those bearing this sin.

Returning to empire (although the same point can be made in other respects), how then is empire to be presented in a way that does more than make sense of it largely in terms of modern values that tell us little about the past? The answer clearly will not be provided in the "decolonization" approach, which is explicitly antithetical to academic methods in that it proclaims its engagement as its rationale, not least in the language of institutional and individual mission statements. In a classic instance of Herbert Butterfield's definition of anachronism—making the study of the past a ratification or attack on the present—the past is to be used, in the form of a supposedly exemplary decolonization, as part of an attempt to recast ideas to match an account of society designed to provide an exemplary future or, at least, to defend the role of universities and the careers and self-image of particular commentators. The decolonizers' view of being historians appears to be of spending their time wishing that people in the past did not think as they in fact did and converting this into a platform for sociopolitical activism in the present designed to ensure that everyone is on what is termed the right side of history. This approach has no analytical substance, and, indeed, both threatens to dissolve the discipline and leaves the student or reader not so much short-changed as totally cheated intellectually and pedagogically, which indeed is an aspect of a current-day malaise in parts of academic history.

Imposing anachronistic value-judgments may well be common but is inherently transient as the fullness of time will, in turn, bring in fresh critiques of present-day values, which, possibly, will also be wrenched out of their historical context, not least by ignoring inconvenient evidence. Yet, the assertion of present-day values and, even more, definitions, as if these are transcendent universals, is possibly part of a religious imperative in a secular milieu, one very much seen with "mission statements." It is an approach that seeks to make history ahistorical by granting a particular perception of it a lasting value. Thus, time is collapsed. There is a substratum of religious eschatology here, to need to believe, secular or otherwise.

The significance of the issue can possibly be seen in the furor in Britain in the summer of 2021 when the government sought to offer some, rather modest, pushback. It was variously accused of meddling for political advantage or provoking a culture war. In practical terms, the governmental response in Britain has been patchy, whereas, in France, President Macron in 2021 was more robust in stigmatizing what he has presented as a challenge to French identity.

Indeed, there is a civilizational dimension. Wallowing in the past, trawling it for grievances, and then using these grievances in trolls is in part an opt-out from the real challenges of the present; they are psychological "displacement" activities. However, that is not how the process is seen by its protagonists. Their call is for a great reset that destroys capitalism and, in their terms, redresses and silences all forms of "white supremacism," a concept that is misleading other than in the racism it propounds. Western liberals should see this approach as a challenge to their civilization, which has always encouraged debate, which indeed is part of its strength. However, the type of criticism that is now at play is deliberately intended as revolutionary: it is not debate, but, instead, aims at the end of discussion.

This is doubly a challenge because the West, its liberal humanism, and the core concept of humane reason are under a grave threat from external changes, notably the rapid rise of the Chinese system and China's energetic attempt to propagate its views around the world. Across the world, China's path is greatly eased by the stigmatization of the West as racist and imperial, a stigmatization made more damaging by the extent to which domestic audiences within leading former colonial powers are willing to endorse this approach. This ignores China's imperial past and present. This situation is a clear indication of a cultural geopolitics that has important political consequences.

Yet, as a reminder of the multivalent nature of history, decolonization, even if attention was solely limited to the West, was scarcely the only, or even always the most significant, current of change in historical argument or context. In particular, the democratization to which reference has already been made was/is not necessarily part of the decolonization just discussed and requires separate consideration. As with other contentious modern usages of history, there was, and is, a contextual offering of accessibility, the public history for a mass age, whatever the formal constitutional type and structure of state and public culture. Democratization offers much to societies.

The democratization of history was about far more than content. Democratization is in part presented as access and deployed accordingly by institutions such as archives that want to argue for their propose, the latter of which is increasingly seen in terms of relevance. Moreover, as with museums, relevance is measured by "footfall" of whatever type. Thus, for example, archives support the digitization of their contents. Moreover, some universities seek to offer MOOCs (massive open online courses, a term that originated in America in 2008), free online courses. These were part of a more general move to online access for history, one that became more prominent with the COVID lockdowns of conventional educational access in 2020–2022.

The democratization of history was always present in the marketplace of gossip, rumor, report, and other constituents of household and community. This democratization became more apparent and different in format over the last quarter millennium as populations rose and urbanized and as literacy increased. This process, a socialization of high-tempo technological and organizational possibilities, can appear to represent a fundamental socioeconomic trend unrelated to politics. In practice, however, governmental structures and ideologies on the one hand, and the pressures arising from contingent political events on the other, ensured both direction and variety in this process. Moreover, this situation contributed greatly to the differing characters and legacies of public histories in particular countries.

The history of this "populist" historical context was, and remains, an important aspect of the context of historiography. This discussion goes back to the classical world, more particularly to the constitution and politics of Athens and Rome, and became newly urgent in the nineteenth century, with controversy focusing on the liberal agenda of an expansion in the franchise. The nature of both authority and power in this developing context became matters of concern to critics. Drawing on long-standing concerns about the "mob" rather than the "people," a distinction still present in discussion about populism, critics worried that those without a due weight in the community would use the vote in order to redistribute wealth to their benefit and to the loss not only of the property owners but also the greater good and goods of society.

At the same time, such populism appeared necessary to governments variously seeking to avoid a repetition of the radicalism associated with the French Revolution, to incorporate subject peoples into imperial or quasi-imperial structures, to provide a return for the duty of military service, and as a corollary to the extension by states of universal education. A new nationalized, social contract was offered, one, in particular, in which power and education were secularized, brought under central government control, and extended and, therefore, held as somehow likely to restrain the risks of popular radicalism.

In turn, differing strategies of democratization were put forward in the twentieth century. In part, there was the ideology designed to use the argument of the interests of the working class in order to advance brutal ideological views, which was the reality of Communism. In part, there were arguments that social welfare was the just desert of the working class or, as with the New Deal, of Americans. In part, there were determined attempts to win the working class from Communism, attempts linked to Christian Democracy in Europe, to the social welfarism variously of the Attlee government in Britain and of Catholic social policies in Western Europe, to post-1945 land reform in Japan, and, to a degree, to the passage of civil rights and Great Society measures in the United States.

All these measures were populist in that their rationale rested on representations of popular, more specifically so-called working-class, interests. They were not, of course, populist in that many popular views were in practice ignored, although generally implicitly rather than explicitly. This was particularly so of popular concern about immigration, social and cultural radicalism, and crime. Indeed, there was a strong antipopulist nature to the development of twentieth-century democratic states, especially so in reaction to the political dangers believed to challenge liberal capitalist states. This antipopulist nature tended to be downplayed, but it was very much part of the practice of government and, frequently, of systems of checks and balances or what were presented as such.

As a consequence, the unpopularity of government could ferment. This unpopularity helped cause a crisis in established political parties, breaking long-established patterns of rule, including in Canada, Israel, Italy, and Japan. There was also the challenge of the restructuring of politics after the Cold War as well as the issues posed by referenda, as in rejections of EU convergence and, eventually, membership.

The ambiguity in the relationship between democracy and populism is taken further at present because of the extent to which populism has become an analytical and rhetorical term. Indeed, there is the danger that presentism will dominate the question and that it will become an aspect of America's culture wars. Populism could become a code word for criticism of Trump, or Modi, or Brexit, or much else, in order both to justify hostility and to provide a supposed parallel between what are in practice and theory very different movements and events from distinct contexts. Populism thus becomes an equivalent to early-modern usage of the term the *mob*, itself a term of questionable meaning, as it covers both social commentary and criticism of those supposedly swayed by emotion, fickle, and prone to violence—everything embodied in what Cicero detested.

There is in practice a lack of precision on the part of both journalists and historians. Is populism just any popular movement, a particular kind of popular movement, or a means to mobilize voters when turnout is falling? Can populism be divided into oppositions, each populist, for example between Sanders and Trump in the United States or between Brexiteers and Corbyn in Britain? Is populism by definition irrational (the modern opiate for the masses), or can it be a legitimate expression of the material and social self-interest of substantial sections of the electorate? And what is the relationship between populism and democracy, and between populism and "majoritarianism"? If Brexit achieves 52 percent support in a referendum in 2016, does that give it democratic legitimacy or disqualify it as "populism"? Are critics really objecting to the prime notions of democracy, those of one person one vote and of the legitimacy of opposing points of view? In the aftermath of the Brexit referendum, some Remainers were doing exactly that, which, possibly, was perhaps not surprising given that the EU structures and philosophy are to a degree antidemocratic.

Moreover, the argument about, and against, populism becomes a form of criticism in terms of the standard left-wing notion of false consciousness. This approach claims that people, especially the working class, allegedly do not or cannot understand their true interests because they are supposedly blinded by manipulation in the shape of being led to support foolish ideas. Populism, which apparently allowed the "unwashed" into elite decision-making processes, could thus be treated with contempt as well as criticism. There is a particularly strong linkage in the case of elite criticism of religious beliefs, notably as superstitious, an approach that joined some eighteenth-century philosophes to later Marxists. The use of language to make a political argument that suits the speaker is very much at issue in the thesis of false consciousness.

Aside from this political and rhetorical convenience, there comes the glib tendency to lump together events and movements for reasons of convenience, and in order to make an argument. What is a monolith such as zeitgeist (spirit of the age) to outsiders, or in this case populism, is far from it to those who look closely. Journalists can be particularly prone to the tendency of reification. In addition to convenience, this tendency reflects often simplistic and self-serving notions of history, time, and causation, notably stadial theories (history through a pattern of stages), as well as explanation in terms of a supposed zeitgeist, a highly convenient approach or, conversely, with reference to apparently immutable socioeconomic tendencies. These instrumentalist and reductionist accounts rob both time of contingency and humans of thought, intention, evaluation, and free action. Populism, therefore, is a term and a concept redolent of past and present thought and controversy about democratization and notably so as mounted in particular environments, variously national, political, and chronological.

Employed critically, the term *populism*, and indeed some of the sanction of modern history, can fail to take adequate note of the public's priorities, concerns, and reticence about policies where this public has reservations about government policy and social change with which elites are comfortable. This process is seen not only in authoritarian societies but also in the West. There, over the last three decades, soi-disant elites in national and supranational bureaucracies, the legal profession, academia, including many historians, and part of the traditional television and print media exemplified by the *New York Times* and the *Financial Times*, appear to think that it is desirable to make progress on agendas that irritate large parts of the electorate. What is seen as an antipatriotic approach to the past is a repeated aspect of this situation. Moreover, this approach is manifested by public sector elites speaking to local communities in an argot that those communities neither understand nor appreciate and evincing a sensibility that is remote from the local communities that they in theory serve. This form of politics sets up the circumstances where an irritable part of the public considers itself to be both ignored and patronized and, therefore, prone to reject imposed norms.

Separately, on the international stage there is the threat to national societies from imperializing powers drawing on narratives seeking popular endorsement. The present manifestations are readily apparent in the case of China and Russia, but these do not exhaust the instances of pressure brought on threatened peoples. In the case of both Russia and China, history is held up as a reason for expansionism, and government control, a necessary part of history, becomes thereby acceptable in the present. In contrast, the liberal tradition of national self-determination, one strongly pronounced from such nineteenth-century causes of Greek independence and Italian unification to twentieth-century counterparts in the aftermath of the world wars and the Cold War, is under assault, whether one looks at Ukraine, Taiwan, or a number of other states.

Social media takes part of the blame in public debate, but it is not appropriate to treat changes in technology in a reductionist fashion. Texts, tweets, Facebook, and the internet have all amplified a change in sensibility that has been in train for two generations. Technology, separately, increases awareness about the world or, at least, distributes information. There is both a benign and a malign account, as there is with populism as a whole. The images of the West transmitted by television, notably to East Germany, are seen as having sapped Soviet and eastern European Communism and contributed to its fall. It is not surprising that Islamic fundamentalists sought to prevent or limit the spread of information about Western life or that the Western model was perceived as a threat to them. Television was banned by the Taliban regime in Afghanistan.

Moreover, the internet offered a range and capacity that were different from those of previous national, transnational, and, in particular, global information and communications systems. The internet also permitted a more engaged and constant consumer response, with, as a result, consumers becoming users, and users becoming producers, as categories were transformed. Media content and software-based products provided platforms for user-driven social interactions and user-generated content (like the dependence of eighteenth-century newspapers on items sent in) rather than being the crucial player in creating content. Wikipedia and Twitter are key instances of user-sourced content.

Democratization, as context rather than necessarily goal, had the overlapping meaning of moving debate on-line, and in doing so, social media became a key medium of the propagation and, in part, exchange of ideas, opinions, and information. The development of this process was rapid and a response to changing practices in social communication, but it also brought to a new fruition the long-standing nature of means and communities of gossip, as well as the tensions inherent in the authorization of news and views. History was only part of the process, but it was an important aspect of it, feeding into and reflecting debates about the present, but also addressing the widespread interest in the past and the need to provide coherence to it. Moreover, the very popularity of the subject made it less credible to contain it within the constraints provided by formal pedagogic and other mechanisms.

In place of any hierarchical network of validation by academic historians, however limited, has come the more diffuse network of other commentators, including novelists and television people, a network that already existed, but far more extensive than in the past, it is now very much a milieux in which there is no particular hierarchy of authorization other than that measured in terms of "hits," which indicate a different focus to that with books on bestsellers, although maybe not so different. Moreover, popular historical work has little to do with the constraints of research-funding and the approved scholarship that is entailed. The latter, for example, has scant to offer as far as accessible biography is concerned, yet biography not only remains of great popularity but also has reached out to become more so as it is a method that can be readily applied, and in a number of milieux, to individuals from a range of categories. The gap between public interest and most academic history has widened greatly. Democratization through the internet and other means provides alternatives to established hierarchies for those interested in history. The existence of those alternatives irritates those in the hierarchies who resent their narrative being challenged or ignored.

Both contexts and consequences have varied. If, in the West, the center left played this changed sensibility in the 1990s, with Bill Clinton and Tony Blair mastering populist techniques, the situation today is more complex.

There has been an international dimension in encouraging and/or limiting or controlling access to the internet as earlier to publications, public history, and historical comment. Thus, Chinese and other efforts to stop Google and Facebook captured an understanding of the potential of this network of media. What this will soon mean on the global scale is unclear, not least because of very different attitudes in non-Western countries, including those of rapidly rising population, particularly India and Nigeria. The authoritarian model offered by China has been given greater strength by its economic growth. The emphasis placed by the Chinese government on soft power focuses on the presentation of the present, but it is likely that the attention already given to the past will become more insistent. Freedom of inquiry accordingly is confined, and the past deployed, in order to provide clarity between heroes and villains.

To some, notably, but definitely not only, in governments, this situation represented information as chaos and crisis. It certainly provided a form and means for populism that was different to the rioting mob but only by so much. Indeed, the application of the word *crowd* to the internet appeared appropriate. Alongside fears of an Orwellian government came those of a Hobbesian chaos. This counterpointing reflected the catastrophism and paranoia that characterized much political debate and discussion by historians and others, and right across the political spectrum. There was also, as separately with consideration of empire, frequently a lack of intellectual and political purchase in terms of an ability to relate specifics to contexts.

At the same time, one of the sad ironies of the information age is that instant access to vast quantities of information and the explosion of competing voices on the internet has given many people merely the illusion of being more informed: when one can readily find "facts" and "expert opinions" to confirm one's biases, it becomes much easier to distrust any competing views. Possibly that is a definition of populism, that of the rush to judgment, with historical works no exception to this process. If so, it is scarcely new or specific to particular values, although this rush has been greatly speeded up by the interacting combination of greater literacy, new technology, and the

ability and willingness of individuals to spend on the latter. It has encouraged an already-existing fast, "in your
face," tabloid approach to all sorts of expression including about history. Thanks in large part to television and
video games and instruments, graphic images are of great
importance as conveyors of information and molders of
taste and opinion. Visual symbols and systems provide
direct links to consumers that are more immediate and
effective than the written word.

The entire issue of information and liberalism is given
fresh importance by the rate of social change, by the increase in population, which brings larger new generations to the fore, and by the way in which technology is
opening up fresh possibilities for a new typology of political space. Populism as means, rhetoric, and a term of
denunciation, both describes and comments on this situation. There is of course the standard approach: "What
I stand for is reasonable, but your approach is crude and
populist," both employed as terms for extreme. The distinction is a nice, not a precise, one, and it is unclear why
historical (or other) views that enjoy widespread popular
support, notably if they give voice to the otherwise voice-
less, are automatically to be dismissed in this fashion.
"Thinking within the box" is, like what is often termed
populism, itself comfortable and uncritical. It is linked,
for example, to the academic definition of certain interests as appropriate for research and research support, a
process that, at the time, receives insufficient critical attention, although it may be judged more critically when
it becomes historical.

The value of a more acute typology and vocabulary is
apparent. In a perspective that certainly would not enjoy

global support, at least at the governmental level, both would benefit from recognizing the strength of nation-states as the basis for identity while, in the democratic and liberal tradition, accepting that the state should be subordinate to the nation and that the nation should be an open community of free individuals. History, repeatedly, is an indication of the contours of this "populism."

The relationship between populism and democracy can be complex. For example, authoritarian tendencies, albeit within a democratic envelope, are seen in Turkey, India, and some other states. In Turkey, under the Erdoğan government, there has been a particularly rigorous suppression of attempts to offer a nonapproved history, whether by Kurds or with reference to discussion of the vicious treatment of Armenians and Greeks in the 1910s and 1920s. In the poll for Istanbul's mayoral election in 2019, Erdoğan's Justice and Development Party sought to discredit the eventually successful opposition candidate, Ekrem Imamoğlu, by claiming that he had a secret Greek heritage and that the opposition wanted to turn Istanbul back into Constantinople, thereby making it less Turkish and Muslim. This "fake news" did not affect the result there but may have been more influential elsewhere. Erdoğan was a happy camper in historical opinion, notably praising past Turkish triumphs, as in his 2013 speech on the anniversary of the major Seljuk Turkish victory over Byzantine forces at Manzikert in 1071. The Ottoman capture of Constantinople in 1453 was part of the approved narrative. In 2022, Turkey's anniversary celebrations of the conquest saw Erdogan say that they should put Greeks, "today's Byzantines[,] . . . in the dustbin of history."[10] It was unclear whether the same was true of Manzikert. Indeed, rather than criticizing solely authoritarianism or populism, it can be noted that, aside from the important lack of debate in authoritarian societies, the commitment practices of liberal societies, as at present, can tend to the same direction, albeit in different political and coercive contexts.

It is more common to find the official view challenged and countered not by those stressing ambiguity and complexity, but by those who are, or consider themselves, defeated in, or by, history. They employ narratives to counter these defeats. Depending variously on context, circumstances, analysis, perception, and emotion, these narratives can be appreciated or condemned. The "revisionist" is the exile regretting past atrocities, for example, Armenians understandably condemning Turkish actions in 1915. The "revisionist" is also those defeated by events that may attract praise from others as well as, or more than, condemnation. This is far from a new process. Indeed, much of past history is a matter of the views of the defeated, who often have more time for their regrets than the victors, who supposedly enjoy the spoils. Although far more was involved, the critique of slavery and the slave trade can be seen in these terms. It was very important in the West in the early 2020s, and so, notably in America, Belgium, and Britain, helping frame other historical issues, especially about race relations and the legacies of empire.

Revisionist narratives vary greatly, as do their popularity and means of transmission. The latter can appear quaint. For example, an important type of revisionism from the past was the idea of rulers surviving in caves or other sites. Examples include the Emperor Frederick I

"Barbarossa" (r. 1152–1190) in the Kyffhäuser legend and similar accounts about, for example, Ogier the Dane (a Danish folklore hero to whom reference was later made during the German occupation of 1940–1945) in Kronborg castle, Genghis Khan, and the legendary Bernardo Carpio in the Philippines. The last was a precolonial legend repurposed for use as an opponent of Spanish rule and subsequently to American and Japanese occupation as well as the rejection of capitalism. In Portugal, legends of the survival of King Sebastian (r. 1557–1578), who had been totally defeated and killed by Moroccan opponents at al-Qasr-al-Kabir/Alcácer-Quibir, circulated for a long time. What was termed Sebastianism led to prophecies of a *Quinto Império* (fifth empire), reflecting the political present of a strong sense of failure and humiliation that was driven home by the unpopularity of Spanish rule in 1580–1640, for Sebastian's death was speedily followed by Philip II of Spain becoming Philip I of Portugal. Sebastianism overlapped with the hunting down and killing of False-Sebastians by Spanish agents.

"Dreaming" can be construed in very different ways. What are explicitly or implicitly dreams, provided a way to order reality, and a form of literature to challenge events. As such, they were an important part of a pattern of historical myth making.[11] Alongside personal records of dreams, there are many literary works, as well as manuals for dream interpretation. Dream culture as a means to present history is not simply a "primitive" phenomenon. Instead, such culture is a continuing and interrelated understanding of views and practices on consciousness, cosmology, and the perception of past, present, and future. It was present both in periods of continuity and at those of abrupt change, as with the fall of the Ming dynasty. The interaction of objectivity and subjectivity was to the fore in this context.[12]

As an aspect of history, dreams can capture an element in motivation, as with Napoleon's retrospective on his successful invasion of Egypt in 1798: "In Egypt, I found myself freed from the obstacles of an irksome civilisation. I was full of dreams. . . . I saw myself founding a religion, marching into Asia, riding an elephant, a turban on my head and in my hand the new Koran that I would have composed to suit my needs. In my undertakings I would have combined the experiences of the two worlds, exploiting for my own profit the theatre of all history."[13] This very revelatory account, which could easily have left no record, raises speculation about similar views on the part of other leaders.

Very differently, urban landscapes, like their rural counterparts, provide opportunities for "dreams" of another reality, such as utopian political, religious, and social speculations. These dreams can be by both governments and peoples. Partly as a result of the latter, authoritarian regimes have sought to discipline these spaces, as in recent governmental destruction of old neighborhoods in Beijing and Mecca, and the earlier plans for city changing by Hitler, Stalin, and Nicolae Ceauşescu, dictator of Romania from 1965 to 1989, who destroyed part of Bucharest.[14] Very differently, one aspect of "dreaming" are the marginal remains of earlier cultural legacies, such as Copts in Egypt or Berber elements in Tunisia.

Government policies about the past often were a part, usually assertive, of popular perception but could also cut across them. As memories were filtered through historical experiences, these perceptions were varied and thus affected differences over the desired future.[15] For example, an aspect of the combination of government policies with personal experience to create collective memories was provided by the idea of amnesties, an idea that generally proved politically contentious, at least in the long term. History is not to be forgotten, and it is difficult to forgive. That is the lesson driven home by partisan debates but also by claims about amnesia.

Thus, in West Germany, Konrad Adenauer, founding chancellor from 1949 to 1963, proved far more sympathetic to active former Nazis, such as Theodor Oberländer, the minister of refugees in 1953–1960, than now, to adopt a presentist position, looks acceptable, let alone comfortable. Hans Globke, the chief of staff of the chancellery from 1953 to 1960, and a key ally of Adenauer, was an active bureaucrat under the Third Reich, not least in drafting antisemitic measures: he wrote the Nuremberg race laws in 1935. Moreover, Adenauer's amnesties, notably of 1949 and 1954, and the 1951 law on the civil service, chimed with a widespread refusal to accept individual and collective responsibility for the actions of the Third Reich of 1933–1945 as well as opposition to what was termed "victors' justice" by the Allies, which, in practice, was very limited. This refusal was an aspect of consensus seeking to ground and run the new state but in a distinctly unpleasant fashion. Those given a green light back into public life included active and prominent SA, SS, and Gestapo members. The Nuremberg verdicts on Nazi war criminals were repeatedly publicly denigrated, not least by church leaders; which underlined the failure of Catholic clerics to speak out about Nazi crimes, a point about historical representation noted by Adenauer in 1946.

However, conspiracy theorists who saw neo-Nazis as very widely active in West Germany, and therefore as a threat, were proved wrong. In line with the standard practice of history as conspiracy, this theme was very much one of the 1950s, the period soon after the war, and led to concern about West German rearmament, but it proved totally mistaken. Indeed, despite interest among refugees from eastern Europe, the relative lack of *revanchism*, and notably so compared to the 1920s and 1930s, was more apparent.

A variety of approaches can be taken to the West German treatment of the Nazi regime, which underlines not only the range of histories on offer to contemporaries (and thus so more generally) but also the subsequent situation. Thus, Adenauer, who urged "allowing the past to be the past," a silence designed to bring stability, was not personally sympathetic to Nazis. Yet, presenting the Germans as victims of the Nazis served to help create distance from the many savage crimes that were perpetrated, although this process could lead to an acceptance of deceitful self-presentation. While only a few Nazis were punished, a "model democracy," with many not called to account for vile crimes, was apparent, and despite concerns about neo-Nazis, the latter situation was not necessary to the former part of the equation. The destruction of some wartime records was also an aspect of the situation.

The American focus on confronting the Soviet Union encouraged the overlooking of Nazi activity. This reflected the more general construction of usable identities from the varied memories on offer in a particularly charged period. World War II exemplified this process, but as part of a more widespread decade of transformation, that of the 1940s, in which public and private histories had to respond to rapidly changing circumstances. Moreover, in most of the world, making the wrong choice could be, at best, detrimental and, at worse, fatal, and what was the wrong choice could change radically during the decade.

Subsequently, the recollection of that specific wartime took on particular prominence, as it has continued to do. The Holocaust played a major role in foregrounding this prominence, which helped ensure that collaboration with Nazi Germany became a historical bellwether for what was really, or supposedly, unacceptable in the present day. In Israel, where the Holocaust, which of course happened elsewhere, became part of national memorialization in the new Jewish state as a searing cataclysm for Jews, Holocaust Martyrs' and Heroes' Remembrance Day has been used in recent years to decry threats to Israel from Iran and from radical Islamic movements such as Hezbollah. Yet, this process has itself been politically contentious within Israel. Whereas certain politicians, most prominently Binyamin Netanyahu, advanced this position, and vociferously so, others, were critical, Reuven Rivlin, as president, denying that "every threat to Israel is existential and every Israel-hating leader is Hitler."

The international resonance is also contentious. Thus, in 2018, Poland criminalized accusations that many Poles collaborated with the Germans. Very differently in context, the Russian foreign minister Sergei Lavrov, seeking to undermine the Ukrainian president, a Jew, and to substantiate the totally unwarranted Russian claim that Ukraine is a neo-Nazi state, declared in 2022 that Hitler was part-Jewish, which was taken in Israel as implying that the Jews were somehow responsible for the Holocaust, a classic instance of blaming the victims.

The Holocaust was uniquely genocidal in the modern world. Separately, on the part of many states, there was a greater interest in minority populations and their histories, although this was often an interest on controlling terms, as with China and both Tibet and Xinjiang. In the West, there was an advance in the understanding of minority populations from the 1960s, and an increase in the willingness to engage with their histories, both in print and visually. The need to engage with the history of areas before Western contact became more overt, although there were also problems in analysis, not least those posed by using Western classifications of ethnicity. Instead, it was important to give agency to native societies. In 1981, Jack Forbes produced in a striking *Atlas of Native History* a rejection of the appropriation of the Native American past. He employed names used by the native people and sought to present real political conditions, rather than the claims of "white governmental units."[16]

The earlier barbarian versus civilization dichotomy was replaced in part, and notably so in the West, by an emphasis on how native peoples cared for the environment and were in touch with it, and in part by a greater general sympathy with the native presence and perspective, as with the presentation of the Wik people of Australia: "This landscape is not a 'wilderness.' It has been humanised and domesticated by the human tendency to intellectualise and to explain, to transpose into religious and artistic imagery the mundane elements around us. . . . The Wik . . . organise and maintain their land with care and affection."[17]

Current environmental concepts are an instance of how far the extent to which modern criteria can and should be imposed on the past remains an issue.

This general point can be seen by the projection on precolonial Africa of concepts of identity and political authority that may be very misleading. In particular, the Western model of the nation-state, while having immediate value for African nationalists, can be flawed. It is possible that the states, and especially the political identities that were first charted in any detail in the nineteenth century, have had their longevity exaggerated by our own assumptions and by the agendas of ethno-genesis that lie at the heart of proximate cultural nationalism. Not simply has tradition been invented, but even possibly so also have states. Furthermore, as more generally across the world, modern concepts of nationality have been used misleadingly, to interpret the polities and politics of the past. Instead, there appears to have been considerable movement for centuries across what have since been constructed as national borders in almost every sphere of human activity. There were multiple civil and sacred identities in precolonial Africa and elsewhere. There are fewer documentary sources for most African history, but that does not mean that processes were different. At the same time, Africa, a continent that stretches from the Cape of Good Hope to the Nile delta is not necessarily an abstraction that is analytically helpful. A similar point can be made about sub-Saharan Africa.

Thus, and more generally, thinking about what we are, and what we belong to, may be ahistorical in its application and also yields something very far short of a universal taxonomy. At the same time, the nation is the key large-scale unit of modern historical consciousness, with its major rivals being "tribal" or would-be national groups in weak states, such as Afghanistan, and religious bodies. Aside from families, the latter two were also the major entities in premodern historical consciousness, however modern may be defined.

This chapter underlines different aspects of the fallacies of modernity and modernization as manifested in the here-and-now. These fallacies dominate the current writing of academic history.

NINE

—⚊—

THE MANY MEANS OF HISTORY

Don't forget. Nothing has ever been given to you.
Everything has always had to be wrested from them [the
ruling class].

—Jean-Luc Mélenchon, radical left-wing French leader,
May 1, 2022, Paris May Day Parade

APOLOGIES ARE AN ORDER OF the day, by or on behalf of many, with demands rising in a crescendo from
past to present, in a hope that this present will somehow
affect the collective experience of the past. Apologies focus, but often misrepresent, the frequently heated debates
over the interpretation and meaning of historical debates.
Both apologies and debates relate to long-established tensions as well as refer to more recent concerns. Thus, in
2020, Bishop Gregor Hanke of Eichstätt, long a German
center of strong Catholicism, described the witch trials
of the sixteenth and seventeenth centuries as a "bleeding
wound in the history of our church" and undertook to
place a memorial plaque in the cathedral. In a campaign
begun in 2011, over fifty German cities have apologized.
The degree of apology allegedly necessary, however, is a

matter of dispute. Moreover, the issue, while part of the current critique of the Catholic Church, ignores the extent to which witch burning reflected not only church policies but also views across local society, including in Protestant territories such as the imperial free city of Nördlingen. Indeed, in 2022, Nicola Sturgeon, the first minister for Scotland, issued a formal apology. In doing so, she linked the 1563 Witchcraft Act to the present day: "Fundamentally, while here in Scotland the Witchcraft Act may have been consigned to history a long time ago, the deep misogyny that motivated it has not. We live with that still. Today it expresses itself not in claims of witchcraft, but in everyday harassment, online rape threats and sexual violence."[1] Some may think the link less clear-cut.

In 2022, a service of "penitence" at Christ Church Oxford saw repentance for antisemitic acts at the Synod of Oxford in 1222 and thereafter. The synod saw the implementation of decrees from Rome obliging Jews to wear badges.

Somewhat differently, and all categorization and comparisons invite caveats, Christopher Columbus has found a place in America's "culture wars." In particular, it has been argued that his voyages of exploration were a background to expropriation, slavery, and genocide. In 2017, the NYPD provided 'round-the-clock protection for the impressive monument in Columbus Circle, Manhattan. In Los Angeles County, the board of supervisors and the city council decided to replace Columbus Day with Indigenous Peoples' Day, allegedly because Columbus was an oppressor. Baltimore's Columbus monument was vandalized. The term *holocaust* has been used, one of the many uses of a word that should be employed with precision in order to avoid what is in effect Holocaust diminishment. The debate has been both politicized and become in America an aspect of the contentious nature of a melting pot society, with claims by some that their heritage is being trashed, while others regard the celebration of Columbus Day, which became a national holiday in 1937, as an offensive step. Certainly, there is no fixed or single account of the past. Indeed, the honoring of Columbus in 1937 was in part a rejection by Democrats of the emphasis, under Republicans, in the 1920s, on a WASP identity for the United States, an emphasis also seen in the limitation of immigration.

In contrast to such a zeal for apology comes denial, most shockingly so with Holocaust denial, which is false history at its most abrupt and striking. There is also the denial or underplaying of undesirable episodes, notably, as with the Soviet Union and China, those in which the state has slaughtered large numbers of its citizens. This is very much the case with the narratives increasingly entrenched in China, Russia, and North Korea. In these, the official version of history is the only one that it is safe to repeat or even to listen to.[2]

Between apology and denial comes the use of the law to wage historical battles. Thus, in India, there is contention over religious sites and how far supposed historical wrongs should be righted. In part, the courts are employed in an attempt to limit the use of direct action, as in 1992 when Hindus destroyed the Babri Masjid, a mosque in Ayodhya that was allegedly built in the sixteenth century on a Hindu site that had been destroyed. In 2019, the Supreme Court permitted the building of a Hindu temple on the site, and this encouraged Hindu activists to energies existing claims, for example to the Gyanvapi mosque in Varanasi, an issue pushed to the fore in 2022, and also to the Taj Mahal. The role of the Archaeological Survey of India is greatly complicated by such political activism.

More generally, the news daily brings accounts of the deployment of the past to support political points and strategies. Furthermore, terms based on past episodes, or what are given coherence as episodes, such as "Appeasement," "Suez," "Vietnam," and "Iraq," are used to present arguments, this vocabulary being readily matched elsewhere by different vocabularies for the same episodes or for similar ones in other societies. Indeed, the frame of historical reference varies as much as does that of geographical reference.

A good example is provided by Spain, where the Civil War (that of 1936–1939, not the many earlier ones) and Francisco Franco, the caudillo (dictator) from 1939 to 1975, provided this frame of reference, replacing the former ones of the early twentieth century, a humiliating defeat by America in 1898 to the ending of monarchy in 1931. Thus, the Catalan crisis of 2017–2018 saw separatists there repeatedly compare the attitudes, policies, and moves of Spain's national government to those of Franco, which was a particularly potent comparison in Catalonia, which was strongly opposed to Franco in the Civil War. In September 2017, efforts to stop a Catalan independence referendum led to frequent references to the past. Protestors repeatedly decried what they saw as a repetition of the Franco years. On September 20, 2017, Carlos Puigdemont, the Catalan president, described the Spanish state as authoritarian and stated that Catalonia would never accept "a return to the darkest times." Pablo Iglesias, leader of the Podemos, a national opposition party, declared it was "shameful" to return to an era with "political prisoners." The Guardia Civil, the national force used to carry out arrests, were associated by many with the Franco years.

In contrast, the government referred to the post-Franco 1978 constitution as its justification, although this constitution was in many senses defined by the attempt to win the support of Francoist elements. Indeed, also on September 20, Alfonso Dastis, the foreign minister, drew attention to Franco having organized two referenda, a method supported by the Catalan separatists, and claimed that some separatists were using a "Nazi" approach of intimidation. A PP (People's Party, conservative) spokesman referred to the fate of Llius Companys, who had declared Catalan independence in 1934 only to be shot by a Civil Guard firing squad in 1940. Companys is a potent legacy in Catalonia, where there are streets, squares, and the main stadium used in the 1992 Olympics named after him, as well as a monument to him in Barcelona (1998).

Deeper history was also in contention. Some Catalan separatists wished to remove the Columbus monument in Barcelona because they saw it as too Spanish.

The possibility of looking deeply, and the need to do so, varies greatly. For example, the use of the battle of Bannockburn (1314) by Scottish nationalists showed that a distant or "deep history" can be made relevant, with the Scottish discussion of the historical merits of independence perforce focusing on the centuries when Scotland had a separate ruler, which ended in 1603. In contrast, there has been no comparable English reference to the historical defiance of foreign invaders, whether Norman in 1066, French in 1216, or Spanish in 1588. Instead, the frame of historical reference in England is far shorter, and focuses on threatened German invasion in 1940. Having won reelection in 2022, President Macron told aides that he needed a modern version of Henry IV (r. 1589–1610) to run the government as prime minister, thus citing the ruler who helped calm the divides of the Wars of Religion. This 2020 reference to an individual able to tackle socioeconomic differences[3] was not intended to refer to the eventual fate of Henry, assassinated in Paris, but was an instance of the more general "historical" usage of past examples.

Such items rush across attention. The speeded-up nature of the offering and discussion of news by social media means that any measurement of items is swamped not only by volume but also by the reproduction of news and opinion across media discussion. There are still some strands that can be distinguished, even if there is generally a considerable degree of overlap. The first is the primacy of individual and family narratives and networks creating history even as they present it. The ease of using systems such as Instagram to offer this, in whole or part, through photography, is part of the more general visualization of news and, therefore, history. Indeed, in so far as contextual change is a key element in the altering nature of history, the linkage of the individual to the visual offered from the nineteenth century by photography has become a cheap and easy digital means.

More importantly, this change is occurring within a global culture in which the man-made visual has become relatively more significant over the last century and certainly more dynamic. In theory, this might be a case of contributing to already-existing means and content of knowledge and opinion, but it is also possible to be less sanguine about the change. Greater interest in the visual on the part of those who consume history as an artifact (as opposed to experiencing it as events) creates problems for forms of historical expression and authority based on the written word. Linked to this, come issues for documentary archives of the conventional form. The implications for the future are unclear, but they pull toward a move away from mediums of historical expression dependent on written text (whether or not digital) and from institutional footfalls, whether educational or not.

Separately, as a pressure for providing a different approach, the primacy of the individual and family may well be the historical locus that leaves less conventional evidence than those of government and education, but that situation does not make these subjects less consequential or less interesting to individuals. Women were confined as a "topic" to social history, which was totally misguided. Separately, "women as historians" is a subject commonly addressed, as with men, with reference to those who wrote what were formally historical works, but as with men, this downplayed the numbers of those who told historical tales and the active role of a wide tranche of society in the historical process. In terms of writing books, the limited political authority of femininity; the nature of institutional support for certain types of male activity, especially in governmental and ecclesiastical bodies; and norms about appointing men to academic positions meant that women in the past were disproportionally present as historical novelists rather than as academic historians.

The locus of the individual and family acts as a way to process information and ideas coming from other bodies. It presents a consumerist account of history. This faces all the difficulties of analysis bound up in consumerism but also the inbuilt intellectual prejudice in favor of producer accounts of phenomena including cultural and intellectual ones. Academic presentations of historiography in terms of the views and writings of past scholars are a classic instance of this prejudice.[4]

This prejudice, however, has serious weaknesses. These are not least in appreciating the issues of producer impact, notably its limitations. Furthermore, there were consumer influences on production. As such, there are parallels with other forms of economic activity and discussion of past episodes, such as the Industrial Revolution. The more, indeed, history is understood as a field in which popular perception is regarded as significant and difficult to mold, if not being completely autonomous, the more a consumerist account appears relevant. Moreover, that account has its own chronology, with relevant continuities and discontinuities, separate to that offered by the producer account focused on academics and other writers.

Technological changes in the means of dissemination are significant in this discussion of consumer factors, but so also are political changes. War, particularly, becomes the context as well as the subject of history, context in the shape of the consumption as well as production of history. War also brings to the fore a destructiveness of history in the shape of the damage of the legacy of the past. That can be deliberate, as with the targeting of religious sites, which attracts more effort than that of governmental records and other scholarly sources. In practice, the destruction of all such elements represent a culture war that is designed to limit the possibility of maintaining historical legacy and identity. The destruction of statues can be part of that process. The brutal struggle in Ethiopia in 2022 provided an instance of such destructiveness, with ancient churches in the province of Tigray, notably those in the town of Lalibela, being targeted by attacking forces in part as a struggle for the symbolic control of history, as was also the case with that of churches and mosques during the conflicts of the 1990s in former Yugoslavia.

The experience of conflict, as well as its after-ordering in the imagination and in public presentation, are defining challenges for understanding and discussion. This helps set the present situation, because of the importance not only of strife within, and between, states but also of comparable senses of difference. Ethnicity and religion are obvious instances of comparable pressures of identity and disagreement, if not strife. Moreover, these elements can be more present in areas where state forms are weak and/or expressions of these pressures. Again, history is expounded as a consequence. Examples include differing Israeli, Palestinian, Indian, and Pakistani narratives, although, in each case, it would be a mistake to see any single narrative, whatever the situation at the level of particular governments. This, indeed, was/is a flaw on the part of those who call for "patriotic education" about history, a call for example made by President Donald Trump (r. 2017–2021), but more frequently in authoritarian states.

The most radical changes in historical work were those in former Communist states. There was a reevaluation of what had been previously covered, both for the history of those states and for that of the world as a whole. There was also the uncovering of omissions. Thus, the focus elsewhere in the Soviet bloc on Russian topics and perspectives ended, as did that on radical social movements in a Marxist historical model. Attention was devoted, instead, both to medieval greatness, for example in Lithuania, and also to the complexities of the 1940s, notably for the Baltic Republics Soviet conquest in 1940.

The opening of archives became a key point in the tension between Communist and anti-Communist histories. It encouraged research by providing access to previously closed material and brought forward the opportunity to study Cold War defeat and collapse. It became possible to research certain topics while also shaping how they would be framed. The chaotic aspects of the process threw a lot of material into view before the Russian archives were closed up again. Projects such as the *Black Book of Communism*, edited by Stephane Courtois, used that evidence with material already in the public domain to indict the Communist record that academic historians and the Western media downplayed.

The Ukraine war of 2022 exemplified both rival narratives between states and the use of historical analogies. The clearest was that of Nazism. President Putin of Russia repeatedly claimed that his invasion was intended as a means to end Nazism, which, in order to bolster support in Russia, he, totally misleadingly, presented as characteristic of Ukraine and notably so of present-day Ukraine, for Ukraine, Russia, and the Soviet Union all had an antisemitic past.[5] This weaponization of history, one that also provided the regime with a rationale, was seen more generally that April with the burial of Major General Vladimir Frolov in St. Petersburg when the governor of the city,

Alexander Beglov, claimed that he had died a heroic death fighting "a new generation of Nazis." Polls indicate that the support for Putin within Russia was closely linked to those, mostly elderly, who understood Russian opponents in terms of this World War II narrative. It was a narrative that Russia had inherited from the Soviet Union, one willed on Communism and Russian nationalism by Germany in 1941–1945. The use of Victory Day in order to deliver a message by Putin, as well as on his behalf, was a means of employing the legacy of one state (the Soviet Union) in one crisis to justify the actions of Russia in another, but with Ukraine cast as the aggressor, which it was not.

Like many leaders, particularly but not only in authoritarian states, Putin likes to present himself in the perspective of history. He is especially prone to see himself in the tradition of Peter the Great (r. 1682–1725) and Catherine the Great (r. 1762–1796), making historical and iconographical references accordingly. Both of these czars greatly expanded Russia territorially, and each was based in St. Petersburg, also Putin's place of birth and where he played a role in city administration from 1990 to 1996. Yet Putin also looked to pan-Slavism, the idea of Russia as uncontaminated by Western concepts of liberalism and individualism, an idea very much developed within the Russian Orthodox Church, with which he is aligned politically.

There is also a use of the "Little Russian" nationalist ideology that developed in Ukraine in the nineteenth century, placing Ukraine as the birthplace of the Rus' faith, and that was encouraged by Russian officials as a way to weaken Polish nationalism.[6] Putin draws on czarist history more generally and has encouraged officials to consider the work of Ivan Ilyin (1883–1954), who regarded royal imperialism, not liberal democracy, as the way to hold Russia together. There was a Christian nationalist Fascism in Ilyin's thought, and it influenced Aleksandr Solzhenitsyn and Aleksandr Dugin. Ilyin was totally opposed to Ukrainian independence and used organic imagery to say that there was no right for individuals or cells to choose their identity. The idea of foreign threat is to the fore. In school, Russians are taught their forbears threw off the yoke of Tatar-Mongol masters in 1480. In 2022, the Kremlin announced that it would reform the Russian school curriculum to teach children as young as seven a "patriotic" version of history.

In turn, although less consistently, the Ukrainians used the same charge against Russia, as when Dmytro Gurin, a Ukrainian member of parliament, said, "I don't see the difference between Mariupol and Auschwitz."[7] This both displayed the rhetorical nature of the appeal to the past and its misleading character, as with the Ukrainian application of the Nazi idea of "the Final Solution," the genocidal fate to be visited on the Jews, as their own plight. Conversely, Putin's construction of a past to argue that Ukraine was not a real nation but, instead, part of Russia is also based on the rhetorical usage of the past, as is the use against Russia of the term genocide as a progression from the treatment of the collectivization famine of the 1930s, the Holodomor in which millions of Ukrainians died, as genocidal in character and intensity. In part, consciously or not, this usage, while a fair description of Stalin's policies and their implementation, is also a way in which to gain attention. The latter is particularly important given not only competing claims but the very volume of discussion over particular issues. Yet, the willingness of prominent Russian propagandists, such as Nikolai Starikov, publicly to deny that there was a famine suggests the continual salience of the issue.[8]

A range of historical parallels was offered in other countries. For example, there is much comparison in Finland, in the media and in public debates, between the Ukraine war in 2022 and the Winter War of 1939–1940, in which Finland bravely and initially successfully opposed invasion by far larger Soviet forces. In Finland, this conflict, in which the Finns fought alone, attracted more attention after World War II than the war with the Soviet Union as German ally in 1941–1944 or that with Germany as Soviet ally in 1944–1945. This was typical, both of the significance of World War II for later national histories and of the need to provide an exemplary account. That of resistance, rather than compromise, was the most important component, as with China and France toward Japanese and German invasion, respectively.

Having earlier deployed charges of appeasement, notably against President Macron of France, British politicians and commentators are also apt to cite World War II with reference to the Ukraine. Thus, when, speaking by Zoom to the Ukrainian Parliament in May 2022, Boris Johnson declared, "This is Ukraine's finest hour, that will be remembered and recounted for generations to come," this was an invocation of Winston Churchill. The author of *The Churchill Factor* (2014), Johnson has repeatedly been keen to link himself to Churchill, not least in his personal narrative. Connections to Churchill have also more generally been drawn in Britain, as in 2010 when

Churchill appeared to help Doctor Who, a popular television character, in *Victory of the Daleks* or in 2012 when his statue in Westminster was animated and given a role in the opening ceremony of the London Olympics. This statue was in turn attacked by protestors in London in 2020, in part due to controversy over Churchill's vigorous support for Britain's imperial mission.

Others used similar language to Johnson in describing the conflict. Edgar Rinkevics, Latvia's foreign minister, attacked Macron in a tweet on Sunday May 15: "In 1939 it was called appeasement, in 2022 it is called face saving, let us not make the same mistakes again."[9] Former president George W. Bush compared Zelensky to Churchill.

Museums provided another source of instant history for the war, offering in one prominent case a polemical contextualization. What until 1998 was Moscow's centrally located Museum of the Revolution and thereafter the Museum of Modern History opened in April 2022 an exhibition entitled *NATO: A Chronicle of Cruelty* that was supported by the Ministries of Defense and Culture as well as Rossiya Segodnya, the principal state news agencies. The starting display reads, "NATO is infamous to the modern world as one of history's most aggressive military-political alliances." The exhibition went back to the [pre-NATO] American use of atomic bombs in 1945 and focused on the American use of violence against civilians and brought the story into the current Ukraine campaign while presenting a pro-Russian account of past and present. This was another version of the Russian inheritance from the Soviet Union.

Reading between the two conflicts was very frequent, with Putin's arguments challenged by the claim that he was discrediting Russia's past. On May 8, 2022, in congratulating former Soviet nations on the seventy-seventh anniversary of German defeat, Putin declared, "As in 1945, victory will be ours. . . . Today, our soldiers, as their ancestors, are fighting side by side to liberate their native land from the Nazi filth with the confidence that, as in 1945, victory will be ours." This narrative was challenged, with President Zelensky telling a G7 meeting via video, "Evil has returned, in a different uniform but for the same purpose. A bloody reconstruction of Nazism." Putin's use of the Soviet effort against Hitler led to much criticism outside Russia. Within conquered areas of Ukraine, such as the city of Kherson, Russian-approved curricula schoolbooks were imposed with their views of Ukrainian history. This was a dramatic demonstration of a key element of history in practice.

The 2022 Ukraine war posed major challenges for many states in developing a workable historical narrative capable of incorporating the combatants or their supporters. Moreover, this difficulty interacted with the extent to which global resonances were in part a matter of the cross-currents of national interests drawing at least in part on historical accounts. Thus, aside from economic and security links, India's care about offending Russia in 2022–2023 in part draws on long-standing uneasiness about Britain and America, a process also seen in South America and Africa. Anticolonialism is an issue, as are Cold War hostilities.

In China, Xi Jinping, the general secretary of the Communist Party from 2012 and president from 2013, is strongly pledged to what is presented as patriotic education. He has a long-standing hostility to what he sees and presents as the anti-Chinese notion of Western commitment to constitutionalism and universal values. His view draws on a very different historical stance, one seen in the online summit on April 1, 2022, between Xi and the heads of European Union institutions who were pressing him over Ukraine as well as over Chinese human rights abuses. Charles Michel, the president of the European Council, claimed that Europeans care greatly about human rights due to their history, not least World War II and the Holocaust, which is a reasonable assessment of the response by European governments and institutions. Xi replied by referring to Chinese mistreatment by colonial powers, notably the nineteenth-century treaties under which China was obliged to open itself up privileged foreign traders. Xi claimed that colonizers displayed signs proclaiming, "No Dogs and Chinese Allowed," although there is no evidence about this much-reported claim. Xi then ran this critique into the very different Japanese massacre of Chinese civilians at Nanjing in 1937, going on to argue that there is therefore Chinese concern about human rights and anger at what he saw as the double standards of foreigners.

National coherence, both political and territorial, is very much the goal of presentist history in China, and nationalism (and history) are intensively employed to that end. The suppression by the government of the prodemocracy demonstrations in 1989, a suppression in which thousands of peaceful protestors were slaughtered (and amnesia then vigorously imposed by the state), was followed by a major effort to use nationalism to support the Communist system. Flag-raising ceremonies became mandatory in schools, museums were presented as "patriotic education bases," and, in 1991, Jiang Zemin, the general secretary, praised patriotic education as a means to stop the young worshipping the West. They were supposed instead to follow the party.

A portrayal of past humiliation for China, notably in the nineteenth century, justified, from then on, an assertion of Chinese values in the present, with the Communist Party, from 1949, as their exponent and protector.[10] Xi has pressed for the fulfilment of a "Chinese Dream," in which national self-assertion is linked to the end of what is presented as historical humiliation. The first mention of his dream of "the great revival of the Chinese nation" was made at the National Museum in Beijing, where the *Road to Revival* exhibit counterpoints humiliation at the hands of colonial powers with revival under the Communists. This is a central theme of Chinese Communist ideology, one to which history contributes. In 2013, Xi returned to the theme when accepting the presidency, and its inclusion in school textbooks was ordered by Liu Yunshan, in effect the party's propaganda head. The theme has also been taken up by figures linked to the military. Abolishing in 2018 the limit on his period as leader, a process followed by many autocrats such as Putin, Xi adopted a strongly nationalist stance.

History was of course to be presented accordingly. Thus, the "New Qing (Manchu) History," an American-led scholarly approach from the mid-1990s, challenged the earlier emphasis on the sinicization of the Qing and, instead, argued that the empire was multiethnic in character and certainly so until the late eighteenth century.[11] This view was attacked by Chinese scholars, notably by Li Zhiting in *Chinese Social Sciences Today* (2015).[12] He argued that "New Qing History" was imperialist both in presenting China in that light and in reflecting Western imperialism as well as damaging to the unity of China. At the same time, the expansion of China under the Qing to include Tibet and Xinjiang encouraged a measure of rehabilitation for the period of the dynasty.

The Opium Wars, the very title of which reflected a reductionist and pejorative account of British motivation that is definitely less than complete, were, and are, seen in China as a national humiliation. They are presented to the public accordingly, as with Xie Jin's film *The Opium War* (1997). The role of the Communist Party in defending China against supposed American and Japanese threats was given historical resonance by stressing the damage done by Western imperialism in the nineteenth century, notably that by Britain. The resulting contrast in effectiveness served to make the Communist Party appear more successful and necessary.[13] The focus on the Opium Wars, rather than the Taiping Rebellion, overlaps with, but is not identical to, that on war with Japan in 1931–1945 rather than civil war within China in the 1920s and 1930s, let alone the appalling human cost of such Communist movements as the Great Leap Forward and the Cultural Revolution. These were multimillion-fatality events, but somehow fail to arouse the revulsion directed at the killings due to British and American action. In 2022, the new textbooks introduced in Hong Kong argued that it had never been legitimately British and could not therefore claim any right to self-determination.

British imperialism therefore has fulfilled a range of official goals in China. It can operate as a surrogate for the United States and has also provided ammunition for a critical focus on particular aspects of modern British policy. This approach is not solely historical. Thus, Britain's alignment with Japan in recent years serves China as a critique of both. To China, this alignment acts as a rejection of the Chinese, an argument, expressed by Liu Xiaoming, the ambassador in Britain, in the *Daily Telegraph* on January 1, 2014, that as the two powers (Britain and China) were "wartime allies" in World War II, they should "join together both to uphold the UN Charter and to safeguard regional stability and world peace."

Given the growing importance of China in the world at present and its determined effort to disseminate state-supported views, the significance of the hostile Chinese account of Western imperialism will grow. It will provide a ready narrative as China pursues alliances and agreements with former British colonies, notably in Africa, but also elsewhere, for example in the West Indies, the Indian Ocean, and the South Pacific.

Such a use of the past is scarcely confined to China, Russia, or Western critics of both. Instead, there is a willingness, amounting to a general situation, to read between past and present that argues for the salience of historical reference but also a failure to offer due contextualization. Academic historians can be apt to feel that they, in contrast, are able to do so. Thus, in a recent British periodical, one observed: "National traditions are built out of collective memory. As the oral historian Alessandro Portelli has said, 'errors, inventions and myths lead us through and beyond facts to their meanings.' But someone has to guide us through the thickets of fact, myth and invention to make sense of those meanings. That's what historians are for, and we need one here."[14]

That somewhat complacent conclusion, however, underplays the degree to which historians can themselves be politicized, particularly (but not only) in authoritarian societies and also where history, and the teaching of history, are seen to have a clear purpose. Moreover, aside from there being no inherent lack of strife in the relations between scholars, there are also "errors, inventions and myths" aplenty.

Returning to popular history (but with this point also being relevant for the academic version), the situation is far easier when conflict is long gone and there is relatively little contention over current policy, including immigration. The current Portuguese response to the period of Muslim rule from 711 to 1249 provides an example. As with earlier periods of Portuguese history, that under the Moors did not have a lasting resonance in terms of Portugal's image of its past. There is a marked contrast with modern Spain, not least with the lack of any significant current Portuguese focus on past cooperation between Moors, Christians, and Jews, a focus that has attracted attention in Spain in terms of the state and culture of al-Andalus. The alternative stress on the Reconquista in Spain is an aspect of the wider extent to which the Middle Ages provides a setting for contention. This was definitely the case with relations between religions, and notably so with the Crusades. Alongside social and other interest and posing, the Middle Ages is also very important for competing images of nationhood. This was not least the case in laying claim to territories for ethnicities that sought a long genesis for a current territorial identity based solely on ethnic extent.[15] The situation in the former Yugoslavia in the 1990s provided a key instance, and notably so with Serbian claims. Somewhat differently, the Middle Ages plays a major role in television and other visual formats.[16]

There are no comparisons in Portugal with the scale and beauty of the sites of Moorish Spain, notably Granada and Córdoba, or with the literature and art later devoted to them by Western writers and artists. Moreover, Moorish Spain lasted until 1492, a quarter-millennium longer than Moorish Portugal, with a major rebellion occurring thereafter near Granada in 1568–1570, and thus had a longer resonance in Spanish history than is the case for Portugal. These points help address the question of whether there is a misleading amnesia as far as Portugal's Moorish past is concerned. While easy to make such statements about popular historiography, like most this one is a less than fair criticism given the extent to which there has not really been an obvious impact of this past to the present. Nor is there a large Islamic minority today in Portugal that needs to be addressed in terms of a historical account or close political or cultural relations with Northwest Africa. Tourists can construct an itinerary focusing on Moorish sites in Portugal, but they are relatively few, and tourists with these interests would be far better advised to turn to southern Spain. In part, that is also a reflection of the extent to which Moorish Portugal was peripheral, not only to the Moorish world as a whole, but also to the Moorish empires whether based in southern Spain or spanning Iberia and Morocco. This marginality understandably directs attention to the independent Christian state that emerged from overturning Moorish Portugal and with scant continuity between them.

Turning to more recent Portuguese history, the over-throw in 1974, with the Carnation Revolution, of the authoritarian Salazarist system led to a new history, in tone, context, and content, a history that was eased by the limited political traction of that system. In part, this new history was because there was, in effect, a pact of forget-ting between the political parties but also because, prefig-uring the situation in former Communist states after the fall of European Communism in 1989–1991, there was no political movement of weight looking back to the Salazar dictatorship. There was no past on offer that was attrac-tive, not least because Portugal's imperial position, which had been significant to the ideology of Salazar's *Estado Novo*, was totally gone. The Salazarist system did not have as strong a political afterglow as Portuguese monarchy had had in the 1910s and 1920. Moreover, unlike in Spain, the military was not the basis for political action from the right. Instead, it was the military that, having helped bring it into existence, toppled the Salazarist system.

Again prefiguring what was to be the situation under former Communist states, the postdictatorial Portuguese governments did see a degree of restitution, notably for the reputation of Humberto Delgado, an opponent of Sala-zar assassinated in 1965 by the Portuguese secret service, with the approval of Salazar. Mário Soares, the Socialist prime minister from 1976 to 1978 and 1983 to 1985, had supported Delgado and had his remains interred in the National Pantheon. Delgado was also retrospectively pro-moted to field marshal. The Lisbon airport was recently named after Delgado. In turn, much that was named by, or after, Salazar was renamed. Thus, the Ponte Salazar over the Tagus at Lisbon, a suspension bridge modeled on the Golden Gate Bridge, was renamed the Ponte 25 de Abril. There are numerous Praças 25 de Abril and the date became a national holiday known as Freedom Day. A very different public art was pushed to the fore, with statues of trade union activists, as in Régua, and of workers. Thus, in Alcochete, on the southern shore of the Tagus estuary, a center of saltpans, a statue of a salt worker was erected in 1985 with the inscription "From Salt to Rebellion and Hope."

Similar points can be made for very different narratives and contexts elsewhere, for example the commemoration of the enslaved and the related attempt to "decommemorate" those seen as enslavers, as well as would-be analogous movements elsewhere. A key element in the latter has been the powerful use by America's civil rights movement of its own history.[17] As with so much popular (and academic) history in America, the differing accounts are readily related by commentators to political differences. In part, this situation is a continuing reflection of divisions in that history from the outset. How far, however, any episode from the past is directly relevant to actions today is a reasonable question but not one that is favored. In practice, the process of a ready transferability of past to present, and vice versa, are not particularly helpful and certainly do not necessarily establish a case.

Thus, it is readily possible to advocate a political situation for Germany today without implying that a similar one was appropriate in 1500, 1700, 1900, or any other date. This is important due to the tendency to present German history both in judgmental terms and with reference to some supposed pattern not only of narrative but also of analysis. Indeed, an understanding of past developments repeatedly demonstrates there was a real lack of patterns, let alone of certainty in developments. To a degree, the transitions of 1866, 1918–1919, 1945, and 1990 in Germany were different stages of the same process, albeit with the dynastic presence, both complication and clarification, absent after 1918. A list in this fashion therefore suggests caution about the ready process of referring to 1990 as a reunification rather than a unification. To do so implies a degree of natural and necessary progression that is pertinent in one perspective as an undoing of the Cold War partition established in the late 1940s but possibly not in another. There was no natural and necessary progression. Thus, to imagine that West and East Germany had to unite is problematic given the need for wariness about similar arguments in 1938 for Germany and Austria, the Anschluss (joining), or indeed for the breakup of that relationship in 1866.

Drawing links across time continues to be insistent. Thus, in March 2013, Jean-Claude Juncker, prime minister of Luxembourg from 1995 to 2013 and president of the European Commission from 2014 to 2019, gave an interview with *Der Spiegel* titled "The Demons Haven't Been Banished" in which he used World War I as his point of reference for issues within the EU, notably the Euro crisis: "I see obvious parallels with regard to people's complacency." Juncker claimed that circumstances were very similar to those of a century earlier as the war neared. He argued, moreover, that, despite the avoidance of large-scale conflict in Europe since 1945, the issues of war and peace there had not been laid to rest. Juncker also argued that sentiments had surfaced that it had been thought had been relegated to the past. Thus, Juncker offered the convenient dichotomy of Euro-federalism or chaos. Transnationalism was deployed to typecase the EU's critics as negative and as grounded in a (misplaced) nationalism that draws on history, an approach taken toward Hungary and Poland.

This critique of nationalism as populism and populism as nationalism is also employed, subliminally or explicitly, to typecast the two world wars as well as to derive a more general political point about the Holocaust. For several decades, this was largely a matter of the experience and collective memory of Jews and was downplayed in the accounts of occupation and brutality by Nazi Germany. In turn, Holocaust memorialization has become a civic activity as part of public commemoration, with national days introduced, including in France in 1993.[18]

There was also the more mundane drawing of links. For example, in February 2020, Matthew Hancock, the British secretary of state for health, referred to the French Maginot Line of 1930s fortifications in terms of the folly of reliance on a stoppage of travel as a means to stop the spread of coronavirus, the analogy being to the German ability to bypass the position when invading in 1940. Hancock was reliant on the use of the example without considering the point that the Maginot Line worked by confining the likely direction of attack, only for the overall strategy to fail because of France's failure to handle the mobile stage of the campaign. A similar misconstruction occurs with the British antiship guns at Singapore, which allegedly pointed in the wrong direction, failing to prevent Japanese conquest in 1942, when, in practice, the guns stopped any Japanese naval assault.

Similarly, with the Vietnam War, it is not helpful in terms of public use of the past to suggest that while tactically and operationally highly problematic for the Americans, the intervention was somewhat different in strategic terms. It ended with America allied to China, the spread of Communism restricted in Southeast Asia, Indonesia securely in the Western camp, the Viet Cong shattered, and the North Vietnamese greatly weakened by the struggle, committed in Cambodia, and facing Chinese hostility.

That was not a view that accorded with the human cost of the war, and the latter resonated with and in response to the general political use of the conflict, as in 2007 when President George W. Bush cited the chaos in Southeast Asia that followed American withdrawal in 1973 as a reason for continuing to persist in Iraq. In part, he was responding to the use of the Vietnam War by his critics. Indeed, the frame of reference for American military activities in Iraq from 2003 had moved from being the rapid success of the Gulf War of 1991 to the commitment of the Vietnam War.

Approached from a different direction, the prioritizations of goals, tasks, and means that are central to strategy are not only inherently political but also necessarily contingent and, as a result, should not be used to set a pattern. Instead, these prioritizations can serve as an analytical device or rhetorical tool in discussion.

Alongside links across time, those across space also invite consideration. On the one hand, there is the global perspective and, within that, attempts to follow a path that links across previous divides. Thus, in place of continental-scale bases for consideration, has come an emphasis on oceans.[19] Yet, while largely effective at the academic level, albeit with omissions or areas underplayed, such as Morocco for Atlantic history, this approach has had less success at the popular level. Globalization is more successful as an academic mantra than as an engagement with collective hopes and fears.[20] Indeed, the extent to which, in 2022, the Ukraine crisis and, separately, national response to economic crises helped drive environmental issues down in attention was noticeable.

More generally, history suggests the unpredictability of developments and events. The past does not set a pattern for the future, clear or otherwise, but neither should it be swept aside in some naive response to the weight of the present and the hope for the future.

INTO THE FUTURE

Few people know anything of the English history but
what they learn from Shakespeare; for our story is rather
a tissue of personal adventures and catastrophes than a
series of political events.

IN HER REFLECTION TO A friend in 1762, the well-
read Lady Elizabeth Montagu captured a precursor, in the
shape of drama, to the modern emphasis on the visual media as the basis for public knowledge and understanding
of history. In the novel *Mansfield Park* (1814), moreover,
Jane Austen described Shakespeare as "part of an Eng-
lishman's constitution. His thoughts and beauties are so
spread abroad that one touches them everywhere; one is
intimate with him by instinct."

Indeed, in light of the historical lodestars of and for the
past, such as Shakespeare, the view sometimes offered today by academics and other commentators that there was
a past golden age of public understanding of history that
has been undermined by "false news," "bad history," and
general ignorance needs to be handled with care. It is an
amusing paradox that this view of a better, if not golden,

age can often be accompanied by scholarly attention to the "invention of tradition" in the past. It is probable that the same situation will be the case in the future and not least in future views of the then past, the latter of course encompassing our present.

The continuation of present-day circumstances and trends seems the most likely scenario in the near term, albeit with frames of historical reference that vary greatly, both within and between societies. The continuation may be affected by the consequences of conflict or of large-scale migration, each of which will pose issues of what to incorporate in new histories and of how best to do so. Indeed, to a degree, the strength, in some countries and certain milieux, of calls for apology and restitution are part of a continuing reading from the past to the present and future, as modernity is redefined in terms of the self-justification of the moment. Thus, a politics of historical reparations will continue to be strong.

These calls are particularly strong around issues of Western-controlled slavery, although those are by no means the sole matters that occasion demands for reparations. The demand for reparations draws in part on material produced by the abolitionist cause from the late eighteenth century. For example, in contrast to the habitual Western emphasis on 1781 as the year of the British surrender to the Americans at Yorktown, the throwing overboard to their death of 142 enslaved people from the *Zong*, a British-owned Dutch slave ship affected by disease and short of water, was not only a cause célèbre of the age, not least because the owners claimed their value on the ship's insurance, but also receives a lot of attention today. In 1840, J. M. W. Turner produced a dramatic painting of the by then historic episode entitled *The Slave Ship*. It has also been featured in media more recently, as in Fred D'Aguiar's novel *Feeding the Ghosts* (1997).

Sir Hilary Beckles, a prominent Barbados historian who chaired the Caricom Reparations Commission, which was established in 2013 and produced a report in 2014, argued:

> This is about the persistent harm and suffering experienced today by the descendants of slavery and genocide that is the primary cause of development failure in the Caribbean. The African descended population in the Caribbean has the highest incidence in the world of the chronic diseases hypertension and type 2 diabetes, a direct result of the diet, physical and emotional brutality and overall stress associated with slavery, genocide and apartheid. . . . The British in particular left the black and indigenous communities in a general state of illiteracy and 70 per cent of blacks in British colonies were functionally illiterate in the 1960s when nation states began to appear.

Indeed, there is a physiological link between descendants of survivors of the trans-Atlantic Middle Crossing and slavery and hypertension and diabetes. So also is the situation of black people in the American Deep South. Thus, in 2020, the blacks of Louisiana were particularly hard hit by coronavirus, in large part due to poverty, less access to healthcare, and a higher rate of underlying health problems, notably diabetes, hypertension, and heart disease, which black people there tend also to acquire at younger ages.

These factors argue for a deep history in terms of health, an approach that is of growing interest in certain milieux as attempts are made to link intractable differences in health outcomes to particular historical events, thus giving those who understand the latter greater traction in present-day "history wars." This approach does not invalidate, or even undermine, more complex accounts to align the issue with Marxist thought, as in Cedric Robinson's *Black Marxism* (1983),[1] and, instead, draw on the literature engaged by such arguments.

A somewhat different approach was taken by the *New York Times* when, in 2019, it sought to reset the foundation date of America as 1619, the first year slaves were brought into the English colonies that were to be the basis for the eventual United States of America as opposed to the customary focus on the Declaration of Independence in 1776. This was an arresting approach, one that attempted to make slavery the original, foundational, moment of colonial history. In practice, that approach underplayed the earlier Hispanic strand of settlement, notably in Florida, but, more particularly, did not engage with Native American society, not least as a source of slaves and of enslavement. Moreover, while crucial to some of the English colonies, slavery was not so to all.

Nevertheless, the notion expressed in a "ladder of civilisation," or other similar images, with progress supposedly set by a Western paradigm, appears increasingly redundant in a Western culture that preaches relative values and is unsure of its own purpose. The "Triumph of the West"[2] is seen as more contingent, partial, troubled and problematic than was the case in the late twentieth century. Ironically, similar views about triumph are now more apparent in the views of some non-Western societies, notably China. Outside the West, more generally, there can be more pride in national histories, a process that can also be observed in former colonies that received a large number of European emigrants. Their sense of their history is now less focused on the mother country. Yet, significant complication still arises in portraying the long-term history of states whose territorial extent and ethnic composition were often the work of European conquerors and therefore relatively recent.

On a different scale, the ambition of the historical gaze, and its deployment to address current concerns, have combined very recently in discerning the idea of a new era, the Anthropocene, a term greatly publicized from 2000 to describe a period of transformative human impact on the environment. This approach is at once global and comprehensive but also without a clear-cut civilizational bias unless seen in terms of the inherent sociocultural assumptions of a new notion of Enlightenment or, at least, perspective of enlightened concern. The threats in 2022 that the Ukraine or Korea crises might lead to nuclear warfare brought the political narrative very much into the Anthropocene, a period sometimes dated from the 1945 nuclear explosions, and vice versa. This is a form of history now at once immediate and of a capacity to reverse time, at least in so far as the latter is measured in terms of the development of civilization.

This situation is different to that with which we started our story but possibly less so than might have been envisaged. History understood as a self-conscious and self-validating academic profession remains essentially source based by method, although both widely different by state contexts and also affected by its own values and prejudices. Academe, however, is but a small part of a historical world defined in part as a playground for the imagination, whether individual or governmental, but, more generally, as an engagement with experience and the desire to explain and represent it.

The pace of change at present in the historical world, understood narrowly as the context within which history is an account or analysis of the past, is very great. This is least true of higher education, where existing institutional structures and practices continue and also enjoy built-in capabilities and advantages. This is due to their existing position within political and social structures, in authoritarian, socialist, and capitalist systems, and also to the norm of going to university as a form of social activity and a means to secure status and opportunities. On the back of this, a host of academic structures continue, such as advanced degrees and scholarly journals. Moreover, many of these structures have adapted to the new technology of mass data and the internet.

At the same time, the extent to which these institutions determine wider practices of historical understanding is very unclear. Anachronism is certainly commonplace across the field of history, from academic to popular, and anachronism involves imposing present-day priorities but also using that to distort our awareness of the past. This is a situation, however, under pressure from technological change, which is not new. The impact of printing was scarcely the sole instance, and that of the cinema was echoed in the preface to the second edition of Clifford and Elizabeth Lord's *Historical Atlas of the United States* (1953):

> The startling rapid growth and development of the United States makes its history particularly susceptible to visual portrayal. The animated cartoon-map is certainly the most

vivid way of showing, for instance, the tentacles of our rail-
road system reaching out year by year across the country,
or of portraying the spread of our crop areas, the development of manufacturing regions, the westward advance of
population.... But movies have their limitations. They may
be seen and heard, but they are difficult to study.... Those
who lack photographic memories ... are more apt to carry
away a vague impression than definite knowledge.[3]

The criticism was well-founded, but that was exactly
what was to be the situation as the visual rose in significance. In addition, the screen cannot readily convey the
interior views of the characters. A story told visually is one
that tends to be on the surface.

Separately, visual processes and data did not inherently mean a move away from research-based learning,
as data could be routinely visualized on screen by the
1980s thanks to powerful desktop computers. Digital information systems became prominent, and the real cost of
computers and their hardware and software fell, while the
introduction of new innovations increased in speed. The
implications for the future are at least more of the same.

A sense of resulting democratization was offered by
Bruce Macdonald in explaining the background to his
individual and exciting *Vancouver: A Visual History* (1992).
He argued that the development of desktop computers
transformed the authorial process: "Persons can bring
their visions to reality without having to compromise
their original ideas."[4] Independent production and publication very much affected the parameters of distribu-
tion. The computer scrutinization of data for patterns
and relationships was no longer restricted to academics
but open to all with computers. A large database makes

it possible to study change over time more convincingly. Moreover, looking to the future, predictive sequencing can be built in.

Data has to be analyzed. Data availability and bias remain significant issues. Historical scholarship requires clarifying generalizations in time, thus limiting perspective, a topic that in August 2022 led to controversy when James Sweet, the president of the American Historical Association, was criticized by some for warning against presentism.[5] Moreover, it is necessary to reconstruct and understand past histories with respect to the attitudes of the period: meanings explain the temporal context of a given subject and period and cannot be assumed in modern terms, which is an anachronistic practice and culture.

Anachronism is differently represented in the very interest in sympathizing with characters, a process that was already much to the fore with historical novels. Visual media provide possibilities and constraints of their own, but the desire for an emotional response has always been present. In part, there is an element of narcissism—a projection of present on past, whether by rulers or by those seeking entertainment from history.

In part, there is the difficulty of thinking of the past as different. It may be obviously so in terms of the visual panoply, notably costume, but there is a marked reluctance to think in terms of different attitudes and values and, instead, an assumption that emotions prevail across time, as well as into the fantasy world. Indeed, this essential similarity of the human experience is the basic historiographical element of modern responses to the past and can be seen as innate and intuitive. That this response is less common in scholarly circles in which, instead, there is a far better understanding both of the specificities and conjunctures of the past, and of the role of changing contexts, does not, however, mean that academics can dictate the contents of historiography. Instead, it is the often untheorized historiographical viewpoints of governments and publics that have more weight and therefore deserve attention.

Technology may well be influencing the context toward a major change in historical consciousness. Human minds may react to stimuli differently as the capacity to do so is altered. Whether that will be a paradigm shift in our understanding of the past, and the meaning in transience and transience in meaning of past experience, is currently unclear. It is probable that there will be a need to rethink history, both to take note of this possible change in historical consciousness and to reflect an awareness of the likely future development of artificial intelligence capabilities able to have a sense of the past and to influence those of humans.

NOTES

PREFACE

1. Julian O'Shaughnessy, "I'm Reconquering Just Like Peter the Great, Insists Vladimir Putin," *The Times*, June 10, 2022. See also Rodric Braithwaite, *Russia: Myths and Realities* (London: Profile, 2022).

1. INTRODUCTION: THE CONTROVERSY OF HISTORY

1. Caroline Hoefferle, *The Essential Historiography Reader* (Boston: Prentice Hall, 2011).
2. Maurice Halbwachs, *On Collective Memory* (French original, 1925; Chicago: University of Chicago Press, 1992).
3. *The Times*, April 28, 2022.
4. K. E. Brashier, *Ancestral Memory in Early China* (Cambridge, MA: Harvard University Press, 2011).
5. Mark Towsey, *Reading History in Britain and America, c. 1750–c. 1840* (Cambridge: Cambridge University Press, 2019).
6. Jane Austen, *Juvenilia* (Cambridge: Cambridge University Press, 2006), 323–34.

7. Yannis Assael, Thea Sommerschield, Brendan Shillingford, Mahyar Bordbar, John Pavlopoulos, Marita Chatzipanagiotou, Ion Androutsopoulos, Jonathan Prag, and Nando de Freitas, "Restoring and Attributing Ancient Texts Using Deep Neural Networks," *Nature* 603 (March 9, 2022), 280–83.

8. Santo Mazzarino, *Il Pensiero Storico Classico* (Rome, Italy: Editori Laterza, 1965–66).

2. ORIGIN ACCOUNTS AND SACRED TIME

1. Beth Spacey, *The Miraculous and the Writing of Crusade Narrative* (Woodbridge, UK: Boydell Press, 2020).

2. Cynthis Camp, ed., *Anglo-Saxon Saints' Lives as History Writing in Late Medieval England* (Cambridge: D. S. Brewer, 2015).

3. Tacitus, *The Histories* II, 1.

4. Denis Twitchett, *The Writing of Official History under the T'ang* (Cambridge: Cambridge University Press, 1992).

5. Jay Rubinstein, *Armies of Heaven: The First Crusade and the Quest for Apocalypse* (New York: Basic Books, 2011).

6. Jay Rubinstein, *Nebuchadnezzar's Dream: The Crusades, Apocalyptic Prophecy, and the End of History* (Oxford: Oxford University Press, 2019).

7. J. Barlow, "Gregory of Tours and the Myth of the Trojan Origins of the Franks," *Frühmittelatter Studien* 29 (1995): 86–95.

8. Martin Brett and D. A. Woodman, eds., *The Long Twelfth-Century View of the Anglo-Saxon Past* (Farnham, UK: Ashgate, 2015).

9. T. Zuidema, "Hierarchy and Space in Incaic Social Organisation," *Ethnohistory* 30 (1983): 49–75.

10. Gary Urton, *The History of a Myth: Pacariqtambo and the Origin of the Inkas* (Austin: University of Texas Press, 1990).

11. Paul Kosmin, *Time and Its Adversaries in the Seleucid Empire* (Cambridge, MA: Harvard University Press, 2018).

12. D. M. Robinson, *In the Shadow of the Mongol Empire: Ming China and Eurasia* (Cambridge: Cambridge University Press, 2020).

13. Nigel Saul, "The Carminows and Their Arms: History, Heraldry and Myth in Late Medieval and Early Modern Cornwall," *English Historical Review* 136 (2021): 1419–49.

14. W. Mark Ormrod, *Edward III* (New Haven, CT: Yale University Press, 2011), 15.
15. Zachary Sayre Schiffman, *The Birth of the Past* (Baltimore: Johns Hopkins University Press, 2012).
16. Peter Russell, *Prince Henry "the Navigator": A Life* (New Haven, CT: Yale University Press, 2000).

3. PRINTING AND NEW UNIVERSAL HISTORIES

1. Peter Burke, *The Renaissance Sense of the Past* (London: Edward Arnold, 1969).
2. Lydia Barnett, *After the Flood: Imagining the Global Environment in Early Modern Europe* (Baltimore: Johns Hopkins University Press, 2019).
3. Ali Anooshahr, *The Ghazi Sultans and the Frontiers of Islam* (London: Routledge, 2009).
4. Peter Fibiger Bang and Dariusz Kolodziejczk, eds., *Universal Empire: A Comparative Approach to Imperial Culture and Representation in Eurasian History* (Cambridge: Cambridge University Press, 2012).
5. Zeynep Yürekli, *Architecture and Hagiography in the Ottoman Empire: The Politics of Bektashi Shrines in the Classical Age* (London: Routledge, 2012).
6. Stefan Bauer, *The Invention of Papal History: Onofrio Panvinio between Renaissance and Catholic Reform* (Oxford: Oxford University Press, 1926).
7. Peter Perdue, *China Marches West: The Qing Conquest of Central Eurasia* (Cambridge, MA: Harvard University Press, 2005).
8. Macabe Keliher, *The Board of Rites and the Making of Qing China* (Oakland: University of California Press, 2019).
9. Pamela Kyle Crossley, *A Translucent Mirror: History and Identity in Qing Imperial Ideology* (Berkeley: University of California Press, 1999).
10. *Collected Novels and Memoirs of William Godwin*, vol. 5 (London, 1805; 2nd ed., 1832), 173.

11. Barry Coward and Julian Swann, eds., *Conspiracies and Conspiracy Theory in Early Modern Europe: From the Waldensians to the French Revolution* (Aldershot: Ashgate Publishing, 2004); Peter R. Campbell, Thomas E. Kaiser, and Marisa Linton, eds., *Conspiracy in the French Revolution* (Manchester: Manchester University Press, 2007).

12. Brendan McConville, *The Brethren: A Story of Faith and Conspiracy in Revolutionary America* (Cambridge, MA: Harvard University Press, 2022).

13. C. Noelle-Karimi, "Afghan Politics and the Indo-Persian Literary Realm: The Durrani Rulers and Their Portrayal in Eighteenth-Century Historiography" in *Afghan History through Afghan Eyes*, ed. Nile Green (London: Oxford University Press, 2015).

14. Edward Gibbon, *The History of the Decline and Fall of the Roman Empire*, ed. J. Bury (London), 4:164–65.

15. A. Musi, "Croce, Napoli e la Spagna," *La Repubblica*, April 24, 2008; A. Musi, *Il Regno di Napoli* (Brescia: Morcelliana, 2016).

16. Auckland to Keith, August 23, 1791, Edinburgh, National Library of Scotland, Acc. 9769 71/2/7.

17. Laurence Echard, *The History of England: From the First Entrance of Julius Cæsar and the Romans, to the End of the Reign of King James the First* (London: 1707–1720) 2:1.

18. Ibid., 2:910.

19. G. Lyttelton, *Letters from a Persian in England*, 4th ed. (London, 1735), 179–98.

20. It is by no means clear therefore whether I should put the Glorious Revolution in quotation marks.

21. London, British Library, Additional Manuscripts, 33126 f. 383.

22. London, British Library, Additional Manuscripts, 35378 f. 20.

4. REJECTING THE PAST

1. Adams, *Works*, edited by C. F. Adams, 3:394–6; J. Boyd, ed., *Papers of Thomas Jefferson*, 9:364–5.

2. K. J. O'Keefe, 'The Dutch Revolt and Historical Memory in the American Revolution,' *International History Review* 43 (2021): 567–78.

3. S. G. Fisher, 'The Twenty-Eight Charges against the King in the Declaration of Independence," *Pennsylvania Magazine of History and Biography* 31 (1907): 257–303; W. L. Hedges, "Telling Off the King: Jefferson's Summary View as American Fantasy," *Early American Literature* 22 (1987): 166–74; S. E. Lucas, "The Stylistic Artistry of the Declaration of Independence," *US National Archives and Records Administration*, January 30, 2005, www .archives.gov.

4. T. H. Breen, *The Will of the People: The Revolutionary Birth of America* (Cambridge, MA: Harvard University Press, 2019).

5. *Archives parlementaires de 1787 à 1860*, 127 vols. (Paris, 1879–1913), 37:491–93.

6. W. Cobbett, ed., *Cobbett's Parliamentary History of England . . . 1066 . . . 1803*, 36 vols. (London, 1806–20), 29:22.

7. Auckland to William, Lord Grenville, foreign secretary, June 8, 1792, London, British Library, Additional Manuscripts, 58920 f. 105.

8. Jean-Pierre Le Glaunec, *The Cry of Vertières: Liberation, Memory, and the Beginning of Haiti* (Montreal: McGill-Queens University Press, 2020).

9. Joan Dayen, *Haiti, History, and the Gods* (Berkeley: University of California Press, 1995).

10. Samuel Horsley, *Sermons*, ed. Heneage Horsley (London: Longman, 1816), 3:293–321; F. C. Mather, *High Church Prophet: Bishop Samuel Horsley (1738–1806) and the Caroline Tradition in the Later Georgian Church* (Oxford: Clarendon Press, 1992), 228–30.

5. NEW PASTS

1. Jeffrey Brooks, *When Russia Learned to Read: Literacy and Popular Literature, 1861–1917* (Princeton, NJ: Princeton University Press, 1985).

2. K. R. Eskildsen, "Leopold Ranke's Archival Turn: Location and Evidence in Modern Historiography," *Modern Intellectual*

History 5 (2008): 425–53. See also K. Kinzel, "Method and Meaning: Ranke and Droysen on the Historian's Disciplinary Ethos," *History and Theory* 59 (2020): 22–41.

3. William Smith, *Dr William Smith's Ancient Atlas* (1874), 11.

4. M. J. S. Rudwick, *Bursting the Limits of Time: The Reconstruction of Geohistory in the Age of Revolution* (Chicago, 2005).

5. William Hughes, *Illuminated Atlas of Scripture Geography* (1840), 3.

6. Hereford Brooke George, *The Relations of Geography and History*, 5th ed. (1924), 295.

7. Hughes, *Illuminated Atlas of Scripture Geography*, 4.

8. Edmund McClure, *Historical Church Atlas* (London: Society for Promoting Christian Knowledge, 1897), 39, 36.

9. James Moorhead, *American Apocalypse: Yankee Protestants and the Civil War, 1860–1869* (New Haven, CT: Yale University Press, 1978); George C. Rable, *God's Almost Chosen Peoples: A Religious History of the American Civil War* (Chapel Hill: University of North Carolina Press, 2011).

10. Richard Gamble, *The War for Righteousness: Progressive Christianity, the Great War, and the Rise of the Messianic Nation* (Wilmington, DE: Intercollegiate Studies Institute, 2003).

11. Alice Y. Tseng, *Modern Kyoto: Building for Ceremony and Commemoration, 1868–1940* (Honolulu: University of Hawai'i Press, 2018).

12. Mark Ravina, *Stand with the Nations of the World: Japan's Meiji Restoration in World History* (Oxford: Oxford University Press, 2017).

13. Yu the Great was founding ruler of the possibly mythical Xia dynasty (if so, died ca. 2025 BCE).

14. Edward Lavington Oxenham, *Historical Atlas of the Chinese Empire* (1888), i, iii.

15. Joshua Bennett, *God and Progress: Religion and History in British Intellectual Culture, 1845–1914* (Oxford: Oxford University Press, 2019).

16. Judith E. Kalb, *Russia's Rome: Imperial Visions, Messianic Dreams, 1890–1940* (Madison: University of Wisconsin Press, 2010).

17. M. M. Austin, "Hellenistic Kings, War and the Economy," *Classical Quarterly* 36 (1986): 455.
18. C. Pearson, *Historical Maps of England* (1869), vi; E. M. Hausteiner, "The Attraction for Rome in the Age of Empire: The *Imperium Romanum* as a Precedence for Imperial Britain," *Mediterraneo Antico* 12 (2009): 31–48.

6. CONTESTING THE NATIONS

1. J. H. Franklin, *George Washington Williams: A Biography* (Chicago: University of Chicago Press, 1985).
2. Robert Goldstein, ed., *The War for the Public Mind: Political Censorship in Nineteenth-Century Europe* (Westport, CT: Praeger, 2000).
3. Helmut Walser Smith, *Germany: A Nation in Its Time, Before, During, and After Nationalism, 1500–2000* (New York: Liveright, 2020).
4. *Times*, April 15, 1905.
5. Paul Cohen, ed., *History and Popular Memory: The Power of Story in Moments of Crisis* (New York: Columbia University Press, 2014).
6. Barbara Gribling, *The Image of Edward the Black Prince in Georgian and Victorian England: Negotiating the Late Medieval Past* (Woodbridge, UK: Boydell Press, 2016).
7. Jiří Kořalka, *František Palacký* (Vienna: Austrian Academy of Sciences, 2007), 370; see also Stuart Kelly, *Scott-Land: The Man Who Invented a Nation* (Edinburgh: Birlinn, 2010).
8. R. W. Slatta, "Taking Our Myths Seriously," *Journal of the West* 40, 3 (2001): 3–5.

7. HISTORY IN THE LONG COLD WAR, 1917–1989

1. Henry Picker, ed., *Hitler's Tischgespräche im Führerhauptquartier*, 4th ed. (Stuttgart: Seewald, 1983), 166, March 31, 1942.

2. Heather Pringle, *The Master Plan: Himmler's Scholars and the Holocaust* (New York: Hachette, 2004).

3. Ronald Ross, "Heinrich Ritter von Srbik and *Gesamtdeutsch* History," *Review of Politics* 31 (1969): 88–107; Klaus Taschweer, *Hochburg des Antisemitismus: Der Niedergang der Universität Wien im 20 Jahrhundert* (Vienna: Czernin, 2015); A. Sked, "Re-Imagining Empire: The Persistence of the Austrian Idea in the Historical Work of Heinrich Ritter von Srbik," *Radovi* 50 (2018), DOI: 10.17234/RadoviZHP.50.1.

4. Franziska Exeler, *Ghosts of War. Nazi Occupation and Its Aftermath in Soviet Belarus* (Ithaca, NY: Cornell University Press, 2022), 234.

5. Polly Jones, *Myth, Memory, Trauma: Rethinking the Stalinist Past in the Soviet Union, 1953–70* (New Haven, CT: Yale University Press, 2013).

6. Leo S. Kleijn, *Soviet Archaeology: Trends, Schools, and History* (Oxford: Oxford University Press, 2012).

7. *National Atlas of Ethiopia* (Addis Ababa, Ethiopia: Ethiopian Mapping Authority, 1988).

8. *Putnam's Historical Atlas* (New York: Putnam's, 1927), xxxii.

9. Richard Aldous, *Schlesinger: The Imperial Historian* (New York: W. W. Norton, 2017).

10. W. H. McNeill, M. R. Buske, and A. W. Roehm, *The World: Its History in Maps* (Chicago, 1963), 8–9.

11. *Times Atlas of World History* (Maplewood, NJ: Hammond, 1978), 69.

12. Samuel P. Huntington, "Conservatism as an Ideology," *American Political Science Review* 51 (1957): 454–73, at 469.

13. Michael E. Latham, *Modernization as Ideology: American Social Science and "Nation Building" in the Kennedy Era* (Chapel Hill: University of North Carolina Press, 2000).

14. Giuliana Chamedes, *A Twentieth-Century Crusade: The Vatican's Battle to Remake Christian Europe* (Cambridge, MA: Harvard University Press, 2019).

8. METHODS FOR A MODERN AGE

1. "In This Issue," *American Historical Review* 117 (2012): xii–xiii.
2. "AHR Exchange on *The History Manifesto*," *American Historical Review* 120 (2015): 527–54.
3. R. Rosenzweig, "Can History Be Open Source? *Wikipedia* and the Future of the Past," *Journal of American History* 93 (2006): 117–46.
4. For example, Joseph L. Locke and Ben Wright, eds., *The American Yawp: A Massively Collaborative Open U.S. History Textbook* (Stanford: Stanford University Press, 2009).
5. I. A. Carbajal and M. Carswell, "Critical Digital Archives: A Review from Archival Studies," *American Historical Review* 12 (2021): 1102–20.
6. As in Britta Schilling, *Postcolonial Germany: Memories of Empire in a Decolonized Nation* (Oxford: Oxford University Press, 2014).
7. Lara Kriegel, *The Crimean War and Its Afterlife: Making Modern Britain* (Cambridge: Cambridge University Press, 2022), 239.
8. Caroline Elkins, *Legacy of Violence: A History of the British Empire* (New York: Knopf, 2022), 679–80.
9. Kriegel, *Crimean War,* 239–43.
10. *The Times,* June 1, 2022.
11. Marko Živković, *Serbian Dreambook: National Imaginary in the Time of Milošević* (Bloomington: Indiana University Press, 2011).
12. Lynn A. Struve, *The Dreaming Mind and the End of the Ming World* (Honolulu: University of Hawai'i Press, 2019).
13. Claire-Elizabeth de Rémusat, *Mémoires de Madame de Rémusat, 1802–1808,* edited by Paul de Rémusat (Paris, 1884), 1:274.
14. Rosie Bsheer, *Archive Wars: The Politics of History in Saudi Arabia* (Stanford: Stanford University Press, 2020).
15. Erik Esselstrom, *That Distant Country Next Door: Popular Japanese Perceptions of Mao's China* (Honolulu: University of Hawai'i Press, 2019).
16. J. Forbes, introduction to *Atlas of Native History* (1981), no pagination.

17. J. R. Cram and J. McQuilton, eds., *Australians: A Historical Atlas* (Broadway, Australia: Fairfax, Syme, and Weldon, 1987), 36–37.

9. THE MANY MEANS OF HISTORY

1. Libby Brooks, "Nicola Sturgeon Issues Apology for 'Historical Injustice' of Witch Hunts," *The Guardian*, March 8, 2022, https://www.theguardian.com/uk-news/2022/mar/08/nicola -sturgeon-issues-apology-for-historical-injustice-of-witch-hunts.

2. Katie Stallard, *Dancing on Bones: History and Power in China, Russia, and North Korea* (Oxford: Oxford University Press, 2022).

3. *The Times*, May 2, 2022.

4. For a perceptive warning, see H. Halstead, "Everyday Public History," *History* 107 (2022): 235–48.

5. Elissa Bemporad, *Legacy of Blood: Jews, Pogroms, and Ritual Murder in the Lands of the Soviets* (Oxford: Oxford University Press, 2019).

6. Faith Hillis, *Children of Rus': Right-Bank Ukraine and the Invention of a Russian Nation* (Ithaca, NY: Cornell University Press, 2013).

7. *Today* program, BBC Radio 4, April 13, 2022.

8. *The Times*, May 20, 2022.

9. *The Times*, May 16, 2022.

10. Peter H. Gries, *China's New Nationalism: Pride, Politics and Diplomacy* (Berkeley: University of California Press, 2004); William Callahan, *China: The Pessoptimist Nation* (Oxford: Oxford University Press, 2010).

11. Ding Yizhuang, "Reflections on the 'New Qing History' School in the United States," *Chinese Studies in History* 43 (2009): 92–96.

12. Translated in "A Righteous View of History," *China Media Project*, April 2015.

13. Albert Feuerwerker, ed., *History in Communist China* (Cambridge, MA: MIT Press, 1968); Jonathan Unger, ed., *Using the Past to Serve the Present: Historiography and Politics in Contemporary China* (Armonk, NY: M. E. Sharpe, 1993).

14. Florence Sutcliffe-Braithwaite, review of Richard King's *Brittle with Relics: A History of Wales, 1962–97* (2022), *London*

Review of Books, April 7, 2022, 10. For similar self-congratulation of historians as making "the past speak to silence," see the editorial by Alex Lichtenstein in *American Historical Review* 126 (2021): xix.

15. Katie Stevenson and Barbara Gribling, eds., *Chivalry and the Medieval Post* (Woodbridge, UK: Boydell Press, 2016); Tommaso di Carpegna Falconieri, *The Militant Middle Ages: Contemporary Politics between New Barbarians and Modern Crusaders*, trans. Andrew M. Hiltzik (Leiden, Netherlands: Brill, 2020).

16. Robert Bartlett, ed., *The Middle Ages and the Movies: Eight Key Films* (London: Reaktion Books, 2022).

17. Claire Whitlinger, *Between Remembrance and Repair: Commemorating Racial Violence in Philadelphia, Mississippi* (Chapel Hill: University of North Carolina Press, 2020).

18. Rebecca Clifford, *Commemorating the Holocaust: The Dilemmas of Remembrance in France and Italy* (Oxford: Oxford University Press, 2013).

19. R. Blakemore, "The Changing Fortunes of Atlantic History," *English Historical Review* 131 (2016): 851–68.

20. Sebastian Conrad, *What Is Global History?* (Princeton, NJ: Princeton University Press, 2016); James Belich et al., *The Prospect of Global History* (Oxford: Oxford University Press, 2016).

10. INTO THE FUTURE

1. Joshua Myers, *Cedric Robinson: The Time of the Black Radical Tradition* (London: Polity, 2021).

2. John Roberts, *The Triumph of the West* (1985), BBC series and accompanying book.

3. Clifford and Elizabeth Lord, *Historical Atlas of the United States*, 2nd ed. (New York: Henry Holt and Company, 1953), iii.

4. Bruce Macdonald, *Vancouver: A Visual History* (Vancouver: Talon Books, 1992), ix.

5. James H. Sweet, "Is History History? Identity Politics and Teleologies of the Present," *Perspectives on History*, August 17, 2022.

SELECTED FURTHER READING

There is a very extensive literature on this subject, and this brief list is necessarily selective. It is focused on recent works. Earlier ones can be approached through the bibliographies and footnotes in these books.

Beiner, Guy. *Forgetful Remembrance: Social Forgetting and Vernacular Historiography of a Rebellion in Ulster.* Oxford: Oxford University Press, 2018.

Bennett, J. *God and Progress: Religion and History in British Intellectual Culture, 1845–1914.* Oxford: Oxford University Press, 2019.

Black, J. *Clio's Battles: Historiography in Practice.* Bloomington: Indiana University Press, 2015.

Black, J. *Contesting History.* London: Bloomsbury Academic, 2014.

Clark, Christopher. *Time and Power: Visions of History in German Politics, from the Thirty Years' War to the Third Reich.* Princeton, NJ: Princeton University Press, 2019.

Gaddis, John Lewis. *The Landscape of History: How Historians Map the Past.* Oxford: Oxford University Press, 2002.

Gerzina, Gretchen, ed. *Britain's Black Past.* Liverpool: Liverpool University Press, 2020.

Hell, Julia. *The Conquest of Ruins: The Third Reich and the Fall of Rome.* Chicago: University of Chicago Press, 2019.

Hoffer, P. C. *Clio among the Muses: Essays on History and the Humanities*. New York: New York University Press, 2014.

Kramer, Lloyd, and Sarah Maza. *A Companion to Western Historical Thought*. Oxford: Blackwell, 2002.

Loud, Graham, and Martial Staub, eds. *The Making of Medieval History*. Woodbridge, UK: York Medieval Papers, 2017.

Matthews, David. *Medievalism: A Critical History*. Cambridge: D. S. Brewer, 2015.

Ng, S. F. *Alexander the Great from Britain to Southeast Asia: Peripheral Empires in the Global Renaissance*. Oxford: Oxford University Press, 2019.

Roehner, Bertrand, and Tony Syme. *Pattern and Repertoire in History*. Cambridge, MA: Harvard University Press, 2002.

Teter, M. *Blood Libel: On the Trail of an Anti-Semitic Myth*. Cambridge, MA: Harvard University Press, 2020.

Woolf, D. R. *A Concise History of History*. Cambridge: Cambridge University Press, 2019.

Woolf, D. R., ed. *The Oxford History of Historical Writing*. Oxford: Oxford University Press, 2011–12.

INDEX

academic historians: *American Historical Review* forum and, 201–2; anachronism and, 219–20, 275, 277; construction of normative and, 9–10; dangers of adopting orthodoxies, 207–9; democratization of access to history and, 205–6, 221–23, 228–30; effect of "history wars" on, 211–13; empiricism and, 11–12; establishment of universities and, 124; Jewish influx from Nazi Germany and, 178–79; military history and, 148; Nazi regime and, 176–77; participation in national narratives and, 159; postmodernism and, 201–2, 207, 215; role for in post–Cold War employment of history, 261–62; role of data and, 277; shift of focus to social/cultural history, 203; as small portion of engagement with history, 274–75
Adams, John, 104–5

Adenauer, Konrad, 237–38
Afghanistan, 228
Afonso I (King of Portugal), 37–38
Africa, 31, 196, 241. *See also individual countries*
afterlife concept, 23
Ainu people, 78–79
Alexander the Great, 31
Alfonso XI of Castile, 38
America: American Revolution, 56–57, 215–16; challenge of to Western ideas of history, 79; frontier and, 166; influence of imperialism on, 143; references to republican Rome, 142; relationship to English ideas and, 91–92; ruralist theme in national narrative, 160. *See also* United States
American Historical Association, 166
American Historical Review, 201–2
American Revolution, 56–57, 215–16

JEREMY BLACK is Emeritus Professor of History
at the University of Exeter, a Senior Fellow of
the Foreign Policy Research Institute, and a Visiting
Fellow of the Oxford Centre for Methodism and
Church History. He is the author of many books,
including *Culture in Eighteenth-Century England:
A Subject for Taste; George III: America's Last King;
England in the Age of Shakespeare;* and *Charting the
Past: The Historical Worlds of Eighteenth-Century
England.* Black is a recipient of the Samuel Eliot
Morison Prize from the Society for Military History.

For Indiana University Press

Lesley Bolton, Project Manager/Editor
Brian Carroll, Rights Manager
Dan Crissman, Trade and Regional
    Acquisitions Editor
Samantha Heffner, Trade Acquisitions Assistant
Brenna Hosman, Production Coordinator
Katie Huggins, Production Manager
Dan Pyle, Online Publishing Manager
Stephen Williams, Marketing Manager
Jennifer Witzke, Senior Artist and Book Designer